Study Guide
DONNA ANDERSON BENTLEY

Understanding Psychology

SECOND EDITION

CHARLES G. MORRIS
UNIVERSITY OF MICHIGAN

Prentice Hall
Englewood Cliffs, New Jersey 07632

Editorial/Production supervision: **Benjamin D. Smith**
Prepress Buyer: **Kelly Behr**
Manufacturing Buyer: **Mary Ann Gloriande**
Supplement acquisitions editor: **Sharon Chambliss**
Acquisitions editor: **Charlyce Jones Owen**

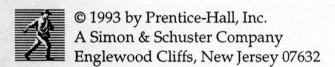 © 1993 by Prentice-Hall, Inc.
A Simon & Schuster Company
Englewood Cliffs, New Jersey 07632

Printed in the United States of America

10 9 8 7 6 5 4 3 2

ISBN   0-13-951542-9

Prentice-Hall International (UK) Limited, *London*
Prentice-Hall of Australia Pty. Limited, *Sydney*
Prentice-Hall Canada Inc., *Toronto*
Prentice-Hall Hispanoamericana, S.A., *Mexico*
Prentice-Hall of India Private Limited, *New Delhi*
Prentice-Hall of Japan, Inc., *Tokyo*
Simon & Schuster Asia Pte. Ltd., *Singapore*
Editora Prentice-Hall do Brasil, Ltda., *Rio de Janeiro*

CONTENTS

SOME THOUGHTS ABOUT LEARNING FOR THE STUDENT

Some Thoughts about Learning for the Student

You might enjoy hearing about Scott. He was a graduate student finishing his last statistics course in pursuit of his doctoral degree. A portion of the final exam was to be done on a computer. Incidentally, in Scott's day there were no PCs and he did not feel comfortable in the big terminal room. For the exam, students were allowed to consult any source for needed information, but they were forbidden to ask assistance from any person.

When Scott confronted the most crucial problem of the test, he found that he had no idea how to do it and he did not know where to look for help. No matter how hard he tried he could not solve the problem. He wasn't even sure whether he had forgotten how to do it or if he had never learned how at all. He had a miserable headache. He felt nauseated and was dizzy. He gave up knowing that his degree was in jeopardy. He began the long walk to his car.

As he crossed the bridge over the campus plaza, his attention was diverted to a commotion below. Some students were having a noisy fight with water guns. As he scanned the area, his eyes came to rest on the windows of the room where his statistics class met. Suddenly it was as if a bright light went on. "I know how to do it!" he shouted. He returned to the computer room and completed the problem with ease. His physical symptoms had disappeared. He felt refreshed, rested, and triumphant.

Some psychologists might explain Scott's experience as "incubation." Others might have a different label for this phenomenon. By whatever name, Scott's experience can work for you too. He learned some vital information, concepts, and skills, but recall had been buried temporarily by anxiety and concern over other matters. Scott inadvertently gave it a rest and it came back. The author of your text briefly includes this marvel of memory somewhere in the chapter on problem solving. Perhaps you will look for it and try to employ it in your own endeavors.

Scott's true story serves to introduce you to the complex and fascinating fields of learning and memory. You will study both of these areas in this introductory psychology course. This study guide is designed to assist you in making your experience more enjoyable, more effective, and more successful.

Scott's narrow escape was chosen to begin this message rather than some other area of psychology because learning is memory and memory is learning, according to the cognitivists. Soon you will learn what cognitivism is. Then you can contrast that model with behaviorism. Behaviorists show that learning occurs as the result of practice. That leads us into a brief discussion of the plan of the study guide.

The guide is based upon prior studying and self-testing. You will begin by recognizing facts in multiple-choice questions. Then you will move to a higher level of thinking and problem solving. The multiple-choice questions will tap your knowledge of facts and your understanding of concepts. The last section of these recognition-type questions will determine if you can apply facts and concepts to real-life situations.

There will be recall questions. You will fill in the blanks. First, the questions will deal with facts. Then you will again move to a higher level of conceptualization, which combines understanding and application.

Your next task is to define the terms and concepts of the chapter in your own words. This activity will set you up to answer some discussion questions to determine if you can integrate your new knowledge. Answers and page number locations for all multiple-choice and recall questions are provided. Page numbers for the short-answer questions are also provided.

It is only fair to mention that some answers may not be obvious. It may be necessary to make some conceptual inferences. Try not to be too upset if an answer does not "jump out at you" from a page in the text. These might be good occasions to ask your professor a question.

Your final task is to respond to some open-ended applications of your new knowledge. You will not find answers to these. Sometimes there is no answer. Here is an opportunity for creativity, for critical thinking, and for self-examination along with the academic aspects of the applications. These situations might spark your curiosity, give you ideas for term papers and class projects, provide a good excuse for asking a question in class, or make a friend of a classmate.

It may become apparent that a majority of the applications throughout the chapters sound too real to be fictional. You will be correct in your assumption. In most cases, the people and the situations are real. Even the dogs are real and their names have not been changed! Some of these scenarios may make you feel sad. Some may help you to solve a problem. Some may give you a little hope or a spark of inspiration. Psychology happens . . . to all of us. It is not a remote science. These experiences are also a part of learning.

This study guide is designed to be an application of research on learning and memory. You will see the rationale unfold when you study these two subfields. Diligent use of this guide will enhance your professor's efforts in the classroom and your studying of the text. Some questions will refer to information you have studied in previous chapters to provide continuity and to illustrate that learning cannot be measured by chapters, but by accumulation, integration, retrieval, and application of knowledge.

This guide is dedicated to all of you who take this course and to my former students at Dalton College who provided so much of the inspiration for completing this project. May all of you benefit from this experience in learning.

Perhaps I might be permitted a few words of gratitude to those who cheerfully and competently assisted in this project. First, all of us are most grateful for the assistance of the reviewers whose thoughtful, perceptive, and knowledgeable comments and corrections greatly enhance the value of this study guide. Many thanks to:

Andre Buteau
Illinois Benedictine College

David Gershaw
Arizona Western College

Paul Lewan
Green River Community College

Laura Thompson
New Mexico State University

The crucial help of Prentice Hall editor, Leslie Carr and editorial assistant, Millie White kept the process moving smoothly in the necessary absence of Sharon Chambliss. It was good to hear Sharon's voice again and to be able to say "congratulations."

None of this would have been possible without the highly competent computer work of Mary Jane Lash of Rochester Hills, Michigan, who somehow produced this beautiful manuscript while tending to the needs of little Kevin. Larry Lash deserves an expression of gratitude, too, for being such a cheerful messenger for our many communications, his help with proofing, and valuable consultations. Many thanks to everyone who had a part in this project.

Donna Anderson Bentley, Ph.D
Auburn Hills, Michigan

THE SCIENCE OF PSYCHOLOGY

1

Chapter Objectives

After you have read and studied this chapter, you should be able to:

1. Define psychology, describe its goals and methods, and distinguish it from other sciences which study human behavior.
2. Describe the early schools of psychology and explain how they contributed to its development.
3. Describe three of the more recent schools of psychology.
4. Describe the major areas of specialization in psychology today.
5. Distinguish between the three basic methods used by psychologists to gather information about behavior. Identify the situations in which each of the methods would be appropriate.
6. Discuss the concerns of ethics in psychology.
7. Distinguish between pure research and applied research.

Multiple-Choice Questions: Recognizing What You Have Learned

These questions ask only that you recognize what you have learned. When you recognize a correct answer, you have accessed that information in memory. A knowledge of facts serves as a framework for later analysis and problem solving.

Remembering the Facts

This group of multiple-choice questions requires that you simply recognize facts from your text book.

1. The processes and changes in human mental and physical growth from before birth through old age are studied by _____ psychologists.

   a. child
   b. physiological

   c. developmental
   d. clinical

2. The processes involved in learning, memory, sensation, perception, cognition, motivation, and emotion are investigated by _____ psychologists.

   a. developmental
   b. physiological

   c. clinical
   d. experimental

3. About half of all psychologists specialize in _____ psychology.

   a. clinical or counseling
   b. personality

   c. experimental
   d. developmental

4. _____ psychologists investigate the influence of people on one another.

   a. Educational
   b. Social

   c. Organizational
   d. Experimental

5. The foundation of contemporary psychology is:

   a. theory
   b. the hypothesis

   c. scientific research
   d. naturalistic observation

6. A central problem in naturalistic observation and case studies is:

   a. insignificant coefficients
   b. observer bias

   c. sample size
   d. lack of subject cooperation

7. Naturalistic observation, case studies, and surveys are particularly valuable as a way to _____ behavior.

   a. predict
   b. explain

   c. modify
   d. describe

8. The relationship between two or more variables is determined by:

a. correlation   c. the survey
b. an experiment   d. an hypothesis

9. Individuals whose reactions or responses are observed in an experiment are called:

a. confederates   c. subjects
b. the data base   d. variables

10. In an experiment, the _____ variable is manipulated to tests its effects.

a. dependent   c. control
b. independent   d. extraneous

11. In a controlled experiment, the group subjected to a change in the independent variable is called the:

a. experimental group   c. confederates
b. control group   d. subjects

12. The selection of cases from a larger population is called a/an:

a. random sample   c. sample
b. experimental group   d. control group

13. In a/an _____ sample, each potential subject has an equal chance of being selected.

a. controlled   c. experimental
b. biased   d. random

14. A sample that does not truly represent a whole population is called:

a. dependent   c. generalized
b. biased   d. uncorrelated

15. Which of the following experimenters, in 1963, caused the profession of psychology to reevaluate its ethical health?

a. Wilhelm Wundt   c. Stanley Milgram
b. W. H. Whyte   d. Susan Chipman

16. In _____, people began to use the scientific method in psychology.

    a. the late 1800's   c. the mid-20th century
    b. Aristotle's time   d. opposition to B. F. Skinner

17. The first formal psychological laboratory was founded in 1879 by:

    a. Edward Bradford Titchener   c. Wilhelm Wundt
    b. William James   d. James R. Angell

18. The school of psychology that stresses the basic units of experience and the combinations in which they occur is called:

    a. functionalism   c. Gestalt
    b. behaviorism   d. structuralism

19. _____ broke experience down into three basic elements: physical sensations, affections or feelings, and images.

    a. Edward Bradford Titchener   c. William James
    b. Wilhelm Wundt   d. John B. Watson

20. The first American born psychologist was:

    a. John B. Watson   c. William James
    b. Edward Bradford Titchener d. Wilhelm Wundt

21. William James was a:

    a. behaviorist   c. Gestalt psychologist
    b. structuralist   d. functionalist

22. The *Principles of Psychology*, published in 1890 is a text authored by:

    a. Charles Morris   c. Edward B. Titchener
    b. William James   d. Wilhelm Wundt

23. Which of the following was the center of the functionalist school of psychology in the late 1800's?

    a. The University of Chicago
    b. Ohio State University
    c. The University of Michigan
    d. The University of California at Davis

24. Which of the following, for John B. Watson, **cannot** be the object of scientific study?

   a. rats
   b. verbal behavior

   c. consciousness
   d. alcoholism

25. Psychology is the study of observable, measurable behavior according to:

   a. Ivan Pavlov
   b. John B. Watson

   c. William James
   d. James R. Angell

26. The famous experiment in which Little Albert learned to fear white rats through classical conditioning was conducted by:

   a. Watson and Rayner
   b. Mary Cover Jones

   c. Ivan Pavlov
   d. Max Wertheimer

27. Wertheimer, Köhler, and Koffka, Gestalt psychologists, were all interested in:

   a. introspection
   b. operant behavior

   c. consciousness
   d. perception

28. B.F. Skinner made the animal an active agent in its own conditioning through the use of:

   a. electric shock
   b. dream interpretation

   c. reinforcement
   d. introspection

29. _____ believed that much of our behavior is governed by hidden motives and unconscious desires.

   a. Mary Cover Jones
   b. Sigmund Freud

   c. B.F. Skinner
   d. Alfred Adler

30. _____ argues that people must learn how to realize their potential.

   a. Behaviorism
   b. Cognitive psychology
   c. Sigmund Freud
   d. Existential and humanistic psychology

31. _____ is/are especially interested in the ways in which people perceive, interpret, store, and retrieve information.

    a.   Cognitive psychology   c.   B.F. Skinner
    b.   The Gestaltists   d.   Jean-Paul Sartre

32. The meaninglessness and alienation of modern life leads to apathy and psychological problems according to:

    a.   B.F. Skinner   c.   the existentialists
    b.   the humanists   d.   Margaret Floy Washburn

Answers for this section:

1. c (2)	7. d (12)	13. d (18)	19 a (23)	25. b (25)	31. a (29)
2. d (4)	8. a (12)	14. b (18)	20. c (24)	26. a (25)	32. c (27)
3. a (4)	9. c (14)	15. c (20)	21. d (24)	27. d (26)	
4. b (5)	10. b (14)	16. a (23)	22. b (24)	28. c (26)	
5. c (8)	11. a (15)	17. c (23)	23. a (24)	29. b (26)	
6. b (11)	12. c (17)	18. d (23)	24. c (25)	30. d (27)	

Understanding the Facts

Now that you have found that you can recognize facts from The Science of Psychology, the next step is to determine if you understand the meaning of the newly-learned information. These multiple-choice questions require a higher level of thinking. They will help you establish more solid connections and provide practice in dealing with higher level concepts.

33. Which of the following statements about naturalistic observation is **not** true?

    a.   Observed behavior is more natural, spontaneous, and varied than in a laboratory.
    b.   It gives psychologists new ideas and suggestions for research.
    c.   It eliminates the danger of observer bias.
    d.   Each natural situation is a one-time-only occurrence.

34. Which of the following statements about case studies is **true**?

    a.   Case studies eliminate the problem of observer bias.
    b.   The researcher can confidently draw general conclusions from a single case.
    c.   Observer bias is less of a problem than in naturalistic observation.
    d.   Sigmund Freud used case studies to develop his theories.

35. Of the following, which method is best suited to explaining psychological phenomena?

    a.   experimentation   c.   the case study
    b.   the survey   d.   naturalistic observation

36. Of the following, which method is best suited to describing behavior?

    a.   correlation   c.   the case study
    b.   experimentation   d.   introspection

37. Which of the following methods is most valuable for prediction?

    a.   surveys   c.   case studies
    b.   correlation   d.   the experiment

38. If a researcher wants to draw conclusions about cause and effect from the data, the researcher uses:

    a.   the survey   c.   naturalistic observation
    b.   correlation   d.   the experiment

39. Which of the following statements about correlation is **not** true?

    a.   Correlation is a mathematical relationship between variables.
    b.   Correlation indicates a cause-effect relationship between variables.
    c.   Correlation can be used for prediction.
    d.   Correlation does not explain the relationships that are discovered.

40. In an experiment, the subjects who receive no treatment are called:

    a.   the control group   c.   confederates
    b.   the experimental group   d.   the biased group

41. If a researcher were to use the names in a telephone directory in the 1940's as a sample for a survey, the sample would be:

a. random
b. accurate
c. biased
d. predictive

42. According to Titchener our most complex thoughts can be reduced to physical sensations, feeling, and memories. He called this approach:

a. functionalism
b. behaviorism
c. cognitivism
d. structuralism

43. The statement, "Sensations without associations simply do not exist," would most likely have been uttered by:

a. Wilhelm Wundt
b. William James
c. B.F. Skinner
d. Kurt Koffka

44. If a person attended school in the 1930's, their education was likely to have been influenced by the application of functional psychology to education by:

a. Angell and Dewey
b. Wundt and Titchener
c. Skinner and Pavlov
d. Freud

45. Of the following concepts, which would be rejected by B.F. Skinner?

a. reinforcement
b. scientific method
c. mind
d. control of variables

46. Which of the following statements about Watson and Rayner's experiment with Little Albert is **true**?

a. Albert was instinctively afraid of furry white rats.
b. Albert learned to fear furry white rats through Pavlovian conditioning.
c. The Watson and Rayner experiment resulted in no change in Albert's behavior.
d. Watson's "loud noise" had no effect on Albert.

47. The statement "the whole is equal to more than the sum of its parts" would apply to which of the following approaches?

a. behaviorism
b. structuralism
c. functionalism
d. Gestalt psychology

48. Watson shared his belief that psychology should study only observable, measurable behavior with:

a. B.F. Skinner
b. The Freudians
c. The Gestaltists
d. John Dewey

49. Early childhood experiences are emphasized in the theory of :

a. B.F. Skinner
b. Carl Jung
c. Sigmund Freud
d. R.D. Laing

50. The question, "Who am I and where am I going?" would most likely be addressed by:

a. cognitive psychology
b. the existentialists
c. Max Wertheimer
d. Ivan Pavlov

51. Mental processes should be studied scientifically, according to the:

a. behaviorists
b. Gestaltists
c. existentialists
d. cognitivists

52. "Reach for the sky," might be a suggestion of:

a. R.D. Laing
b. the humanists
c. the existentialists
d. Sigmund Freud

Answers for this section:

33. c (11)	37. b (13)	41. c (18)	45. c (26)	49. c (27)
34. d (11)	38. d (15)	42. d (23)	46. b (25)	50. b (27)
35. a (14)	39. b (13)	43. b (24)	47. d (26)	51. d (29)
36. c (11)	40. a (15)	44. a (24)	48. a (26)	52. b (27)

Applying the facts

The learning of facts and concepts is of little value unless it can be applied and employed to solve problems. The next group of multiple-choice questions reflects applications of your learning.

53. You would like to know if there is a relationship between college entrance exam scores and high school grade-point average. Which of the following methodologies would you use to answer this question?

    a. conduct an experiment
    b. survey your classmates
    c. calculate a correlation
    d. send a questionnaire to the college registrar

54. The State Patrol is interested in knowing if there is a relationship between alcohol consumption and driving ability. They plan an experiment. In this example, amount of alcohol is the _____ variable.

    a. independent   c. control
    b. dependent   d. biased

55. To determine if alcohol consumption affects driving ability, the researcher would use which of the following methodologies?

    a. correlation   c. naturalistic observation
    b. a survey   d. an experiment

56. If you are curious about the relationship between the distance of your residence from the campus and grade-point average, which of the following methods would you use to determine this relationship?

    a. experiment   c. survey
    b. correlation   d. a case study

57. You want to determine the average intelligence of the population of the small town you live in. You cannot test everyone so you test a sample. For your findings to have any value, the sample must be:

    a. made up of people who are being paid to cooperate
    b. selected by a computer
    c. all high school graduates
    d. random and representative

58. A 5-year-old dog does a counter-clockwise turn every time her master presents her food bowl. When she was a puppy, her master accidentally dropped a food bowl on the dog's head. The dog turned counter-clockwise. This behavior can best be explained by;

a. R.D. Laing
b. Pavlovian conditioning
c. B.F. Skinner's reinforcement
d. Sigmund Freud

59. Jean Piaget employed a type of naturalistic observation to study the development of thought processes in children. He observed the growth of mental functions. From this information, you can conclude that Jean Piaget is a:

a. behaviorist
b. humanist
c. cognitivist
d. psychoanalyst

60. You have decided to major in psychology with the hope of going on to graduate school. You have always been fascinated with how memory works and are curious about persons with impaired memory. Which of the following fields of psychology would be the most likely choice for you?

a. experimental
b. physiological
c. personality
d. clinical

61. Joan has a Ph.D in experimental psychology. Whenever her friend George, a musician, gets angry with her he accuses her of not "using psychology" and says he is a better psychologist than she is. Which of the following statements best describes information that George needs to learn?

a. George should find out how effective Joan is as a college professor.
b. Psychologists rely on scientific method to obtain answers to questions.
c. George needs to find out how Joan copes with a crisis.
d. George should learn to teach Joan how to "use psychology."

62. An anthropologist goes to live with a tribe of Indians for 2 years in an effort to learn about their culture and behavior. Which of the following methodologies would be most suited for this project?

a. naturalistic observation
b. a survey
c. a case study
d. the experimental method

63.   An anthropologist who goes to live with a tribe of Indians to study their culture and behavior should bring a team along. This approach might help to prevent:

        a.   extraneous variables entering the experiment
        b.   danger to the researcher
        c.   observer bias
        d.   insignificant correlations

Answers for this section

53. c (12)   56. b (14)   59. c (29)   62. a (12)
54. a (14)   57. d (18)   60. b (4)   63. c (12)
55. d (14)   58. b (25)   61. b (6)

Fill-in-the-Blank Questions: Recalling What You Have Learned

By now, there should be a considerable amount of new information about the Science of Psychology in long-term-memory. The following questions of recall rather than recognition will show if you are becoming more comfortable with the material.

Remembering the Facts

1.   Psychology is the _____ study of _____ and _____.

2.   Scientific method includes _____ testing of hypotheses.

3.   A central problem in naturalistic observation is _____ _____.

4.   Naturalistic observation, case studies, and surveys are best suited for _____ behavior.

5.   Correlational research is best suited for finding relationships and for _____.

6.   The variable in an experiment that is manipulated to see what effects it has is called the _____ variable.

7.   The group subjected to a change in the independent variable is called the _____ group.

8.   Expectations by the experimenter that might influence the results of an experiment is called _____ _____.

9. A sample in which each potential subject has an equal chance of being selected is called a/an _____ _____.

10. A sample that does not truly represent a whole population is called a/an _____ _____.

11. The first formal psychological laboratory was founded in 1879 by _____ in _____.

12. Wundt and his co-workers trained themselves in _____ _____in an effort to find the atoms of thought.

13. Wundt's student, _____, brought objective introspection to America.

14. Wundt and Titchener's school of psychology is known as _____.

15. _____ concluded that pure sensations without associations do not exist.

16. William James' approach is called _____.

17. For John Watson, psychology was the study of _____, _____ behavior.

18. What famous psychologist would be **most** likely to say, "If you cannot see it and measure it, forget it"? _____

19. Roughly translated, the word Gestalt means _____ or _____.

20. B.F. Skinner added a new element to behaviorism. It is called _____.

21. _____ was the founder of psychoanalysis.

22. A concern with the meaninglessness and alienation of modern life is addressed by _____ psychology.

23. Finding ways to realize one's full human potential is the concern of _____ psychology.

24. Cognitive psychology studies human _____ _____.

Answers for this section:

1. scientific, behavior, mental process (6)
2. empirical (6)
3. observer bias (11)
4. describing (12)
5. prediction (13)
6. independent (15)
7. experimental (15)
8. experimenter bias (15)
9. random sample (18)
10. biased sample (18)
11. Wundt, Germany (23)
12. objective introspection (23)
13. Titchener (23)
14. structuralism (23)
15. James (24)
16. functionalism (24)
17. observable, measurable (25)
18. Watson (25)
19. whole, form (26)
20. reinforcement (26)
21. Freud (26)
22. existential (27)
23. humanistic (27)
24. mental process (29)

Understanding and Applying the Facts

As you previously did with recognition-type questions, you will now move to a higher level of recall. The following questions will determine if you understand the facts.

25. In order to determine a cause-effect relationship the researcher must use a/an _____ as the method.

26. In order to determine the relationship between intelligence test scores and college grade-point average, a researcher would use a/an _____.

27. A cause-effect relationship (can-cannot) be determined by correlation.

28. The outcome of an experiment is called the _____ variable.

29. Subjects in an experiment who receive no treatment are called the _____ group.

30. A researcher is getting a list of students' names for a potential sample for an experiment. It is a small university and most students live in dormitories. A person in the registrar's office gave the researcher a representative sample of dorm residents. Therefore, the sample is not _____ and is _____.

31. _____ percent of Stanley Milgram's subjects gave the highest level of shock.

32. Stanley Milgram hired people to help him with a learning experiment, but Milgram was not investigating learning. He was investigating _____.

33. The factor in the 1963 Milgram experiment that caused the APA to reformulate its ethical code was _____.

34. Perhaps the greatest contribution made by Wundt and his followers is that they introduced _____ and _____ into psychology.

35. The phrase "learning by doing" is most in keeping with the application of functionalism to education by _____.

36. In Watson and Rayner's experiment with Little Albert, the child learned to fear a/an _____ by association with a/an _____ _____.

37. If we see just the tail of a cat, we perceive the entire cat. This situation is of special interest to the _____ psychologists.

38. According to Skinner an animal will increase its behavior as a result of _____.

39. According to _____ people can become "fixated" because of early conflict and can carry feelings of anxiety into adulthood.

40. Perhaps abnormal behavior is a normal response to an abnormal world. This is the position of _____ who is a/an _____.

41. The way in which you, as a student, go about retrieving this new information is of special interest to _____ psychologists.

Answers for this section:

25.	experiment (14)	34.	measurement, experiment (23)
26.	correlation (12)	35.	John Dewey (23)
27.	cannot (13)	36.	rat, loud noise (25)
28.	dependent (14)	37.	Gestalt (26)
29.	control (15)	38.	reinforcement (26)
30.	random, biased (18)	39.	Freud (27)
31.	65 (20)	40.	R.D. Laing, existentialist (27)
32.	obedience (20)	41.	cognitive (29)
33.	deception (20)		

Testing Yourself for Mastery

The following terms and concepts are found in bold face or italics in the chapter. The time has come to determine if you can define and discuss your new learning in your own words, then check your work against the text.

psychology

scientific method

naturalistic observation

case studies

surveys

subjects

experiment

independent variable

dependent variable

experimental group

control group

experimenter bias

sample

random sample

representative sample

biased sample

structuralism

functionalism

conditioning

Gestalt psychology

behaviorism

reinforcement

psychoanalysis

psychotherapy

existential psychology

humanistic psychology

cognitive psychology

Integrating Your Newly Learned Information

Now that you have recognized, recalled, and given definition to The Science of Psychology you are ready to try to integrate your knowledge in a definitive discussion through short-answer questions.

1. How does experimental psychology differ from physiological psychology? (3, 4)

2. What are the goals of psychology? (6)

3. What factors are involved in scientific method? (6, 8)

4. Explain a disadvantage of naturalistic observation and case studies. (11)

5. What is the central concern in interpreting a correlation? (13)

6. How does an experiment differ from correlation? (12-14)

7. Give an example of an independent variable and a dependent variable in a hypothetical experiment. (14)

8.   How does a researcher avoid a biased sample? (17, 18)

9.   Compare structuralism and functionalism. (23, 24)

10.   What was the "new element" added to behaviorism by B.F. Skinner? (26)

Applications

You have worked through a section of recognition-type and recall questions to determine if you can apply information to real-life situations. It is time to try to respond to some applications. Some are based upon those questions. Answers to this section will not be given. Your questions concerning these applications will serve as a basis for classroom discussion and ideas for class projects throughout the course.

1.   You want to find out if there is a relationship between college entrance exam scores and high school grade-point average. You would do a correlation. How would you go about carrying out this project?

2.   If you want your dog to come to you when your call his name, how would you begin his training in puppyhood? Would you use Watson's or Skinner's behaviorism?

3.   Your project for a statistics course is to determine the average intelligence of the student body on your campus. What are the necessary steps (remember this is a scientific investigation)? How would you handle the ethical considerations?

4.   Do you think it is possible to redesign the Milgram experiment on obedience and find what you were looking for without violating current ethical standards of the APA?

Return to Chapter Summary

Now that you have concluded these exercises, you should go back and reread the chapter summary in your textbook. It provides you with a framework that integrates all of this newly-learned information. By reviewing the chapter summary, you will strengthen the many connections between the various new pieces of information.

PHYSIOLOGY AND BEHAVIOR

2

Chapter Objectives

After you have read and studied this chapter, you should be able to:

1. Describe the structure of neurons. Trace the path of a neural impulse and explain how it transmits messages from cell to cell.
2. Explain how neurons communicate. Identify the roles of neurotransmitters and receptors. Describe the effects of drugs on the synapse.
3. Describe the divisions and structures of the brain and explain the role of each.
4. Identify the functions of the sensory and motor projection areas. Describe the abilities of the two hemispheres of the cerebral cortex.
5. Describe the structure and function of the reticular formation, limbic system, and spinal cord.
6. Identify the divisions of the peripheral nervous system, and the autonomic nervous system and explain how they work together to regulate the glands and smooth muscles of the body.
7. Describe the functions of the endocrine system. Explain how hormones released by the endocrine system affect metabolism, blood-sugar level, sex characteristics, and the body's reaction to stress.
8. Summarize the concerns of behavior genetics.
9. Describe the structure of chromosomes and the role they play in inherited traits and characteristics.
10. Explain the concepts of dominant and recessive genes.

11. Identify several approaches to studying heritability of a trait.
12. Discuss some social implications of behavior genetics.

Multiple-Choice Questions: Recognizing What You Have Learned

These questions ask only that you recognize what you have learned. When you recognize a correct answer, you have accessed that information in memory. A knowledge of facts serves as a framework for later analysis and problem solving.

Remembering the Facts

This group of multiple-choice questions requires that you simply recognize facts from your textbook.

1. The smallest units of the nervous system are called:

    a. axons   c. dendrites
    b. neurons   d. chromosomes

2. Short fibers that branch out from the cell body and pick up incoming messages are called:

    a. neurons   c. nerves
    b. axons   d. dendrites

3. A single long fiber extending from the cell body that carries outgoing messages is called a/an:

    a. dendrite   c. nerve
    b. axon   d. myelin sheath

4. Some axons have a fatty covering on them. That cover is called:

    a. synapsis   c. dopamine
    b. ACh   d. myelin

5. Neurons that carry messages from sense organs to the spinal cord or brain are called _____ neurons.

    a. sensory or afferent   c. motor or efferent
    b. polarized   d. association

6. Neurons that carry messages from the spinal cord or brain to the muscles and glands are called _____ neurons.

   a. inter
   b. sensory or afferent
   c. motor or efferent
   d. ionized

7. The condition of a neuron at rest is called:

   a. ionization
   b. refraction
   c. its potential
   d. polarization

8. Electrically charged particles found both inside and outside of the neuron are called:

   a. inhibitors
   b. ions
   c. synaptics
   d. synaptic pulse

9. The firing of a nerve cell caused by depolarization of the neuron is called a/an:

   a. refractory period
   b. neural potential
   c. neural impulse
   d. synaptic pulse

10. A period after firing when the neuron will not fire again no matter how strong the incoming messages may be is called the:

    a. relative refractory period
    b. absolute refractory period
    c. neural action potential
    d. ionization state

11. A shift in the electrical charge in a tiny area of the neuron is called the:

    a. graded refractory period
    b. graded potential
    c. action potential
    d. potential refraction

12. Another term for the synaptic knob is:

    a. axon terminal
    b. vesicle
    c. cleft
    d. the gap

13. The tiny gap between the axon terminal of one neuron and the dendrite or cell body of the next neuron is called the:

    a. all-or-none space
    b. vesicle space
    c. synaptic space or synaptic cleft
    d. transmission gap

14. The area composed of the axon terminal of one neuron, the synaptic space, and dendrite of the next neuron is called a:

    a. synapse   c. reception
    b. vesicle   d. transmitter site

15. Chemical released by the synaptic vesicles that affect the next neuron are called:

    a. neuroactivators   c. endorphins
    b. endocrines   d. neurotransmitters

16. Which of the following are chemical substances involved in the reduction of pain?

    a. endorphins   c. myelins
    b. hormones   d. norepinephrines

17. The central nervous system is made up of the:

    a. brain only
    b. brain and spinal cord
    c. brain and peripheral connections
    d. brain, spinal cord, and endocrine system

18. The forebrain region that relays most incoming messages from the sense receptors is the:

    a. thalamus   c. pons
    b. medulla   d. corpus callosum

19. The medulla, pons, and cerebellum are located in the:

    a. hindbrain   c. forebrain
    b. midbrain   d. brainstem

20. The _____ connects the cerebral cortex at the top of the brain to the cerebellum.

    a. thalamus   c. hypothalamus
    b. medulla   d. pons

21. Breathing, heart rate, and blood pressure are controlled by the:

    a. pons   c. medulla
    b. thalamus   d. hypothalamus

22. The _____ is important for sight and hearing and is one of the places where pain is registered.

   a. thalamus
   b. midbrain
   c. hindbrain
   d. cerebellum

23. Motivation and emotional responses are governed by a forebrain region called the:

   a. thalamus
   b. corpus callosum
   c. cerebral cortex
   d. hypothalamus

24. Complex behavior is regulated in two hemispheres of the forebrain called the:

   a. association areas
   b. cerebral cortex
   c. corpus callosum
   d. motor projection areas

25. The _____ is a band of nerve fibers that connects the two hemispheres of the brain and coordinates their activities.

   a. corpus callosum
   b. limbic system
   c. reticular formation
   d. hippocampus

26. The _____ lobe receives and interprets visual information.

   a. frontal
   b. parietal
   c. temporal
   d. occipital

27. The _____ lobe responds to sensations of touch and bodily position.

   a. frontal
   b. temporal
   c. occipital
   d. parietal

28. A ring of structures around the brain stem that plays a role in learning and emotional behavior is called:

   a. the limbic system
   b. the hypothalamus
   c. temporal formation
   d. reticular formation

29. The primary function of _____ is to alert and arouse the higher parts of the brain.

   a. the amygdala
   b. the hippocampus
   c. reticular formation
   d. the limbic system

30. The _____ division of the autonomic nervous system prepares the body for quick action in any emergency.

    a.   sympathetic   c.   somatic
    b.   central   d.   parasympathetic

31. The hormone that regulates the rate of metabolism is:

    a.   insulin   c.   glucogen
    b.   vasopressin   d.   thyroxin

32. Levels of calcium and phosphate in the blood and tissue fluids are regulated by the _____ gland(s).

    a.   pineal   c.   parathyroid
    b.   pituitary   d.   adrenal

33. The _____ is/are known as the "master gland(s)."

    a.   anterior pituitary   c.   posterior pituitary
    b.   adrenals   d.   thyroid

34. The main ingredient of chromosomes and genes is:

    a.   RNA   c.   DNA
    b.   hormones   d.   ACTH

Answers for this section:

1. b (37)	7. d (38)	13. c (41)	19. a (46)	25. a (52)	31. d (63)
2. d (38)	8. b (38)	14. a (41)	20. d (47)	26. d (48)	32. c (63)
3. b (38)	9. c (39)	15. d (42)	21. c (46)	27. d (48)	33. a (64)
4. d (38)	10. b (40)	16. a (42)	22. b (47)	28. a (55)	34. c (67)
5. a (38)	11. b (40)	17. b (45)	23. d (47)	29. c (55)	
6. c (38)	12. a (41)	18. a (47)	24. b (47)	30. a (60)	

Understanding the Facts

Now that you have found that you can recognize facts from Physiology and Behavior, the next step is to determine if you understand the meaning of newly-learned information. These multiple-choice questions require a higher level of thinking. They will help you establish more solid connections and provide practice in dealing with higher level concepts.

35. Myelin is to axon as:

    a. leaf is to tree
    b. door knob is to door
    c. thermal underwear is to body
    d. fire is to furnace

36. If you could take hold of the bottom of a nerve cell body and pull it downward as far as it would go, you would be holding a/an:

    a. dendrite
    b. axon
    c. myelin sheath
    d. ion

37. A neural impulse or action potential can be compared with:

    a. lightning hitting a tree
    b. a house on fire
    c. a fuse burning from one end to the other
    d. an extinguished candle

38. A polarized neuron is similar to a:

    a. loaded gun
    b. gun with no ammunition
    c. firecracker with no fuse
    d. lighted match

39. Impulses traveling on non-myelinated axons resemble:

    a. a frog leaping across the lawn
    b. fire moving down a fuse
    c. a duck landing on a pond
    d. a car racing on a track

40. Alzheimer's disease may be attributable to a reduction of _____.

    a. myelin
    b. dopamine
    c. acetylcholine (ACh)
    d. norepinephrine

41. Which of the following neurotransmitters appears to be a more powerful painkiller than morphine?

    a. the endorphins   c. ACh
    b. dopamine   d. serotonin

42. Which of the following neural transmitters seems to play an important role in schizophrenia?

    a. serotonin   c. ACh
    b. norepinephrine   d. dopamine

43. In the spring of 1992, a baby in Florida was "born without a brain." This statement was not entirely true, for she could breathe with no artificial assistance. Which of the following brain structures or regions did she have?

    a. thalamus   c. hypothalamus
    b. medulla   d. corpus callosum

44. Although Phineas Gage survived the tamping iron accident with no apparent impairment of memory and skills, he lacked goal directed behavior and was prone to emotional outbursts. Which lobe of his brain was damaged?

    a. temporal   c. frontal
    b. parietal   d. occipital

45. Which of the following statements about hemispheric specialization is **true**?

    a. Business and industry should promote a "right-brain movement."
    b. Not everyone shows the same differences between left and right hemispheres.
    c. In most people, the right hemisphere is dominant in verbal tasks.
    d. The left hemisphere excels at visual and spatial tasks.

46. Severe damage to the amygdala and hippocampus would result in which of the following conditions? The person:

    a. would go into a coma
    b. would not be able to pay attention to relevant stimuli
    c. would not remember names and faces learned before the injury
    d. cannot form new memories

47. When a person is frightened or angry, which of the following divisions of the nervous system is in command? The _____ nervous system.

    a. sympathetic division of the autonomic
    b. somatic
    c. parasympathetic division of the autonomic
    d. peripheral

48. Recently there has been an increase in new businesses offering special light treatments to people who suffer from depression during the dark winter months. These questionable enterprises are attempting to capitalize on the function of which of the following glands?

    a. parathyroid   c. pineal
    b. adrenal   d. pituitary

49. Which of the following theorists would be **most** likely to attack Francis Galton's conclusions about the heritability of genius?

    a. John B. Watson   c. Sigmund Freud
    b. Charles Darwin   d. John Dewey

50. Characteristics such as intelligence, height, and weight:

    a. are controlled by single genes
    b. are produced by dominant genes
    c. result from the process of polygenic inheritance and environment
    d. are produced by recessive genes

51. Although it is difficult to devise methods of determining the heritability of behavioral traits in humans, progress was made in the last decade through:

    a. selection studies   c. strain studies
    b. the Human Genome Project d. a closer look at Galton's research

52. In attempting to find the relative influence of heredity and environment on human behavior, psychologists have traditionally employed:

    a. Galton's techniques   c. selection studies
    b. strain studies   d. twin studies and family studies

Answers for this section

35. c (38)	41. a (43)	47. a (60)
36. b (38)	42. d (42)	48. c (63)
37. c (39)	43. b (46)	49. a (67)
38. a (38)	44. c (49)	50. c (68)
39. b (39)	45. b (54)	51. b (70)
40. c (42)	46. d (55, 57)	52. d (70, 71)

Applying the Facts

The learning of facts and concepts is of little value unless it can be applied and employed to solve problems. The next group of multiple-choice questions reflects applications of your learning.

53. Suzette is a filing clerk in an office. She opens most of the mail and puts it in the proper places, but has no idea what to do with it beyond that activity. You have a brain structure that is analogous to Suzette's job. It is called the:

   a. medulla
   b. pons

   c. thalamus
   d. corpus callosum

54. Your psychology class has just begun. You are a little sleepy and are not paying much attention. Suddenly your professor announces a test for Tuesday you quickly noted that information. Which brain region or structure assisted you in paying attention?

   a. reticular formation
   b. limbic system

   c. thalamus
   d. hippocampus

55. Jimmie, a 2-year-old, accidentally puts his finger into a light socket. He instantaneously pulled his hand away. He did not have to learn to do this. Which structure enabled him to do this?

   a. the spinal cord
   b. the autonomic nervous system

   c. reticular formation
   d. the hippocamus

56. You are walking in the forest. You hear a noise and turn to see a coiled rattlesnake. Which part of your nervous system takes control of you? The:

    a.   somatic nervous system
    b.   parasympathetic division of the autonomic nervous system
    c.   sympathic division of the autonomic nervous system
    d.   cerebral cortex

57. Lafitte is a poodle who travels with his master. He got out of the car to take a walk and collapsed. His master forced some corn syrup into Lafitte's mouth and within a few minutes he was back to normal. Which endocrine gland is not functioning properly?

    a.   pineal   c.   the adrenals
    b.   thyroid   d.   pancreas

58. Mollie, age 18, was diagnosed as having a benign tumor in her brain. Among other problems, she had symptoms of menopause. The tumor had grown around the _____ gland, making it impossible for the other glands to function.

    a.   thyroid   c.   pituitary
    b.   ovaries   d.   pineal

59. Amanda's parents both have brown eyes, but she was born with blue eyes. Which of the following explanations is correct?

    a.   The gene for blue eyes is dominant.
    b.   She received B genes from both parents.
    c.   She received b genes from both parents.
    d.   She receive a B gene from one parent and a b gene from the other.

60. It is important that there is fat in the diet of a pregnant woman and in the diet of the newborn and for many months after birth. From what you know about the central nervous system, fat is especially crucial to the development of which of the following?

    a.   reticular formation   c.   axons
    b.   dendrites   d.   myelin sheath

61. Professor Smith was forced to retire early because of Parkinson's disease. Which of the following neurotransmitters is **most** likely involved?

    a.   dopamine   c.   norepinephrine
    b.   serotonin   d.   endorphins

62. Your friend contracted botulism. There was some paralysis, but he survived. Which of the following situations is the correct explanation for the paralysis?

    a.   The inhibitory serotonin was reduced.
    b.   Chemicals leaked out of the synaptic vesicles.
    c.   Botulism prevented the release of ACh.
    d.   Too much ACh poured into the synapses.

Answers for this section:

53. c (47)	58. c (64)
54. a (55)	59. c (68)
55. a (59)	60. d (38)
56. c (60)	61. a (42)
57. d (64)	62. c (43)

Fill-in-the-Blank Questions: Recalling What You Have Learned

By now, there should be a considerable amount of new information about Physiology and Behavior in long-term memory. The following questions of recall rather than recognition will show if you are becoming more comfortable with the material.

Remembering the Facts

1. Individual cells that are the smallest unit of the nervous system are called
_____.

2. A single long fiber extending from the cell body is termed a/an _____.

3. A group of axons bundled together is called a/an _____.

4. The fatty covering around some axons is called the _____
_____.

5. Short fibers that branch out from the cell body and pick up incoming messages are the _____.

6. The condition of a neuron at rest is called _____.

7. A period after firing when the neuron will not fire again is called the
_____ _____ period.

8. _____ and _____ are chemical substances involved in the reduction of pain.

9. The central nervous system consists of the _____ and _____ _____.

10. The _____ connect(s) the cerebral cortex at the top of the brain to the cerebellum.

11. The part of the hindbrain that controls breathing, heart rate, and blood pressure is called the _____.

12. The forebrain region that governs motivation and emotional responses is called the _____.

13. Most complex behavior is regulated by the _____ _____.

14. A band of nerve fibers that connects the two hemispheres of the brain is called the _____ _____.

15. The part of the cerebral cortex that responds to sensations of touch and bodily position is called the _____ lobe.

16. A network of neurons whose primary function is to arouse the higher parts of the brain is called _____ _____.

17. A ring of structures around the brain stem that plays a role in learning and emotional behavior is called the _____ _____.

18. The _____ nervous system carries messages between the central nervous system and the internal organs.

19. The _____ system is composed of glands that release hormones into the bloodstream.

20. _____ is a hormone that controls the level of calcium and phosphate in the blood and tissue fluids.

21. _____ is a hormone secreted by the adrenal glands that activates the sympathetic nervous system.

22. The study of the relationship between heredity and behavior is called _____ _____.

23. The main ingredient of chromosomes and genes is _____.

24. Pairs of threadlike bodies within the cell nucleus that contain the genes are called _____.

25. The member of a gene pair that controls the appearance of a certain trait is called a/an _____ gene.

26. The process in which several genes interact to produce a certain trait is called _____ _____.

27. _____ studies can be used with animals to estimate heritability.

28. _____ twins develop from a single ovum.

Answers to this section:

1. neurons (37)
2. axon (38)
3. nerve (38)
4. myelin sheath (38)
5. dendrites (38)
6. polarization (38)
7. absolute refractory (40)
8. endorphins, enkephalins (42)
9. brain, spinal cord (45)
10. pons (47)
11. medulla (46)
12. hypothalamus (47)
13. cerebral cortex (47)
14. corpus callosum (52)

15. parietal (48)
16. reticular formation (55)
17. limbic system (55)
18. autonomic (60)
19. endocrine (62)
20. parathormone (63)
21. epinephrine (66)
22. behavior genetics (67)
23. deoxyribonucleic acid or DNA (67)
24. chromosomes (67)
25. dominant (68)
26. polygenic inheritance (68)
27. selection (70)
28. identical (71)

Understanding and Applying the Facts

As you previously did with recognition-type questions, you will now move to a higher level of recall. The following questions will determine if you understand the facts.

29. The _____ _____ is pinched at intervals which make the _____ resemble a string of microscopic sausages.

30. Like a loaded gun, a _____ neuron is ready to fire when it is properly triggered.

31. Some neurotransmitters are destroyed by other chemicals in the synapse, but others are recycled. An example of this is _____.

32. We jump across the synaptic space and hook up at the proper place on the next neuron. They call us _____.

33. If you have a toothache, you might hope that your brain would produce more _____ and _____.

34. The effects of the venom of a black widow spider and the effects of _____ are the same, for they both speed up the release of transmitters into the synaptic space.

35. The reason that the 2 to 3 square foot cerebral cortex can fit inside of the skull is because it is _____.

36. Jim lost his sense of touch because of a head injury. The damage is most likely in the _____ lobe.

37. The cerebral cortex accounts for about _____ percent of human brain weight and contains _____ percent of the neurons in the central nervous system.

38. When the doctor taps your knee with a rubber mallet, you kick. This is an example of a _____ and it is processed in the _____ _____.

39. Spinal reflexes enable the body to avoid serious damage, therefore they are called _____ reflexes.

40. Spinal reflexes would not work without help from the _____ nervous system.

41. If you become depressed during the dark winter months, there is speculation (not yet supported by research) that too much _____ is released by the _____ gland in response to reduced light.

42. The two integrating systems that are constantly in action in human and animal life are the _____ system and the _____ system.

43. Just as you are getting out of your car you see someone coming toward you with a gun. Instantly your heart beats faster, digestion stops, the pupils of your eyes enlarge, and you run faster than ever before to safety. You were able to do this because of the hormone _____ secreted by the _____ gland(s).

Answers for this section:

29. myelin sheath, axon (38)
30. polarized (38)
31. dopamine (43)
32. neurotransmitters (42)
33. endorphins, enkephalins (42)
34. amphetamines (44)
35. convoluted (47)
36. parietal (48)

37. 80, 70 (47)
38. reflex, spinal cord (59)
39. protective (59)
40. peripheral (59)
41. melatonin, pineal (63)
42. endocrine, nervous (62)
43. epinephrine, adrenal (66)

Testing Yourself For Mastery

The following terms and concepts are found in boldface or italics in the chapter. The time has come to determine if you can define and discuss your new learning in your own words, then check your work against the text.

endocrine system

neuron

cell body

dendrites

axon

nerve

myelin sheath

sensory or afferent neurons

motor or efferent neurons

ions

polarization

neural impulse or action potential

graded potential

absolute refractory period

relative refractory period

nodes

axon terminal or synaptic knob

synaptic space or synaptic cleft

synapse

synaptic vesicles

neurotransmitters

receptor site

acetylcholine (ACh)

dopamine

serotonin

norepinephrine

enkephalins and endorphins

central nervous system

peripheral nervous system

hindbrain

medulla

pons

cerebellum

brain stem

midbrain

forebrain

thalamus

hypothalamus

cerebral cortex

convolutions

sensory projection areas

motor projection areas

association areas

four brain lobes

corpus callosum

reticular formation (RF)

limbic system

hippocampus

somatic nervous system

autonomic nervous system

sympathetic division

parasympathetic division

hormones

endocrine glands

thyroid gland

thyroxin

parathyroids

parathormone

pancreas

insulin and glucogen

pituitary gland

posterior pituitary

posterior pituitary

anterior pituitary

gonads

adrenal glands

adrenal cortex

adrenal medulla

beta endorphin

ACTH

epinephrine

behavior genetics

genetics

genes

chromosomes

deoxyribonucleic acid (DNA)

dominant gene

recessive gene

polygenic inheritance

strain studies

selection studies

family studies

twin studies

identical twins

fraternal twins

adoption studies

amniocentesis

Integrating Your Newly Learned Information

Now that you have recognized, recalled, and given definition to Physiology and Behavior, you are ready to try to integrate your knowledge in a definitive discussion through short-answer questions.

1. Draw a picture of a neuron and label all of its components. (37)

2. Describe how a neuron carries messages. Include the terms: polarization, action potential, absolute refractory period, relative refractory period, and the all-or-none law in your answer. (38-40)

3. Discuss the function of the synapse. Include the proper terminology and incorporate the role of neurotransmitters. (40-43)

4. Describe the cerebral cortex and discuss its major characteristics. (47, 48 & 50)

5. Outline the function of the four lobes of the cerebral cortex. (40, 49)

6. Summarize the research findings on hemispheric specialization. (51-54)

7. Describe the functions of reticular formation and the limbic system. (55, 57)

8. Discuss the functions of the peripheral nervous system and its divisions. (59-62)

9. Choose two of the glands of the endocrine system. Indicate the hormone or hormones released by each and explain how they regulate a body function. (63-66)

10. Discuss the methods used by psychologists to attempt to determine the heritability of behavioral traits. (69-72)

Applications

You have worked through a section of recognition-type and recall questions to determine if you can apply information to real-life situations. It is time to try to respond to some applications. Some are based upon those questions. Answers to this section will not be given. Your questions concerning these applications will serve as a basis for classroom discussion and ideas for class projects throughout the course.

1. Because of advances in behavior genetics, there is an improved ability to predict birth defects in babies not yet conceived. What might be some of the positive effects of this new knowledge? Think of at least two serious ethical considerations that must be addressed by this new ability.

2. Evan was born in Wales. He has blue eyes. He says that if a person claims to be Welsh, but does not have blue eyes, that person is not pure Welsh. Is Evan just telling a story or is it possible that his statement is true? Try to find an explanation for this.

3. Why would it be unwise, if not dangerous, to give skim milk to a baby under two years of age?

4. You have responded to a question about Mollie who had a brain tumor that had grown around the pituitary gland. The gland could not function. She had symptoms of menopause at age 18. Explain why this would happen.

Return to Chapter Summary

Now that you have concluded these exercises, you should go back and reread the chapter summary in your textbook. It provides you with a framework that integrates all of this newly-learned information. By reviewing the chapter summary, you will strengthen the many connections between the various new pieces of information.

SENSATION AND PERCEPTION

3

After you have read and studied this chapter, you should be able to:

1. Trace the path of light from the time it enters the eye until it reaches the receptor cells.
2. Distinguish between rods and cones, and list their characteristics and functions with respect to light, color, and how they connect to other cells.
3. Describe the process of adaptation, including the phenomenon of afterimages.
4. Explain how messages entering the eye are processed in the brain.
5. Describe the three basic properties of color. Distinguish between additive and subtractive color mixing.
6. Describe the two main theories of color vision.
7. Identify the characteristics of sound.
8. Describe the structure of the ear and explain the functions of the various parts.
9. State the two theories of pitch discrimination.
10. Explain the importance of the vestibular senses and describe the functions of the two divisions.
11. Summarize the theories which explain how the sense of smell is activated by chemical substances.
12. Explain the processes involved in the sense of taste and name the four primary qualities of taste.
13. Explain how the sensations of pressure, warmth, and cold originate and how people respond to them.
14. Describe three theories of pain.

15. Discuss the problems of deafness and tinnitus.
16. Discuss the principles of perceptual organization identified by the Gestaltists.
17. Define perceptual constancy and identify four kinds.
18. Describe four observer characteristics which can affect perception.
19. Identify the contributions of both monocular and binocular cues of depth.
20. Explain real movement. Define and give three examples of apparent movement.
21. Describe two kinds of visual illusions.

Multiple-Choice Questions: Recognizing What You Have Learned

These questions ask only that you recognize what you have learned. When you recognize a correct answer, you have accessed that information in memory. A knowledge of facts serves as a framework for later analysis and problem solving.

Remembering the Facts

This group of multiple-choice questions requires that you simply recognize facts from your textbook.

1. Light enters the eye through the:

   a. pupil   c. cornea
   b. iris   d. lens

2. The colored part of the eye is the:

   a. pupil   c. retina
   b. cornea   d. iris

3. The opening in the center of the iris is called the:

   a. pupil   c. lens
   b. cornea   d. retina

4. The lining of the eye containing light sensitive receptor cells is called the:

   a. fovea   c. iris
   b. retina   d. cornea

5.   Rods and cones are located in the:

a.   retina   c.   lens
b.   fovea   d.   iris

6.   People who have normal color vision are called:

a.   monochromats   c.   fullchromats
b.   dichromats   d.   trichomats

7.   The ability to see colors is nonexistent in:

a.   cats   c.   rodents
b.   tree shrews   d.   apes

8.   The number of cycles per second in a wave is called:

a.   frequency   c.   pitch
b.   Hz   d.   amplitude

9.   The height of the wave represents its:

a.   pitch   c.   amplitude
b.   frequency   d.   decibel

10. The unit of measurement for the loudness of sounds is the:

a.   bell   c.   Hz
b.   bel   d.   decibel

11. The unit of measurement for the frequency of waves is the:

a.   hertz (Hz)   c.   bell
b.   decibel   d.   bel

12. Tones that result from sound waves that are multiples of the basic tone are called:

a.   decibels   c.   timbres
b.   Hz's   d.   overtones

13. The quality or texture of a sound caused by overtones is called:

a.   pitch   c.   timbre
b.   amplitude   d.   richness

14. A structure on the surface of the basilar membrane that contains receptor cells for hearing is called the:

   a. organ of Corti   c. cochlea
   b. auditory nerve   d. oval organ

15. The part of the inner ear containing fluid that vibrates is called the:

   a. round window   c. cochlea
   b. oval window   d. organ of Corti

16. A double bass can reach down to about:

   a. 50 Hz   c. 10 Hz
   b. 20 Hz   d. 5 Hz

17. The human ear responds to frequencies from about _____ Hz to _____ Hz.

   a. 50, 5,000   c. 25, 35,000
   b. 20, 20,000   d. 50, 10,000

18. The bundle of neurons that carries signals from each ear to the brain is called the:

   a. vestibular nerve   c. cochlea
   b. organ of Corti   d. auditory nerve

19. Nasal membranes containing receptor cells sensitive to odors are called olfactory:

   a. pheromones   c. bulbs
   b. epithelium   d. mercaptan

20. A/an _____ is a chemical that communicates information to other organisms through smell.

   a. anosmia   c. pheromone
   b. mercaptan   d. papillae

21. Small bumps on the tongue that contain taste buds are called:

   a. papillae   c. pheromones
   b. anosmias   d. nodes

22. _____ sacs in the inner ear are responsible for sensing gravitation and movement.

   a.   Semicircular   c.   Vestibular
   b.   Sensory   d.   Rotational

23. Pressure, temperature, and pain are called the _____ senses.

   a.   cutaneous   c.   vestibular
   b.   paradoxical   d.   kinesthetic

24. According to gate control theory, pain is transmitted to the brain through a "neurological gate" in the:

   a.   limbic system   c.   spinal cord
   b.   hypothalamus   d.   parietal lobe

25. The process of putting meaning into raw sensory information is called:

   a.   sensation   c.   deception
   b.   conception   d.   perception

26. The German word Gestalt, roughly translated, means:

   a.   whole   c.   figure
   b.   shape   d.   contour

27. Visual cues requiring the use of one eye are called _____ cues.

   a.   binocular   c.   linear
   b.   monocular   d.   superposition

28. Objects are perceived in their true magnitude even when the viewer is far away from them because of:

   a.   size constancy and experience
   b.   an illusion
   c.   a hallucination
   d.   shape constancy and genetic influence

29. Superposition is a/an _____ cue for depth perception.

   a.   innate   c.   binocular
   b.   monocular   d.   linear

30. Texture gradient is a/an _____ cue for depth perception.

   a. binocular   c. monocular
   b. ineffective   d. superpositioned

31. The combination of two retinal images to give a three-dimensional perceptual experience is called:

   a. motion parallax   c. aerial perspective
   b. shadowing   d. stereoscopic vision

32. The difference between the two images the eyes receive is known as:

   a. retinal disparity   c. convergence
   b. retinal parallax   d. monocular disparity

33. Convergence of the eyes is a/an _____ due to distance.

   a. learned   c. binocular
   b. monocular   d. inaccurate

34. Sound localization requires us to determine both distance and:

   a. direction   c. timbre
   b. depth   d. intensity

35. The perception that a stationary object is actually moving is known as:

   a. a physical illusion   c. an autokinetic illusion
   b. the phi phenomenon   d. stroboscopic motion

36. A distortion of information reaching receptor cells is called a/an:

   a. hallucination   c. delusion
   b. physical illusion   d. perceptual illusion

37. Stroboscopic motion is a/an:

   a. delusion   c. illusion
   b. allusion   d. hallucination

38. Stroboscopic motion causes a perceptual illusion known as:

a. the phi phenomenon
b. an autokinetic illusion
c. binocular disparity
d. monocular disparity

39. Misleading cues that cause us to create perceptions that are inaccurate or impossible are called:

a. perceptual illusions
b. phi's
c. physical illusions
d. autokinetic illusions

Answers for this section:

1. c (83)   8. a (95)   15. c (98)   22. c (105)   29. b (119)   36. b (125)
2. d (83)   9. c (96)   16. a (95)   23. a (107)   30. c (119)   37. c (125)
3. a (83)   10. d (96)   17. b (95)   24. c (108)   31. d (121)   38. a (125)
4. b (83)   11. a (95)   18. d (98)   25. d (109)   32. a (121)   39. a (125)
5. a (84)   12. d (96)   19. b (102)   26. a (109)   33. c (122)
6. d (92)   13. c (96)   20. c (103)   27. b (119)   34. a (123)
7. c (94)   14. a (98)   21. a (104)   28. a (115)   35. c (125)

Understanding the Facts

Now that you have found that you can recognize facts from Sensation and Perception, the next step is to determine if you understand the meaning of newly-learned information. These multiple-choice questions require a higher level of thinking. They will help you establish more solid connections and provide practice in dealing with higher level concepts.

40. The tick of a watch from 20 feet in quiet conditions, a drop of perfume diffused throughout a three-room apartment, and a candle flame seen from 30 miles on a clear dark night are all examples of:

a. the difference threshold
b. a jnd
c. the absolute threshold
d. an experience threshold

41. Turning on a light at sunset is more noticeable than turning on the same light at noon on a sunny day. This is an example of the _____ threshold.

a. difference
b. sensory
c. perceived
d. absolute

42. Retina is to eye as:

   a.   shutter is to camera
   b.   film is to camera
   c.   ammunition is to gun
   d.   light bulb is to lamp

43. When we focus on an object that is very close to the eyes, the muscles around the lens contract and make the lens:

   a.   flatter   c.   fatter
   b.   thicker   d.   rounder

44. When we focus on an object that is far away, the muscles around the eye make the lens:

   a.   rounder   c.   flatter
   b.   bigger   d.   thicker

45. The depressed spot on the retina directly behind the lens is called the:

   a.   fovea   c.   cornea
   b.   receptor cell   d.   iris

46. Images that pass through the lens are in sharpest focus in the:

   a.   retina   c.   fovea
   b.   rods   d.   cones

47. The _____ occupy/occupies the center of the visual field.

   a.   retina   c.   pupil
   b.   fovea   d.   lens

48. _____ respond(s) to varying degrees of light and dark, but not to color.

   a.   Cones   c.   The retina
   b.   Receptor cells   d.   Rods

49. Which of the following statements is **true**?

   a. There are no cones in the fovea.
   b. The fovea contains rods and cones.
   c. Cones are found mainly in the fovea.
   d. Toward the edges of the retina, rods and cones predominate.

50. The one-to-one connection between cones and bipolar neurons:

   a. diminishes the ability to distinguish fine details
   b. allows for maximum visual acuity
   c. makes dim light vision possible
   d. eliminates the need for intense light

51. Axons of the ganglion cells join to form the:

   a. optic nerve   c. cones
   b. rods   d. fovea

52. The colors red, white, blue, and green, used in color television, are an example of:

   a. color purity   c. saturation of wavelengths
   b. subtractive color mixing d. additive color mixing

53. Young-Helmholtz theory says that:

   a. Cones are sensitive to one of three colors red, green, or blue.
   b. The retina has 319 different kinds of cones.
   c. The human eye can discriminate 319 different colors.
   d. Rods are sensitive to one of three colors red, green, or blue.

54. We can never see a yellowish blue or reddish green light. This statement comes from:

   a. trichromatic theory
   b. the work of Thomas Young
   c. the work of Hermann von Helmholtz
   d. opponent-process theory

55. The hammer, anvil, and stirrup are located in the:

   a. inner ear   c. oval window
   b. middle ear   d. organ of Corti

56. Which of the following statements about theories of hearing is **not** true?

   a. Neither place theory nor frequency fully explains pitch discrimination.
   b. The volley principle explains the ear's response to frequencies up to about 4,000 Hz.
   c. Place theory fully explains pitch discrimination.
   d. A combination of place theory and frequency theory is needed to explain pitch discrimination.

57. The only neurons known to be replaced in the human body are those:

   a. with myelated axons
   b. in the brain stem
   c. in the olfactory bulbs
   d. in the olfactory epithelium

58. A door viewed from an angle casts a trapezoidal image on the retina, but it is perceived as a rectangle. This is an example of:

   a. shape constancy
   b. an illusion
   c. perceptual error
   d. a perceptual expectation

59. Which of the following statements about perception is **not** true?

   a. Past experience is a powerful factor in perception.
   b. Preconceptions influence perception.
   c. Both eyes are needed for perception of depth and distance.
   d. One's desires and needs may strongly influence perception.

60. A pygmy from the Mbuti of Zaire saw a herd of buffalo at a distance on the plain. He asked what kind of insects they were. This is an example of the influence of _____ on perception.

   a. retinal disparity
   b. cultural background
   c. cognitive style
   d. motivation

61. A basketball is perceived as a spherical object. Without _____ it might be perceived as a flat disk.

   a. shadows
   b. texture gradient
   c. binocular cues
   d. superposition

62. Superposition, aerial perspective, shadowing, elevation, and texture gradient:

    a.   are binocular cues for distance and depth
    b.   are combinations of binocular and monocular cues for distance and depth
    c.   employ retinal disparity in perceiving depth
    d.   are monocular cues for distance and depth

63. Slight movements of eye muscles which usually go unnoticed are responsible for:

    a.   the phi phenomenon   c.   perceptual illusions
    b.   physical illusions   d.   the autokinetic effect

64. The bent appearance of a stick when placed in water is an example of:

    a.   a perceptual illusion   c.   a physical illusion
    b.   the phi phenomenon   d.   induced movement

Answers for this section:

40. c (81)	45. a (84)	50. b (86)	55. b (98)	60. b (118)
41. a (82)	46. c (84)	51. a (88)	56. c (99, 100)	61. a (120)
42. b (83)	47. b (84)	52. d (91)	57. d (102)	62. d (119, 120)
43. d (84)	48. d (84)	53. a (92)	58. a (115)	63. d (125)
44. c (84)	49. c (84)	54. d (93)	59. c (115-119)	64. c (125)

Applying the Facts

The learning of facts and concepts is of little value unless it can be applied and employed to solve problems. The next group of multiple-choice questions reflects applications of your learning.

65. An unscrupulous carpet manufacturer produced samples with a certain fiber density, but when the actual product was shipped to the customer, the density was slightly lower, giving the manufacturer a handsome profit. It is possible that he had knowledge of:

    a.   cutaneous perception   c.   adaptation
    b.   the difference threshold   d.   the absolute threshold

66. Hypothetically, if a researcher examined the eye of an animal and found no cone cells in the retina, a conclusion might be made that the animal:

a. was color-blind c. could not perceive color
b. had night blindness d. had retinal disparity

67. You noticed that your dog will not eat the green biscuits in the multi-flavor box of dog goodies. Which of the following explanations is the **most** valid? The dog:

a. does not like the color green
b. does not like the flavor of the green biscuits
c. once choked on a green biscuit
d. once became sick after eating a green biscuit

68. The Lahser Road exit on an Interstate highway through metropolitan Detroit is misspelled. It reads "Lasher Road," but it apparently causes no great confusion. This is an example of:

a. perceptual feedback c. cognitive leveling
b. superposition d. perceptual generalization

69. Joe is blind in one eye. Which of the following statements about Joe's vision is **true**? He:

a. does not have retinal disparity
b. cannot experience motion parallax
c. cannot perceive depth
d. cannot experience texture gradient

70. None of us would be enjoying the "movies" if it were not for the phenomenon of:

a. phi c. perceptual illusions
b. the autokinetic illusion d. stroboscopic motion

71. Evan, the Welshman, has blue eyes. When we notice the color, we are responding to which part of the visual system? The:

a. pupil c. lens
b. iris d. cornea

72. You bought an expensive cage for your pet hamster. It has multi-colored fittings and exercise devices. The color of these trappings:

    a.   is lost on the hamster because he is color-blind
    b.   causes your hamster to be more active
    c.   will improve the hamster's visual acuity
    d.   will improve your hamster's intelligence

Answers for this section:

65. b (82)	67. b (118)	69. a (125)	71. b (83)
66. c (84)	68. d (122)	70. d (83)	72. a (94)

Fill-in-the-Blank Questions: Recalling What You Have Learned

By now, there should be a considerable amount of new information about Sensation and Perception in long-term memory. The following questions of recall rather than recognition will show if you are becoming more comfortable with the material.

Remembering the Facts

1. The least amount of energy that can be detected as a stimulation 50 percent of the time is called the _____ threshold.

2. The smallest change in stimulation that can be detected 50 percent of the time is called the _____ threshold.

3. The depressed spot on the retina is called the _____.

4. The transparent protective coating over the front part of the eye is called the _____.

5. The _____ is the colored part of the eye.

6. The transparent part of the eye that focuses light onto the retina is called the _____.

7. The _____ is the lining of the eye containing light-sensitive receptor cells.

8. _____ are receptor cells in the retina responsible for night vision.

9. Receptor cells in the retina responsible for color vision are called _____.

10. The ability to distinguish fine details is termed visual _____.

11. _____ is the adjustment of the senses to stimulation.

12. A sensory experience that occurs after a visual stimulus has been removed is known as a/an _____.

13. _____ cells join to form the optic nerve which carries messages from each eye to the brain.

14. The place on the retina where the axons of all the ganglion cells leave the eye and where there are no receptors is called the _____ _____.

15. Some fibers in the optic nerve from each eye cross to the other side of the brain at a point near the base of the brain called the _____ _____.

16. The aspect of color that corresponds to names such as red, green, and blue is termed _____.

17. _____ is the vividness or richness of a hue.

18. The nearness of a color to white as opposed to black is called _____.

19. _____ color mixing is the process of mixing lights of different wavelengths to create new hues.

20. The process of mixing pigments, each of which absorbs some wavelengths of light and reflects others is called _____ color mixing.

21. _____ theory holds that all color perception derives from three different color receptors in the retina.

22. People who have normal color vision are called _____.

23. _____ - _____ theory holds that three sets of color receptors respond in an either/or fashion to determine the experienced color.

24. The primary determinant of pitch is _____.

25. A/an _____ is the unit of measurement for the frequency of waves.

26. _____ is an auditory experience corresponding primarily to frequency of sound vibrations.

27. _____ is the magnitude of a wave.

28. The unit of measurement for the loudness of sounds is termed a/an _____.

29. _____ result from sound waves that are multiples of the basic tone.

30. The quality or texture of a sound caused by overtones is called _____.

31. Three small bones in the middle ear that relay vibrations of the eardrum to the inner ear are the _____, _____, and _____.

32. A part of the inner ear that contains vibrating fluid that causes the basilar membrane to vibrate is called the _____.

33. The organ of _____ on the surface of the basilar membrane contains the receptors cells for hearing.

34. Pitch is determined by the location of greatest vibration of the basilar membrane according to _____ theory.

35. Nasal membranes containing receptor cells sensitive to odors are called the olfactory _____.

36. A chemical that communicates information to other organisms through smell is called a/an _____.

37. _____ are small bumps on the tongue that contain taste buds.

38. Structures in the inner ear that are particularly sensitive to body rotation are called _____ _____.

39. The _____ receptors give us our sense of equilibrium and body position in space.

40. The four perceptual constancies are _____, _____, _____, and _____ constancy.

41. Superposition is a _____ cue for distance perception.

42. Shadowing is a _____ cue for distance and depth perception.

43. _____ vision results from a combination of two retinal images to give a three-dimensional perceptual experience.

44. Retinal disparity is a _____ cue for distance.

45. The perception that a stationary object is actually moving is the definition for a/an _____ _____.

46. The _____ phenomenon is apparent movement caused by flashing lights in sequence.

Answers for this section:

1. absolute (81)
2. difference (82)
3. fovea (84)
4. cornea (83)
5. iris (83)
6. lens (83)
7. retina (83)
8. rods (84)
9. cones (84)
10. acuity (86)
11. adaptation (86)
12. afterimage (87)
13. ganglion (88)
14. blind spot (88)
15. optic chiasm (88)
16. hue (90)
17. saturation (90)
18. brightness (91)
19. additive (91)
20. subtractive (92)
21. trichromatic (92)
22. trichromats (92)
23. opponent-process (93)
24. frequency (95)
25. hertz (Hz) (95)
26. pitch (95)
27. amplitude (96)
28. decibel (96)
29. overtones (96)
30. timbre (96)
31. hammer, anvil, stirrup (98)
32. cochlea (98)
33. Corti (98)
34. Place (99)
35. epithelium (102)
36. pheromone (103)
37. papillae (104)
38. semicircular canals (105)
39. vestibular (105)
40. size, shape, brightness, and color (115)
41. monocular (119)
42. monocular (120)
43. stereoscopic (121)
44. binocular (121)
45. autokinetic illusion (125)
46. phi (125)

Understanding and Applying the Facts

As you previously did with recognition-type questions, you will now move to a higher level of recall. The following questions will determine if you understand the facts.

47. In very bright light, the muscles in the _____ contract to make the _____ smaller and protect the eye from damage.

48. You have probably noticed that the most difficult time of day to drive an automobile is at "dusk." It may be that neither the _____ nor the _____ is/are fully operative under those conditions.

49. The much greater incidence of highway accidents at night can be partially accounted for by problems with _____ _____.

50. _____ perceive as quite separate the colors that humans see as shades of the same color.

51. Above 4,000 Hz _____ theory provides the best explanation for pitch discrimination.

52. You have a friend who suffers from tinnitus. You might suggest that your friend seek relief through a treatment called _____, but to avoid _____ treatment.

53. Sue had open-heart surgery. After she came home from the hospital, her sister gave her a gift of perfume she had never used before. She used it during the recovery period. Five years later, Sue found the perfume in the back of a drawer, opened it, and found herself overwhelmed by emotions and memories of a very difficult time. Neural messages had been sent not only to the temporal lobe, but to the _____ and _____ in the lower brain centers.

54. The profession of dentistry is experimenting with devices that are a direct application of _____ _____ theory.

55. Loud sounds are perceived to be closer than faint sounds. This is an example of a _____ cue to sound location.

56. We do not have to have vision in both eyes to perceive distance and depth because of the existence of _____ _____.

57. The tendency to create three-dimensional perceptual experiences that agree with past experience despite sensory information to the contrary is known as _____ _____ _____.

58. _____ are better able to locate sounds that are on the same level with them, while _____ are better able to locate sounds below them.

59. Flashing lights in a sequence produces the illusion of movement. This is known as the _____ _____.

60. You can deal with the illusion of _____ _____ by looking down at the ground.

Answers for this section:

47. iris, pupil (83)
48. rods, cones (84)
49. dark adaptation (86)
50. monkeys (95)
51. Place (100)
52. masking, drug (101)
53. amygdala, hippocampus (103)
54. gate control (108)
55. monaural (123)

56. monocular cues (119)
57. binocular depth inversion (122)
58. humans, birds (123)
59. phi phenomenon (125)
60. induced movement (129)

Testing Yourself For Mastery

The following terms and concepts are found in boldface or italics in the chapter. The time has come to determine if you can define and discuss your new learning in your own words, then check your work against the text.

absolute threshold

difference threshold

just noticeable difference (jnd)

cornea

pupil

iris

lens

retina

retinal disparity

convergence

binocular depth inversion

sound localization

monaural cue

binaural cue

autokinetic illusion

stroboscopic motion

phi phenomenon

physical illusion

perceptual illusion

fovea

receptor cells

rods

cones

bipolar neurons

visual acuity

adaptation

dark adaptation

light adaptation

afterimage

ganglion cells

optic nerve

blind spot

optic chiasm

hue

saturation

brightness

additive color mixing

complementary colors

primary colors

subtractive color mixing

trichromatic theory

opponent-process theory

trichromats

monochromats

dichromats

frequency

hertz (Hz)

pitch

amplitude

decibel

overtones

timbre

hammer, anvil, stirrup

oval window

round window

cochlea

basilar membrane

organ of Corti

auditory nerve

Place theory of hearing

frequency theory of hearing

volley principle

olfactory epithelium

olfactory bulb

taste buds

papillae

vestibular senses

semicircular canals

vestibular sacs

paradoxical heat

gate control theory

figure

ground

perceptual constancy

size constancy

shape constancy

brightness constancy

color constancy

monocular cues

binocular cues

superposition

linear perspective

aerial perspective

elevation

texture gradient

shadowing

motion parallax

stereoscopic vision

Integrating Your Newly Learned Information

Now that you have recognized, recalled, and given definition to Sensation and Perception, you are ready to try to integrate your knowledge in a definitive discussion through short-answer questions.

1.   Discuss the difference between sensation and perception. (80, 109)

2.   Differentiate between rods and cones and include the physical location and
      function of each. (84)

3.   Contrast trichromatic and opponent-process theories of color vision. (92, 93)

4.   How would a psychologist answer the following well-known question? "If a tree
      falls in the forest and there is no one there, is there a sound?" (95)

5.   Define perceptual constancy and explain two examples of the
      constancies. (113-115)

6.   There are four observer characteristics that influence perception. Explain two of
      them and try to give an example of each. (116-118)

7.   If you had vision in only one eye, could you perceive depth and distance?
      Why? (119-121)

8.   Explain the process of sound localization. (123)

9.   Explain the difference between physical illusion and perceptual illusion. (125)

10.   Explain how we can perceive movement when the objects we are looking at
      remain stationary? (124-125)

Applications

You have worked through a section of recognition-type questions to determine if you can apply information to real-life situations. It is time to try to respond to some applications. Some are based upon those questions. Answers to this section will not be given. Your questions concerning these applications will serve as a basis for classroom discussion and ideas for class projects throughout the course.

1. During the next five days, try to be alert to odors around you and see if you come across one that triggers a memory. Explain why this phenomenon occurs and describe the memory. Is the memory emotional?

2. Frostie, the Bichon, has a favorite toy. It is a blue "ducky." He constantly chases it and carries it around. He also has a green "wart hog" that he totally ignores. There could be many other reasons for this behavior, but for now try to analyze the behavior in terms of what you know about perception.

3. If you are a deer hunter, you know you should wear fluorescent orange for your own protection. Is there any advantage of your wearing fluorescent orange for the deer? If there is, explain why.

4. Pretend that you are Max Wertheimer and explain to the class the reasons why camouflage works.

5. You are the owner of a pet supply store. You took a psychology course. How might you apply your knowledge of human and animal perceptual abilities to increase sales?

Return to Chapter Summary

Now that you have concluded these exercises, you should go back and reread the chapter summary in your textbook. It provides you with a framework that integrates all of this newly-learned information. By reviewing the chapter summary, you will strengthen the many connections between the various new pieces of information.

STATES
OF CONSCIOUSNESS

4

Chapter Objectives

After you have read and studied this chapter, you should be able to:

1. Define sensory deprivation. List three responses of subjects to sensory deprivation.
2. Define altered states of consciousness. List at least six characteristics of them and describe three socially acceptable ones.
3. Identify the various forms of meditation. List the physiological changes that result from meditation.
4. Describe how hypnosis was popularized and why some scientists question whether hypnosis can be characterized as an ASC.
5. Describe three daydream patterns. Identify three views held by different psychologists of the function or purpose of daydreaming.
6. Describe the four stages of sleep.
7. Define REM sleep. Outline the cycle of REM periods.
8. List and describe three sleeping disorders.
9. Differentiate among the dreams of children and men and women. Explain how external stimuli affect dreams.
10. List the general effects of lack of sleep and the specific effects of loss of REM sleep.
11. List the ways drugs are used to alter consciousness. Identify two conditions that can determine the effects of drugs.

12. List two characteristics and two negative effects of each of the following drugs: alcohol, marijuana, amphetamines, barbiturates, the opiates, cocaine, and the hallucinogens.

Multiple-Choice Questions: Recognizing What You Have Learned

These questions ask only that you recognize what you have learned. When you recognize a correct answer, you have accessed that information in memory. A knowledge of facts serves as a framework for later analysis and problem solving.

Remembering the Facts

This group of multiple-choice questions requires that you simply recognize facts from your textbook.

1. About _____ percent of people are considered *fantasy-prone*.

   a. 10   c. 25
   b. 4   d. 2

2. We spend about _____ of our lives in sleep.

   a. 1/3   c. 1/5
   b. 1/10   d. 1/2

3. Stage 4 sleep is marked by:

   a. high blood pressure   c. slow delta waves
   b. rapid eye movements   d. high body temperature

4. The first REM period lasts about:

   a. 30 minutes   c. 1 hour
   b. 10 minutes   d. 5 minutes

5. Over the course of a night, about _____ to _____ percent of the time is spent in stage 2 sleep.

   a. 2, 8   c. 10, 15
   b. 25, 35   d. 45, 50

6. Thoughts, feelings, and perceptions that occur while we are awake and are reasonably alert are called:

   a. waking consciousness
   b. fantasies
   c. an ASC
   d. sensations

7. Altered states such as daydreaming, sleep, and dreaming:

   a. are normal and spontaneous
   b. are deliberate attempts to alter normal consciousness
   c. are categorized as "the unconscious"
   d. do not occur spontaneously

8. Most vivid dreaming occurs during:

   a. NREM
   b. stage 2 sleep
   c. paradoxical sleep
   d. stage 3 sleep

9. On the average, people dream about _____ every night.

   a. 2 hours
   b. 1 hour
   c. 30 minutes
   d. 4 hours

10. Vivid images that occur primarily during REM periods are called:

    a. hypnagogics
    b. fantasies
    c. dreams
    d. illusions

11. Difficulty in falling asleep or remaining asleep throughout the night is called:

    a. apnea
    b. insomnia
    c. narcolepsy
    d. REM rebound

12. _____ is a sleep disorder characterized by breathing difficulty during the night and exhaustion during the day.

    a. Narcolepsy
    b. Insomnia
    c. REM rebound
    d. Apnea

13. Concentration on respiration is a characteristic of:

    a. Zen
    b. TM
    c. Sufism
    d. daydreaming

14. Frenzied dancing and the use of prayer are characteristics of:

    a.   Transcendental Meditation   c.   Zen
    b.   Sufism   d.   mantras

15. Concentration on a mantra is central in:

    a.   sensory deprivation   c.   Sufism
    b.   hypnosis   d.   TM

16. An early term for hypnosis was:

    a.   trance   c.   mesmerism
    b.   mantra   d.   daydreaming

17. Which of the following substances is classified as a depressant?

    a.   opium   c.   cocaine
    b.   alcohol   d.   novocaine

18. Physical and psychological problems that appear if a person reduces or stops using a substance are called:

    a.   tolerance   c.   withdrawal
    b.   dependence   d.   addiction

19. Dependence is sometimes called:

    a.   addiction   c.   tolerance
    b.   a crutch   d.   abuse

20. When increasing amounts of a drug are needed to achieve the same effect, the situation is known as:

    a.   intolerance   c.   addiction
    b.   substance abuse   d.   tolerance

21. Alcohol is a factor in more than _____ of all fatal automobile accidents.

    a.   2/3   c.   1/2
    b.   1/5   d.   3/4

22. The "drug of choice" among Americans of all ages is:

    a.   cocaine   c.   alcohol
    b.   marijuana   d.   tobacco

23. About _____ Americans either abuse alcohol or are dependent upon it.

    a.   10 million   c.   20 million
    b.   350,000   d.   20 percent of

24. Which of the following cultural groups have low rates of alcoholism?

    a.   Jews and Muslims   c.   South Americans
    b.   the British   d.   the Japanese

25. Barbiturates are popularly known as:

    a.   minor tranquilizers   c.   stimulators
    b.   "downers"   d.   "uppers"

26. Amytal, Nembutal, and Seconal are all:

    a.   euphorics
    b.   drugs used to treat schizophrenia
    c.   barbiturates
    d.   minor tranquilizers

27. _____ is the best known of the opiates.

    a.   Heroin   c.   Caffeine
    b.   Amphetamine   d.   Marijuana

28. During most of the nineteenth century and for the early part of this century opium was a widely used ingredient in a patent medicine known as:

    a.   morphine   c.   the "joy plant"
    b.   laudanum   d.   xanthine

29. Which of the following drugs dulls the senses and induces feelings of euphoria?

    a.   cocaine   c.   amphetamines
    b.   nicotine   d.   heroin

30. Which of the following drugs stimulates the sympathetic nervous system?

a. cocaine   c. heroin
b. opium   d. laudanum

31. Amphetamines are chemically similar to which of the following neurotransmitters?

a. dopomine   c. epinephrine
b. norepinephrine   d. serotonin

32. Which of the following has/have, since the 1970's, become popular as "diet pills?"

a. barbiturates   c. hallucinogens
b. amphetamines   d. marijuana

33. Among the most famous users of cocaine was:

a. Charles Darwin   c. B.F. Skinner
b. Timothy Leary   d. Sigmund Freud

34. The most popular illegal drug in use today is:

a. marijuana   c. LSD
b. cocaine   d. PCP

35. LSD, PCP, mescaline, peyote, and psilocybin are classified as:

a. hallucinogens   c. amphetamines
b. barbiturates   d. "downers"

Answers for this section:

1. b (143)   7. a (140) 13. a (158) 19. a (162) 25. b (169) 31. c (172)
2. a (144)   8. c (147) 14. b (158) 20. d (163) 26. c (169) 32. b (172)
3. c (146)   9. a (150) 15. d (159) 21. a (164) 27. a (169) 33. d (173)
4. b (148) 10. c (150) 16. c (159) 22. c (164) 28. b (169) 34. b (174)
5. d (148) 11. b (155) 17. b (163) 23. c (166) 29. d (170) 35. a (174)
6. a (140) 12. d (156) 18. c (163) 24. a (169) 30. a (173)

Understanding the Facts

Now that you have found that you can recognize facts from States of Consciousness, the next step is to determine if you understand the meaning of newly-learned information. These multiple-choice questions require a higher level of thinking. They will help you establish more solid connections and provide practice in dealing with higher level concepts.

36. Although psychology had its early roots in the study of consciousness, the science had to battle the work of _____ to bring the study of consciousness back into favor in the 1950's and 1960's.

    a.   Freud   c.   Dewey
    b.   James   d.   Watson and Skinner

37. Which of the following situations or conditions was **not** a factor in the renewed interest in the scientific study of consciousness?

    a.   the development of electroencephalography
    b.   the death of B.F. Skinner
    c.   the 1960's experimentation with psychedelic drugs
    d.   the widespread use of computers

38. The hallmark of normal waking consciousness is the:

    a.   highly selective nature of attention
    b.   ability to fantasize creatively
    c.   ability to sleep without interruption
    d.   ability to remember the content of dreams

39. Which of the following altered states of consciousness seemingly occurs without effort?

    a.   hypnosis   c.   daydreaming
    b.   meditation   d.   drug use

40. Which of the following statements is **not** true about the daydreams of people who score high on measures of anxiety?

    a.   Their daydreams are related to worrying.
    b.   They take pleasure in their daydreams.
    c.   Their daydreams are loosely connected.
    d.   Their daydreams are not concerned with guilt.

41. A study of fantasy by Lynn and Rhue (1988) found that *fantasy-prone* people:

    a. spend 4 percent of their time lost in elaborative memories
    b. are highly intelligent
    c. felt lonely and isolated as children
    d. are low in creativity

42. Which of the following statements about the reason we need to sleep is the **most** valid?

    a. There is no completely satisfactory explanation for the role of sleep.
    b. The body is depleted of certain chemicals that are restored during sleep.
    c. Protein depletion is the cause of sleep.
    d. A buildup of s-factor is reduced during sleep.

43. During which stage of sleep are the body's voluntary muscles essentially paralyzed?

    a. NREM   c. REM
    b. Stage 4   d. Stage 2

44. According to Freudian theory, dreams take on a highly illogical character because:

    a. they occur only during REM stage
    b. most wishes have been fulfilled in reality
    c. people are consciously aware of their motives
    d. of the process of censorship and symbolic transformation

45. According to Crick and Mitchison (1983), dreaming:

    a. reflects the brain's efforts to free itself of irrelevant thoughts
    b. is generated by random outbursts of nerve cell activity
    c. represents wishes that have not been fulfilled in reality
    d. is an effort to preserve all previous memory associations

46. Which of the following statements about the length of dreams is **true**?

    a. They flash on your mental screen just before waking.
    b. Dreams last about as long as the events would be in real life.
    c. Only external stimuli can modify the length of a dream.
    d. Only internal stimuli can modify the length of a dream.

47. Narcolepsy is thought to be caused by:

    a. drug abuse
    b. over-use of sleeping pills
    c. a defect in the central nervous system
    d. inability to enter into REM sleep

48. Which of the following conditions remained relatively unimpaired for subjects of sleep deprivation studies?

    a. visual acuity and perception of brightness
    b. olfactory perception
    c. patterns of sleep and wakefulness
    d. perceptions of movement

49. Which of the following statements about meditation is **not** true?

    a. It is an altered state of consciousness.
    b. Meditation is a product of the 1960's.
    c. Meditation reduces the activity of the sympathetic nervous system.
    d. Alpha brainwaves increase noticeably during meditation.

50. Which of the following statements about hypnosis is **not** true?

    a. Clinical and therapeutic uses of hypnosis are universally effective.
    b. Hypnosis has been found to be more effective than morphine in alleviating certain types of pain.
    c. Dentists have been successful in using hypnosis as an anesthetic.
    d. Hypnosis has been effective as an aid in quitting smoking.

51. Current research about the effects of drug use and abuse is most often carried out:

    a. through anecdotal reports of drug experiences
    b. with the use of naturalistic observation
    c. in carefully controlled scientific experiments
    d. with the help of surveys and questionnaires

52. Alcohol continues to be a popular drug because:

    a. of its long-term effects
    b. of its short-term effects
    c. there are no withdrawal symptoms
    d. it does not increase aggression

53. Research has indicated that alcohol causes an increase in aggression, hostility, violence, and abusive behavior because it:

 a. dulls the effects of environmental cues to proper behavior
 b. triggers the person's innate propensity to be violent
 c. makes a person feel more courageous
 d. is a stimulant

54. The amount of alcohol reaching the bloodstream depends on:

 a. how slowly or how fast alcohol is consumed
 b. a hormone triggered by the endocrine system
 c. an enzyme in the stomach
 d. whether or not the drinking is accompanied by food

55. A mental illness attributed to long-term heavy use of alcohol is:

 a. Klinefelter's syndrome   c. Down syndrome
 b. Korsakoff syndrome   d. clinical depression

56. Drinking alcohol on an empty stomach has more pronounced effects on:

 a. men   c. Orientals
 b. adolescents   d. women

57. In the spring of 1990 it was reported that a single gene had been found that puts people at risk of alcoholism. Which of the following statements relating to this report is **true**?

 a. Subsequent research has confirmed that finding.
 b. Subsequent research has failed to confirm that finding.
 c. It has been confirmed that nonbiological factors alone are responsible for alcoholism.
 d. An "alcoholic personality" has, at last, been identified.

58. The effects of barbiturates are very similar to those of:

 a. alcohol   c. nicotine
 b. valium   d. caffeine

59. Restlessness, fits of yawning, chills, and hot flashes are the first symptoms of withdrawal from:

a. cocaine   c. heroin
b. alcohol   d. valium

60. Amphetamine psychosis is similar to which of the following mental disorders?

a. paranoid schizophrenia   c. clinical depression
b. mania   d. catatonic schizophrenia

61. Which of the following is the only legitimate medical use for cocaine?

a. to help induce hypnotic suggestion
b. to induce free-association in psychoanalysis
c. to add to cola drinks to soothe an upset stomach
d. as a local anesthetic

62. The use of which of the following drugs has declined since the 1970's?

a. alcohol   c. LSD
b. marijuana   d. laudanum

63. In most cultures LSD is taken episodically rather than habitually because:

a. of its high cost
b. of the rapid development of tolerance for it
c. the withdrawal effects are extremely severe
d. the induced experiences are too frightening

Answers for this section:

36. d (138)	43. c (148)	50. a (160, 161)	57. b (167)
37. b (139, 140)	44. d (151)	51. c (163)	58. a (169)
38. a (141)	45. a (152)	52. b (164)	59. c (170)
39. c (142)	46. b (153)	53. a (165)	60. a (173)
40. b (142)	47. c (157)	54. c (166)	61. d (173)
41. c (143)	48. a (158)	55. b (166)	62. c (175)
42. a (146)	49. b (158)	56. d (166)	63. b (176)

Applying the Facts

The learning of facts and concepts is of little value unless it can be applied and employed to solve problems. The next group of multiple-choice questions reflects applications of your learning.

64. You are sitting in your English class, but in place of listening to the lecture you are thinking about autographing the novel you are going to write someday. You are engaged in:

a. REM sleep   c. planning
b. daydreaming   d. creative hypnosis

65. John is a high school senior taking classes for the intellectually gifted. According to research results, his daydreams are **most** likely to:

a. be concerned with fear of failure
b. be frightening because of feelings of guilt
c. contain less guilt than his less gifted peers
d. reflect his emotional problems

66. Your grandmother is 77 years old. Therefore, she:

a. spends less time in Stage 3 and 4 sleep than you do
b. spends more time in Stage 3 and 4 sleep than you do
c. does not have rapid eye movements during sleep
d. sleeps less well than your grandfather

67. If you wanted to burglarize an occupied house, you would want to catch the occupants at which stage of sleep?

a. NREM   c. Stage 4
b. Stage 1   d. REM

68. If you wanted to burglarize an occupied house, you would want to catch the occupants during the REM sleep stage because during that stage:

a. when awakened, the victims would not remember what you look like
b. when awakened, they would be paralyzed
c. the brain is relatively insensitive to outside sensory input
d. their dreams would render them unable to care about the intrusion

69. Someone has sold you an expensive series of audio tapes that are intended to teach you psychology while you are asleep. Which of the following statements about this situation is **true**?

    a. Early experiments designed to teach sleepers simple word pairs were successful.
    b. Rudimentary forms of learning while sleeping are not possible.
    c. You will learn this way, but the process causes frightening dreams.
    d. No learning of complex material during sleep has ever been demonstrated.

70. You have been studying for a psychology exam all week. The exam is on Monday. Since you studied so hard, you decide to reward yourself by "partying" all night during the weekend. Research suggests that:

    a. your learning will be enhanced by eliminating REM stages
    b. you are likely to forget about one-third of the material because REM sleep was prevented
    c. the dreaming from previous REM stages will enhance your memory
    d. since you have learned so much, REM sleep will diminish for several days

71. Lately you have had a problem with insomnia. You buy some patent sleeping pills. This is counterproductive because the pills:

    a. can cause REM rebound   c. interfere with Stage 3 sleep
    b. can cause NREM rebound   d. cause delusions

Answers for this section:

64. b (142)   68. c (150)
65. c (143)   69. d (154)
66. a (148)   70. b (152)
67. d (148)   71. a (155)

Fill-in-the-Blank Questions: Recalling What You Have Learned

By now, there should be a considerable amount of new information about States of Consciousness in long-term memory. The following questions of recall rather than recognition will show if you are becoming more comfortable with the material.

Remembering the Facts

1. Thoughts and feelings that occur when we are awake and reasonably alert are called _____ consciousness.

2. A state of awareness that differs noticeably from states we experience when we are awake and alert is called a/an _____ _____ of consciousness.

3. To escape momentarily from the demands of the real world we might _____.

4. Our most vivid dreams occur during REM or _____ sleep.

5. Vivid images that occur primarily during REM periods of sleep are called _____.

6. _____ is a sleep disorder characterized by difficulty in falling asleep.

7. A sleep disorder characterized by breathing difficulty during the night and feelings of exhaustion during the day is called _____.

8. _____ is a hereditary sleep disorder. Victims of it nod off during the day and there is a sudden loss of muscle tone following moments of emotional excitement.

9. Extreme reduction of sensory stimuli is called _____ _____.

10. _____ is any of various methods of concentration, reflection, or focusing thoughts to reduce sympathetic nervous system activity.

11. In Transcendental Meditation, the sound selected for a student is called a/an _____.

12. _____ is a trance-like state in which the subject responds readily to suggestion.

13. A strong physical need for a substance such as a drug is called _____.

14. _____ is a term used for the phenomenon whereby higher doses of a drug are required to produce its original effects.

15. The unpleasant physical or psychological effects that follow the discontinuance of a dependence-producing substance is called _____.

16. A chemically inactive substance used for comparison with active drugs in experiments on the effects of drugs is called a/an _____.

17. Chemicals that slow down behavior or cognitive processes are categorized as _____.

18. The intoxicating ingredient in fermented or distilled liquors is _____.

19. Barbiturates are known as _____.

20. _____ is the best known of the opiates.

21. Amphetamines and cocaine are drugs classified as _____.

22. Among the most famous users of cocaine was _____ _____.

23. Drugs that distort visual and auditory perception are called _____.

24. _____ is a hallucinogen that produces hallucinations and delusions similar to those occurring in a psychotic state.

25. _____ is a plant that contains a mild hallucinogen.

Answers to this section:

1. waking (140)
2. altered state (140)
3. daydream (142)
4. paradoxical (148)
5. dreams (150)
6. insomnia (155)
7. apnea (156)
8. narcolepsy (156)
9. sensory deprivation (157)
10. meditation (158)
11. mantra (158)
12. hypnosis (159)
13. dependence (162)
14. tolerance (163)
15. withdrawal (163)
16. placebo (163)
17. depressants (163)
18. alcohol (164)
19. "downers" (164)
20. heroin (169)
21. stimulants (170)
22. Sigmund Freud (173)
23. hallucinogens (174)
24. LSD (175)
25. marijuana (176)

Understanding and Applying the Facts

As you previously did with recognition-type questions, you will now move to a higher level of recall. The following questions will determine if you understand the facts.

26. Because of the behaviorism of John Watson and B.F. Skinner psychology suffered a "loss of _____." But the loss was recovered in the (years) _____ and _____.

27. Introspection has been replaced by _____ and _____ as means of studying consciousness.

28. Very slow delta waves is a characteristic of Stage _____ sleep.

29. Heart rate, breathing rate, blood pressure, and body temperature are as low as they will get during the night during Stage _____ sleep.

30. The fact that voluntary muscles are essentially _____ during _____ sleep makes this period safer for us.

31. There is evidence that there is a greater rate of _____ synthesis during REM sleep compared to NREM sleep.

32. Your grandmother is the victim of a sleep disorder that causes breathing difficulties during the night. Sometimes she actually stops breathing after she falls asleep. Her condition is called _____ and it affects _____ to _____ percent of the population.

33. You are concentrating on a "song" with the words: zimwa zeeoo jemwadoo because your "teacher" suggested it. You are practicing _____ _____ and your "song" is called a/an _____.

34. Zen concentrates your attention on _____.

35. If you practiced "frenzied dancing" and focused on prayer, you would be engaged in a type of meditation called _____.

36. Meditation takes many forms, but its purpose is to reduce activity of the _____ nervous system.

37. Peace of mind, a sense of well being, and total relaxation are among the benefits reported from engaging in _____.

38. Meditation produces a (lower/higher) rate of metabolism.

39. A hypnotist begins by focusing on a willing subject's _____.

40. Using Hilgard's Stanford Susceptibility Scale, about _____ percent of the people tested show almost no response to hypnosis.

41. The evidence strongly suggests that clinical and therapeutic uses of hypnosis (will, will not) be universally effective.

42. To eliminate sources of error in drug research, a _____ _____ procedure is used.

43. A chemically inactive substance used for comparison with active drugs in experiments on the effects of drugs is called a/an _____.

44. The National Institute on Alcohol Abuse and Alcoholism found that more than 40 percent of all heavy drinkers died before age _____.

45. The McKim (1986) research on motor responses and reaction time under the effects of alcohol concluded that only _____ mg of alcohol is enough to impair ability to drive an automobile.

46. Alcohol consumption affects the central nervous system, but it can also have effects due to a person's _____.

47. Although _____ have potentially deadly effects, they are used to treat insomnia, anxiety, epilepsy, arthritis, and bedwetting.

48. The _____ nervous system is stimulated by drugs such as amphetamines and cocaine.

49. The mind-altering drug that is best known for its ability to maintain wakefulness and alertness is _____.

50. A mind-altering drug that may cause skin to wrinkle and age fast is _____.

51. Only _____ percent of smokers are able to quit permanently.

52. Amphetamines are chemically similar to the neurotransmitter _____.

53. The original formula for _____ _____ included chemically active coca leaves as a substitute for alcohol.

54. You should be careful what kind of mushrooms you eat because they may contain natural _____.

55. The term "psychedelic", originated by Humphrey Osmund and Aldous Huxley means "_____ _____."

56.   An estimated _____ million Americans have tried marijuana at least once.

Answers for this section:

26. consciousness, 1950's, 1960's (138)
27. electroencephalography, computers (139, 140)
28. 4 (146)
29. 4 (146)
30. paralyzed, REM (148)
31. protein (146)
32. apnea, 2, 4 (156)
33. Transcendental Meditation, mantra (158)
34. respiration (158)
35. Sufism (158)
36. sympathetic (158)
37. meditation (158)
38. lower (158)
39. attention (159)
40. 10 (160)
41. will not (160)

42. double-blind (163)
43. placebo (163)
44. 65 (164)
45. 50 (165)
46. expectations (166)
47. barbiturates (169)
48. sympathetic (170)
49. caffeine (171)
50. nicotine (172)
51. 15 (172)
52. epinephrine (172)
53. Coca Cola (173)
54. hallucinogens (174)
55. mind expanding (175)
56. 50 (176)

Testing Yourself For Mastery

The following terms and concepts are found in boldface or italics in the chapter. The time has come to determine if you can define and discuss your new learning in your own words, then check your work against the text.

consciousness

waking consciousness

altered state of consciousness

daydreaming

REM (or paradoxical) sleep

non-REM (NREM) sleep

REM rebound

dreams

insomnia

apnea

narcolepsy

sensory deprivation

meditation

hypnosis

double-blind procedure

placebo

depressants

alcohol

barbiturates

opiates

dependence

tolerance

withdrawal

stimulants

amphetamines

cocaine

hallucinogens

LSD (lysergic acid diethylamide)

marijuana

caffeine

nicotine

Integrating Your Newly Learned Information

Now that you have recognized, recalled, and given definition to States of Consciousness, you are ready to try to integrate your knowledge in a definitive discussion through short-answer questions.

1. Discuss the reasons why the study of consciousness lost favor among behavioral scientists in the 1920's, 1930's, and 1940's and explain the factors during the 1950's and 1960's that sparked a renewed interest in research on consciousness. (138-140)

2. Describe the characteristics of a "fantasy prone" person. (143)

3. What are some of the purposes of daydreaming or fantasy? (142, 143)

4. Although there is, as yet, no satisfactory explanation for the role of sleep, list at least three possible explanations for our need to sleep. (146)

5. Why is REM sleep also called paradoxical sleep? (148)

6. Although you have not studied Sigmund Freud's theory yet, perhaps you could briefly explain his view on the purpose of dreams. (151)

7. What is the neurological interpretation for the illogical and disjointed nature of many dreams offered by Hobson and McCarley in their 1977 research? (151)

8. List the general effects of sleep deprivation. (154, 155)

9.   List three situations in which people have been helped with a problem through the use of hypnosis. (160)

10.   What is the difference between "substance use" and "substance abuse" according to the American Psychiatric Association? (162)

Applications

You have worked through a section of recognition-type questions to determine if you can apply information to real-life situations. It is time to try to respond to some applications. Some are based upon those questions. Answers to this section will not be given. Your questions concerning these applications will serve as a basis for classroom discussion and ideas for class projects throughout the course.

1.   It may be valid to assume that everyone daydreams occasionally. For two days, try to catch yourself in this state of consciousness when it happens. Write down the content of your fantasies. Try to determine how much time during these two days was spent in fantasy. Were you a "conquering hero" or a "suffering hero"? Later, when you study about abnormal behaviors refer back to these notes and interpret them in light of your new knowledge.

2.   Go to the library and check out two or three books by Aldous Huxley. You probably won't have time to read them all, but see if you can find evidence of or references to the use of hallucinogens and "psychedelic" experiences in his writing.

3. Your roommate likes to "party," watch television, and play tennis. These activities leave little time for studying, so your roommate takes "diet pills" to stay awake in an attempt to study for exams. What could you tell this person in an effort to change that behavior and why should you try?

4. As part of a term paper or to satisfy your own curiosity, go to the library and find evidence of Sigmund Freud's personal use of cocaine, his views on the subject, and some of the results of his recommendations of its use. Later, when you study Freud's theory, relate what you found to aspects of his theory.

5. Joan had wanted to be a writer for as long as she could remember. She majored in English with a journalism minor and subsequently worked with newspapers and corporate public relations. Joan was a dedicated student and a diligent worker. Her days were filled with goal-directed thinking. But she had a fantasy. Occasionally, she would allow herself a daydream: she was a guest on the *Today Show* being interviewed upon the publication of her first book, a best-seller. Analyze Joan's behavior in terms of what research and discussion in the chapter provides. Soon you will study adjustment. Then you can look back at your analysis and try to determine more about Joan's personal functioning.

6. Tom is a middle-aged veteran of the Vietnam war. His family insists that he has symptoms of Post-Traumatic Stress Syndrome, although there has never been a diagnosis. He has no regular job, but works occasionally doing odd jobs. He cannot support himself and must live at home with his widowed father. He is addicted to television and watches shows and reruns indiscriminately. Could this be a form of fantasy? Analyze his behavior in terms of your new knowledge of fantasy and daydreaming.

7.	You were introduced to William James and functionalism in the first chapter. Perhaps you have been exposed to the literature of Henry James. Now you know that they were brothers. Find a book by Henry James and see what he meant by the phrase "stream of consciousness" and try to find parallels between his ideas and those of his brother. Try to write a few pages of your own "stream of consciousness".

Return to Chapter Summary

Now that you have concluded these exercises, you should go back and reread the chapter summary in your textbook. It provides you with a framework that integrates all of this newly-learned information. By reviewing the chapter summary, you will strengthen the many connections between the various new pieces of information.

LEARNING

5

Chapter Objectives

After you have read and studied this chapter, you should be able to:

1. Describe how classical conditioning was discovered. Define: unconditioned stimulus, unconditioned response, conditioned stimulus, and conditioned response.
2. Describe the experiment with little Albert. Describe desensitization therapy.
3. List the factors necessary for the success of learning in classical conditioning.
4. Explain these processes: extinction, spontaneous recovery, inhibition, stimulus generalization, discrimination, and higher-order conditioning.
5. Distinguish between classical and operant conditioning.
6. Explain the principle of reinforcement. Define primary reinforcer and secondary reinforcer and give examples of each.
7. Explain the effects of delay of reinforcement.
8. Identify four schedules of reinforcement and the pattern of response associated with each.
9. Define positive reinforcement.
10. Explain how to use punishment successfully.
11. Define negative reinforcement. Explain the process of avoidance training.
12. Summarize the principles of stimulus and response generalization, discrimination, extinction, and spontaneous recovery.
13. Summarize the arguments which minimize each of the four differences originally thought to distinguish classical from operant conditioning.

14. Distinguish between cognitive learning and traditional theories of conditioning. Explain contingency theory.
15. Discuss social learning theory and its implications for human learning.
16. Define learning set and describe the phenomenon of insight learning.

Multiple-Choice Questions: Recognizing What You Have Learned

These questions ask only that you recognize what you have learned. When you recognize a correct answer, you have accessed that information in memory. A knowledge of facts serves as a framework for later analysis and problem solving.

Remembering the Facts

This group of multiple-choice questions requires that you simply recognize facts from your textbook.

1. Classical conditioning was discovered by accident by:

   a.   Ivan Pavlov   c.   John B. Watson
   b.   B.F. Skinner   d.   Joseph Wolpe

2. The type of learning in which an organism transfers a natural response from one stimulus to another, previously neutral stimulus is called:

   a.   operant conditioning   c.   classical conditioning
   b.   insight learning   d.   cognitive learning

3. A stimulus that invariably causes an organism to respond in a specific way is called a/an:

   a.   learned stimulus   c.   learning set
   b.   unconditioned stimulus   d.   conditioned stimulus

4. A response that takes place in an organism whenever an unconditioned stimulus occurs is called a/an:

   a.   unconditioned response   c.   innate set
   b.   learned response   d.   conditioned response

5. A response an organism learns to produce when a conditioned stimulus is presented is called a/an:

    a. classical response   c. unconditioned response
    b. conditioned response   d. insight solution

6. A conditioning technique designed to reduce anxiety about a particular object or situation is called:

    a. token reinforcement   c. conditioned aversion
    b. aversive conditioning   d. desensitization therapy

7. The time lapse between the presentation of the conditioned stimulus and the unconditioned stimulus is called:

    a. a gap   c. interstimulus interval
    b. interstimulus space   d. interspace

8. Pairing the CS and US on only a portion of the learning trials is termed:

    a. partial pairing   c. intermittent pairing
    b. partial reinforcement   d. conditioned association

9. _____ is the decrease in the strength or frequency of a learned response due to failure to continue pairing the US and CS or the withholding of reinforcement in operant conditioning.

    a. Discrimination   c. Spontaneous recovery
    b. Extinction   d. Spontaneous discrimination

10. The reappearance of an extinguished response after the passage of time, without further training is called:

    a. spontaneous recovery   c. generalized recovery
    b. disextinction   d. discriminative recovery

11. The transfer of a learned response to different but similar stimuli is called:

    a. generalized learning   c. stimulus generalization
    b. response generalization   d. similarization

12. Learning to respond to only one stimulus and inhibit responses to all other stimuli is called:

   a. generalized discrimination
   b. discriminative set
   c. selectivity
   d. stimulus discrimination

13. Higher order conditioning is the term given to:

   a. conditioning based on previous learning
   b. abstract thinking
   c. backward pairing
   d. discriminative learning

14. Behavior designed to operate on the environment so as to gain something desired or avoid something unpleasant is called:

   a. reinforced action
   b. operant behavior
   c. operate behavior
   d. elicited behavior

15. A type of learning in which the likelihood of a behavior is increased or decreased by the use of reinforcement or punishment is called:

   a. classical or instrumental conditioning
   b. reward and punishment learning
   c. operative learning
   d. operant or instrumental conditioning

16. To present a stimulus that increases the probability that the preceding response will occur in the future is to:

   a. punish
   b. teach
   c. reinforce
   d. present an operant

17. The reinforcement of successive approximations to a desired behavior is called:

   a. shaping
   b. chaining
   c. token reward
   d. contouring

18. The law of _____ says that behavior that consistently results in a reward will be "stamped in" as learned behavior.

   a. the good Gestalt
   b. effect
   c. diminishing returns
   d. affect

19. Any event whose presence increases the likelihood that ongoing behavior will recur is termed a _____ reinforcer.

   a. negative   c. secondary
   b. primary   d. positive

20. Any event whose reduction or termination increases the likelihood that ongoing behavior will recur is termed a _____ reinforcer.

   a. negative   c. positive
   b. primary   d. secondary

21. A reinforcer that is rewarding itself is called a _____ reinforcer.

   a. secondary   c. primary
   b. natural   d. innate

22. A reinforcer whose value is learned through association with primary reinforcers is called a/an _____ reinforcer.

   a. associative   c. jointed
   b. linked   d. secondary

23. The rule for determining when a reinforcer will be delivered is termed a _____ of reinforcement.

   a. schedule   c. rate
   b. law   d. plan

24. In a _____ schedule, reinforcement is given for a correct response after a fixed length of time.

   a. variable-interval   c. fixed-ratio
   b. fixed-interval   d. variable-ratio

25. Reinforcement is given for the first correct response after various lengths of time in a _____ schedule of reinforcement.

   a. fixed-ratio   c. variable-interval
   b. variable-ratio   d. fixed-interval

26. In which of the following schedules of reinforcement is reinforcement presented after a varying number of correct responses have occurred?

a. fixed-ratio
b. variable-interval

c. fixed-interval
d. variable-ratio

27. Any event whose presence decreases the likelihood that ongoing behavior will occur is termed:

a. aversion
b. punishment

c. negative reinforcement
d. scheduled reinforcement

28. The learning of a desirable behavior to prevent an unpleasant condition from occurring is called:

a. escape learning
b. threat reduction

c. avoidance learning
d. negative learning

29. Giving a response that is somewhat different from the response originally learned to that stimulus is called:

a. response generalization
b. response discrimination

c. generalized responding
d. similarity responding

30. Learning that depends on mental processes that are not directly observable is called:

a. insight
b. association

c. latent learning
d. cognitive learning

31. _____ learning is learning that is not immediately reflected in behavior change.

a. Cognitive
b. Latent

c. Operant
d. Contingency

32. A learned mental image of a spatial environment that aids in problem solving when stimuli in the environment change is called a/an:

a. cognitive map
b. insight image

c. operant structure
d. schema

33. _____ learning occurs rapidly as a result of understanding all the ingredients of a problem.

    a.   Latent   c.   Schematic
    b.   Insight   d.   Operant

34. The ability to become increasingly more effective in solving problems as more problems are solved is called a/an:

    a.   learning set   c.   operant set
    b.   contingent map   d.   flexibility trend

35. When prior conditioning prevents conditioning to a second stimulus even when the two stimuli are presented simultaneously it is called:

    a.   shaping   c.   response deterioration
    b.   closure   d.   blocking

36. Apathy and passivity learned in a situation where one's behavior has no effect on reward and punishment is termed:

    a.   learned withdrawal   c.   learned helplessness
    b.   depressed helplessness   d.   powerlessness

Answers for this section:

1. a (187)	7. c (191)	13. a (195)	19. d (202)	25. c (205)	31. b (213)
2. c (187)	8. c (192)	14. b (195)	20. a (202)	26. d (207)	32. a (214)
3. b (188)	9. b (194)	15. d (197)	21. c (203)	27. b (207)	33. b (215)
4. a (188)	10. a (194)	16. c (197)	22. d (203)	28. c (209)	34. a (216)
5. b (188)	11. c (195)	17. a (199)	23. a (205)	29. a (210)	35. d (217)
6. d (190)	12. d (195)	18. b (201)	24. b (205)	30. d (213)	36. c (218)

Understanding the Facts

Now that you have found that you can recognize facts from Learning, the next step is to determine if you understand the meaning of newly-learned information. These multiple-choice questions require a higher level of thinking. They will help you establish more solid connections and provide practice in dealing with higher level concepts.

37. For Pavlov's dogs, in the classical conditioning experiments, food was the
_____ and the bell was the _____.

    a.   US, CS   c.   US, CR
    b.   CS, US   d.   UR, CR

38. In classical conditioning, the unconditioned response and the conditioned response:

    a.   cannot be elicited   c.   are the same
    b.   extinguish quickly   d.   are different

39. Babies 5 to 10 days old in the Lipsitt (1971) research, learned to blink their eyes when they heard a tone. In this experiment, the unconditioned stimulus was:

    a.   the sound of a tone   c.   the odor of meat
    b.   a puff of air   d.   a tap on the knee

40. Babies 5 to 10 days old in the Lipsitt (1971) research learned to blink their eyes when they heard a tone. In this experiment, the conditioned stimulus was:

    a.   a puff of air   c.   blinking the eyes
    b.   closing their eyes   d.   a tone

41. In the Watson and Rayner (1920) experiment with Albert, the baby's **initial** reactions to the white rat were all but which of the following?

    a.   he was afraid of it   c.   he wanted to play with it
    b.   he crawled toward it   d.   he displayed no fear

42. In the Watson and Rayner (1920) experiment with Albert, the white rat was the _____ stimulus and the loud noise was the _____ stimulus.

    a.   conditioned, unconditioned   c.   natural, learned
    b.   unconditioned, conditioned   d.   neutral, learned

43. In the Watson and Rayner (1920) experiment with Albert the loud noise was a/an:

    a.   conditioned response   c.   unconditioned stimulus
    b.   conditioned stimulus   d.   neutral stimulus

44. Which of the following was the first to demonstrate a method by which children's fears can be unlearned using classical conditioning?

   a. Ivan Pavlov   c. John Watson
   b. Mary Cover Jones   d. Joseph Wolpe

45. Joseph Wolpe adapted the method of Mary Cover Jones to the treatment of anxiety and called his method:

   a. psychoanalysis   c. systematic extinction
   b. operant therapy   d. desensitization therapy

46. Presenting the US before the CS in classical conditioning is called:

   a. interconditioning   c. backward conditioning
   b. forward conditioning   d. serial presentation

47. Presenting the unconditioned stimulus before the conditioned stimulus in classical conditioning:

   a. results in strong responses
   b. seldom results in effective learning
   c. causes the response to extinguish
   d. makes learning complete in one trial

48. The most effective interstimulus interval is:

   a. between a fraction of a second and a few seconds
   b. not yet known
   c. between 1 and 2 seconds
   d. between a fraction of a second and 15 seconds

49. Pavlov found that if the interval between the sound of the bell and the presentation of food was too long, dogs:

   a. became vicious   c. would not eat
   b. would not learn   d. became apathetic

50. When learning takes more than one trial, the irregular pairing of the CS and US is called intermittent pairing and it:

   a. makes new learning impossible
   b. creates anxiety in the learner
   c. reduces the rate of learning and the learning level achieved
   d. increases the rate of learning and the learning level achieved

51. Although most learning through classical conditioning requires more than one trial, which of the following can be accomplished with only one trial?

   a. phobias   c. fear of rats
   b. anxiety   d. conditioned food aversion

52. The phenomenon of spontaneous recovery tells us that:

   a. learning is not permanently lost
   b. conditioned food aversion extinguishes rapidly
   c. Albert will cease to be afraid of white rats
   d. Wolpe's desensitization is not effective

53. Which of the following results in extinction in classical conditioning?

   a. no further reward
   b. no reinforcement after the response
   c. punishment for emitting a response
   d. no further pairing of the CS and US

54. Pavlov's dogs originally salivated to the sound of a bell, but would also salivate when they heard a buzzer. This phenomenon is explained by:

   a. stimulus generalization   c. stimulus discrimination
   b. response generalization   d. Joseph Wolpe

55. The reverse of generalization is:

   a. spontaneous recovery   c. discrimination
   b. extinction   d. aversion

56. Marlin's (1983) research shows how it is possible to use conditioning as a building block for further learning. This procedure is known as:

   a. instrumental conditioning   c. higher-operant conditioning
   b. higher-order conditioning   d. reinforced learning

57. Reinforcement in classical conditioning could be defined as:

    a.   the pairing of the CS and the US
    b.   coming after the response
    c.   the meat in the Pavlovian experiments
    d.   the pairing of the CS and the CR

58. Operant conditioning is based upon which of the following?

    a.   insight   c.   consequences of behavior
    b.   trial and error   d.   instinctive responses

59. Operant conditioning is accomplished by all but which of the following?

    a.   associating a CS and US   c.   punishment
    b.   reward   d.   ignoring

60. Which of the following neural components or regions is necessary for classical conditioning to occur?

    a.   limbic system   c.   a reflex
    b.   myelin   d.   reticular formation

61. One of the most common ways of getting a desired behavior to occur in operant conditioning is:

    a.   to associate the CS and US
    b.   to wait for the desired behavior to occur
    c.   to wait for a conditioned response to occur
    d.   to withhold reinforcements

62. A laboratory device most widely used today for speeding up operant conditioning is the:

    a.   "puzzle box"   c.   shaping crate
    b.   visual cliff   d.   Skinner box

63. Which of the following procedures was used to get the severely disturbed boy named Dickey to wear his glasses?

    a.   shaping   c.   blocking
    b.   chaining   d.   desensitization

64. A positive reinforcer is roughly equal to a/an:

    a. intrinsic payment   c. temptation
    b. bribe   d. reward

65. A negative reinforcement is effective because it:

    a. serves as a punishment for undesirable behavior
    b. extinguishes a conditioned response
    c. subtracts something unpleasant from the situation
    d. adds something pleasant to the situation

66. Which of the following is **not** a primary reinforcer?

    a. money
    b. a glass of lemonade on a hot day
    c. a candy bar
    d. an aspirin tablet

67. Chimpanzees have learned to work for poker chips. Why?

    a. Poker chips are a primary reinforcer.
    b. They like the color of the poker chips.
    c. They like to play with the poker chips.
    d. Poker chips are a secondary reinforcer.

68. Which of the following schedules of reinforcement is **most** resistant to extinction?

    a. fixed-interval   c. fixed-ratio
    b. variable-ratio   d. variable-interval

69. Which of the following schedules of reinforcement is **least** resistant to extinction?

    a. fixed-ratio   c. variable-ratio
    b. variable-interval   d. fixed-interval

70. Which of the following procedures tends to **decrease** behavior?

    a. negative reinforcement   c. token reinforcement
    b. reward   d. punishment

71. Cognitive learning is also called _____ learning.

    a.   internal   c.   insight
    b.   conscious   d.   trial and error

72. One of the pioneers in cognitive learning was:

    a.   Edward Lee Thorndike   c.   Edward C. Tolman
    b.   William James   d.   Kurt Koffka

73. In 1930, Tolman and Honzik conducted a famous experiment showing that learning may not be immediately reflected in a behavior change. They called this phenomenon:

    a.   insight learning   c.   the latency period
    b.   latent learning   d.   preoperant learning

74. The concept for which Edward C. Tolman is best known is:

    a.   his agreement with Thorndike's Law of Effect
    b.   the concept of the "good Gestalt"
    c.   aversive control of behavior
    d.   latent learning

75. Which of the following statements reflects what is, perhaps, the **most** important insight coming from the work of Tolman and subsequent related research?

    a.   Learning seems to involve more than just a change in observable behavior.
    b.   They confirmed much of Freud's evidence about the unconscious.
    c.   The "suddenness" of some kinds of learning was discovered.
    d.   Cognitive maps do not exist.

76. " . . . from unsuccessful trial and error to instant success" is one description for:

    a.   latent learning   c.   insight learning
    b.   a learning set   d.   operant shaping

77. On the basis of findings of research generally under the heading of *contingency* theory, we now know that:

  a. Pavlovian conditioning does not happen automatically when a CS and US are paired
  b. operant conditioning does not happen automatically when reward is presented
  c. shaping behavior does not work
  d. insight learning does not occur

78. While Rescola and Kamin have uncovered cognitive processes related to classical conditioning, Seligman and his colleagues have found an important cognitive process in operant conditioning called:

  a. blocking   c. modeling
  b. vicarious learning   d. learned helplessness

79. Albert Bandura is famous for research on a kind of learning that occurs when we watch what happens to other people or when we are told about something. This kind of learning is called:

  a. introspection   c. self-analysis
  b. vicarious learning   d. performance modeling

Answers for this section:

37. a (188)	48. a (191)	59. a (197)	70. d (207)
38. c (188)	49. b (191)	60. c (189)	71. a (213)
39. b (189)	50. c (192)	61. b (197)	72. c (213)
40. d (189)	51. d (192)	62. d (198)	73. b (213)
41. a (189)	52. a (194)	63. a (199)	74. d (213)
42. a (189)	53. d (194)	64. d (202)	75. a (215)
43. c (189)	54. a (195)	65. c (202)	76. c (215)
44. b (189)	55. c (195)	66. a (203)	77. a (218)
45. d (190)	56. b (195)	67. d (203)	78. d (218)
46. c (191)	57. a (188)	68. b (207)	79. b (219)
47. b (191)	58. c (196)	69. a (207)	

Applying the Facts

The learning of facts and concepts is of little value unless it can be applied and employed to solve problems. The next group of multiple-choice questions reflects applications of your learning.

80. Frostie, the Bichon, comes running when he hears his master rattle his food box. In this case, the sound of the food in the box is a/an:

    a. CR   c. UR
    b. CS   d. US

81. Susan suffers from allergies. When she first saw a picture of goldenrod in her botany text she began sneezing. Theoretically, the picture was a/an _____ and the sneeze was a/an _____.

    a. US, CS   c. US, CR
    b. CS, UR   d. CS, CR

82. Hilde, the Weimeraner, always took a counter-clockwise turn each time her master put her food bowl down. Her master had dropped the bowl on her head when she was a puppy. The bowl was never dropped again, but Hilde continued this behavior all her life. The behavior could be explained by the concept of:

    a. instinct   c. extinction
    b. spontaneous recovery   d. spontaneous reflex

83. Since extinction does not totally destroy a response it is most probable that if little Albert grew up and married, he did not buy his wife a:

    a. convertible   c. white fur coat
    b. diamond necklace   d. black ermine stole

84. Frostie, the Bichon, is 5 years old. He has never begged for "handouts" at the dinner table. In fact, he never comes near the table when his family is eating. Which of the following is the **best** explanation for this behavior?

    a. He was never given any food from the table.
    b. He saw his sister punished for begging.
    c. His master extinguished early begging behavior.
    d. He does not like food that humans eat.

85. A rat is placed in a box, the floor of which gives a mild electric shock. The rat accidentally presses a bar in the box and the shock stops. When the rat is put in the box again, it immediately presses the bar and the shock stops. This is an example of:

   a. aversive control
   b. punishment
   c. shaping
   d. negative reinforcement

86. You have a headache. You learn that taking an aspirin will relieve that headache. This is an example of:

   a. negative reinforcement
   b. extinction
   c. positive reinforcement
   d. response

87. Joe carries a plastic sack with him to all of his classes. He picks up discarded soft drink bottles and cans. The bottles and cans are _____ reinforcers.

   a. social
   b. secondary
   c. primary
   d. delayed

88. Pop quizzes in your psychology class are an example of which of the following schedules of reinforcement?

   a. fixed-ratio
   b. variable-interval
   c. fixed-interval
   d. variable-ratio

89. Phil is an avid fisherman. He enjoys the relaxation the sport gives him, but he gets really excited when he catches a fish. For this activity, Phil is on which of the following schedules of reinforcement?

   a. fixed-ratio
   b. variable-interval
   c. fixed-interval
   d. variable-ratio

90. Sue was walking through the shopping mall on her way to a lunch date. She passed by many inviting store displays, but was not paying attention. Two weeks later she was invited to a special party and "didn't have a thing to wear." Suddenly she remembered a dress in a store window she had passed and went back to the mall to see if it was still available. This is an example of:

   a. latent learning
   b. a cognitive map
   c. latent cognition
   d. insight

112

91. Martha's friend was a patient in a large metropolitan hospital. Martha visited her friend almost every day. Martha was "lost" for the first two or three trips, but after that she went directly to the room without thinking about the twist and turns. Which of the following is the **best** explanation for the behavior?

    a. latent learning
    b. Martha resolved the cognitive dissonance.
    c. Martha had formed a cognitive map.
    d. Martha was reinforced for every correct turn and incorrect turns were ignored.

92. You have just become the proud owner of a new puppy. From your knowledge of operant conditioning, which of the following techniques would be **most** effective in "house training" the puppy?

    a. Put newspapers all over the floor and wait until he uses them.
    b. When he "potties" on the floor, swat him gently with a rolled-up newspaper.
    c. Rub his nose in it when he is "naughty".
    d. Take the puppy outside often. Wait for him to "potty", then love him and tell him "good boy".

Answers for this section:

80. b (188)	84. a (194)	88. b (205)	92. d (197)
81. d (188)	85. d (202)	89. d (207)	
82. b (194)	86. a (202)	90. a (213)	
83. c (194)	87. b (203)	91. c (213)	

Fill-in-the-Blank Questions: Recalling What You Have Learned

By now, there should be a considerable amount of new information about Learning in long-term memory. The following questions of recall rather than recognition will show if you are becoming more comfortable with the material.

Remembering the Facts

1. The process by which experience or practice results in a relatively permanent change in behavior is called _____.

2. The acquisition of fairly specific patterns of behavior in the presence of well-defined stimuli is called _____.

3. _____ conditioning is a type of learning in which an organism learns to transfer a natural response from one stimulus to another, previously neutral stimulus.

4. A/an _____ stimulus invariably causes a certain reaction.

5. A/an _____ stimulus was originally neutral, then was paired with a/an _____ stimulus to produce the desired response when presented alone.

6. A conditioning technique designed to gradually reduce anxiety about a particular object or situation is called _____ therapy.

7. The time-lapse between the presentation of the CS and the US is called the _____ _____.

8. Presenting the US before the CS is called _____ conditioning.

9. Pairing the CS and the US on only a portion of the learning trials is called _____ _____.

10. A decrease in the strength or frequency of a learned response due to the absence of reinforcement is called _____.

11. _____ _____ is the term for the reappearance of an extinguished response after the passage of time.

12. The transfer of a learned response to different but similar stimuli is called _____ _____.

13. Responding to only one stimulus and inhibiting response to all other stimuli is called _____ _____.

14. _____ _____ conditioning is conditioning based on previous learning.

15. To _____ is to present a stimulus that increases the probability that the preceding response will recur in the future.

16. Reinforcing successive approximations to a desired behavior is called _____.

17. The law of _____ says that behavior that is consistently rewarded will be "stamped in" as learned behavior.

18. An event whose presence increases the likelihood that ongoing behavior will recur is called a/an _____ _____.

19. A _____ reinforcer is an event whose reduction or termination increases the likelihood that ongoing behavior will recur.

20. A _____ reinforcer is rewarding in itself.

21. The value of a _____ reinforcer is learned through association with primary reinforcers.

22. Any event whose presence decreases the likelihood that ongoing behavior will recur is called _____.

23. Learning a desirable behavior to prevent an unpleasant condition from occurring is called _____ _____.

24. Giving a response that is somewhat different from the response originally learned to that stimulus is called _____ _____.

25. _____ learning is the term given to learning that depends on mental processes that are not directly observable.

26. Learning that is not immediately reflected in behavior change is called _____ learning.

27. A learned mental image of a spatial environment that may be called on to solve problems when environmental stimuli change is called a/an _____ _____.

28. _____ learning occurs rapidly as a result of understanding all the ingredients of a problem.

29. A/an _____ _____ develops as a person or animal becomes more effective in solving problems as more problems are solved.

30. _____ occurs when prior conditioning prevents conditioning to a second stimulus even when two stimuli are presented together.

31. _____ theory proposes that for learning to take place, the stimulus must provide the learner with information about the likelihood of other events occurring.

32. Apathy and passivity learned in a situation where one's behavior has no effect on reward and punishment is called _____ _____.

33. _____ or _____ learning occurs through observing other people's behavior.

Answers for this section:

 1. learning (186)
 2. conditioning (186)
 3. classical (187)
 4. unconditioned (188)
 5. conditioned, unconditioned (188)
 6. desensitization (190)
 7. interstimulus interval (191)
 8. backward (191)
 9. intermittent pairing (192)
10. extinction (194)
11. spontaneous recovery (194)
12. stimulus generalization (195)
13. stimulus discrimination (195)
14. higher order (195)
15. reinforce (197)
16. shaping (199)
17. effect (201)

18. positive reinforcer (202)
19. negative (202)
20. primary (203)
21. secondary (203)
22. punishment (207)
23. avoidance training (209)
24. response generalization (210)
25. cognitive (213)
26. latent (213)
27. cognitive map (214)
28. insight (215)
29. learning set (216)
30. blocking (217)
31. contingency (218)
32. learned helplessness (218)
33. observational, vicarious (219)

Understanding and Applying the Facts

As you previously did with recognition-type questions, you will now move to a higher level of recall. The following questions will determine if you understand the facts.

34. Reinforcement in classical conditioning can be defined as the pairing or association of the _____ and the _____.

35. Reinforcement in operant conditioning comes _____ _____ _____.

36. Classical conditioning is dependent upon the elicitation of a _____.

37. In operant conditioning, the organism emits a response, then the response is either _____, _____, or _____.

38. When Lipsitt (1971) taught babies to blink their eyes when they heard a tone, the eye blink was a _____ or elicited response to a specific stimulus and is called a/an _____ response.

39. In classical conditioning a _____ or reflexive stimulus is associated with a _____ stimulus so that, eventually, the organism responds in the same manner to the _____ stimulus when the _____ stimulus is removed.

40. Although learning in classical conditioning is cumulative, it eventually reaches a point of _____ _____.

41. Sam ordered a corned beef sandwich in a restaurant. The meat was spoiled and it made him ill. He never ate corned beef again. He was a victim of _____ _____ _____.

42. Each species is preprogrammed for certain types of learning that are important for its survival. This preprogramming is called _____.

43. Your dog has been begging at the dinner table for two years with good results for him. You want him to stop begging, so you refuse to feed him from the table. You are using a procedure known as _____.

44. Your dog's begging at the table increases at first, then diminishes slightly because of your new program, but soon he is begging as strongly as before. This behavior can be explained by _____ _____.

45. Little Albert, originally conditioned to fear a white rat, was also afraid of a Santa Claus mask although that fear was never deliberately conditioned. The fear came about through _____ _____.

46. George is afraid of snakes, but not all snakes. He fears only dangerous snakes because of _____ _____.

47. Two ways to speed up the acquisition of a response in operant conditioning are to _____ _____ and _____ the _____.

48. A way to use operant conditioning to teach complex behavior is _____ behavior.

49. Positive reinforcement _____ something rewarding to the environment while negative reinforcement _____ something unpleasant from the environment.

50. Tokens are _____ reinforcers.

51. One reason why people continue to gamble even though they don't win is because gambling devices are set on a _____ _____ schedule of reinforcement.

52. Kicking and pounding a vending machine that did not deliver your product illustrates the characteristic _____ in response that follows _____.

53. In the past, psychologists referred to the mind as "the black box." Behaviorists are interested in the stimuli going into "the black box" and the responses coming out, while _____ are interested in the contents of "the black box."

54. As a parent, you must be very careful of the behavior you display around your children, for they learn not only through classical and operant conditioning, insight and trial and error but also by _____. This valuable knowledge comes from the work of _____.

Answers for this section:

34. CS, US (188)
35. after the response (197)
36. reflex (189)
37. reinforced, punished, ignored (197)
38. natural, unconditioned (189)
39. natural, neutral, neutral, natural (189)
40. diminishing returns (192)
41. conditioned food aversion (192)
42. preparedness (193)
43. extinction (194)
44. spontaneous recovery (194)

45. stimulus generalization (195)
46. stimulus discrimination (195)
47. increase motivation, restrict environment (197)
48. shaping (199)
49. adds, subtracts (202)
50. secondary (203)
51. variable-ratio (207)
52. increase, extinction (211)
53. cognitivists (213)
54. observation, Bandura (219)

Testing Yourself for Mastery

The following terms and concepts are found in boldface or italics in the chapter. The time has come to determine if you can define and discuss your new learning in your own words, then check your work against the text.

learning

conditioning

classical conditioning

unconditioned stimulus

conditioned stimulus

unconditioned response

conditioned response

desensitization therapy

backward conditioning

interstimulus interval

intermittent pairing

conditioned food aversion

extinction in classical conditioning

spontaneous recovery

stimulus generalization

discrimination in classical conditioning

higher-order conditioning

operant behavior

operant conditioning

reinforcement

Skinner box

shaping

Law of effect

negative reinforcer

positive reinforcer

primary reinforcer

secondary reinforcer

four schedules of reinforcement

punishment

response generalization

extinction in operant conditioning

discrimination in operant conditioning

cognitive learning

latent learning

cognitive map

insight

learning set

contingency theory

blocking

learned helplessness

social learning theory

vicarious learning

Integrating Your Newly Learned Information

Now that you have recognized, recalled, and given definition to Learning, you are ready to try to integrate your knowledge in a definitive discussion through short-answer questions.

1. Try to explain the differences between classical and operant conditioning, incorporating the nature of the responses in each, the source of these responses and how reinforcement differs in each of these models of learning. (187-200)

2. Explain why intermittent pairing reduces both the rate of learning and the level of learning. (192)

3. We know that humans and animals learn through both classical and operant conditioning. Which model do you think is responsible for the most learning? Explain the reasons for your choice. (187-200)

4. Why is it necessary to understand the concept of preparedness in attempting to teach animals new behavior? (201)

5. Explain the four schedules of reinforcement and present an example for each that is not in the book. (205-207)

6.   Describe the conditions that make punishment effective. (208)

7.   Describe the negative effects of punishment. (208)

8.   Describe some learned behavior that cannot be accounted for by classical or operant conditioning and indicate the theoretical model that explains that behavior. (213-223)

9.   Briefly explain Robert Rescorla's contingency theory and how it adds new knowledge to former findings in classical conditioning. (217, 218)

10.   Explain the main factors of Bandura's social learning theory. (219-223)

Applications

You have worked through a section of recognition-type questions to determine if you can apply information to real-life situations. It is time to respond to some applications. Some are based upon those questions. Answers to this section will not be given. Your questions concerning these applications will serve as a basis for classroom discussion and ideas for class projects throughout the course.

1.   Joyce has a 9-month-old nephew who is afraid of her. She came in to the baby's house one day and yelled, "Hi!" The baby's head was turned away from her. Choose the most obvious model of learning and explain the process that led to the baby's fear. Then explain how Joyce might reverse this learning.

2. The Watson and Rayner experiment with little Albert took place in 1920. Analyze this experiment in light of today's APA ethical standards.

3. A college professor, fully aware of the ethical standards for research with human subjects, always defended Watson and Rayner's work with little Albert, insisting that the experiment was not unethical, nor did it do Albert any harm. Can you think of any reasons for the professor's point of view? Do you think he was right or wrong?

4. Your friend is phobic about elevators. You will learn later that phobias are not serious as long as they do not interfere with life functioning. But your friend's office is on the tenth floor. Can you find anything in the Learning chapter that could help your friend? Can you recommend a type of therapy? Would you like to try it yourself?

5. Why do some people continue to push buttons and kick and hit vending machines when the machines put them on extinction? Use your new technical knowledge in your answer.

6. You have just acquired a new puppy. You do not want the puppy to get on the furniture. Choose the proper model of learning and explain how you would achieve the behavior you desire.

7. Big dogs dig holes in yards. Hilde, the Weimaraner, dug only one hole in her yard during her 10 years of life. Can you think of how this desired behavior was achieved?

8.   Someone once said, "the world is just one big Skinner box". Can you think of why someone would say that?

9.   Ask your professor if you can do this when shaping behavior is explained: Write "shaping behavior" on the chalkboard. Be sure an eraser is nearby. Ask for a volunteer. Take the volunteer out of the room and tell him/her that there is a target behavior. The only reinforcement the volunteer gets is a hand clap (or use a clicker if you can get one) when a response is correct. Tell the class to be very quiet. Bring your volunteer in and reinforce every step toward the goal, which is to erase "shaping behavior" from the chalkboard. Most of the time it works and the class will not forget the concept.

10.   Students (and some professionals who should know better) often confuse negative reinforcement with punishment. Devise a way to explain the difference, use an example, and explain it to a classmate who is having difficulty with the concept.

Return to Chapter Summary

Now that you have concluded these exercises, you should go back and reread the chapter summary in your textbook. It provides you with a framework that integrates all of this newly-learned information. By reviewing the chapter summary, you will strengthen the many connections between the various new pieces of information.

6

MEMORY

Chapter Objectives

After you have read and studied this chapter, you should be able to:

1. Describe the path information takes from the environment to long-term memory.
2. Explain the characteristics of short-term and long-term memory.
3. Explain coding in both short-term and long-term memory.
4. Understand storage and retrieval in long-term memory.
5. Discuss explanations for forgetting.
6. Describe the different types of memory, and their characteristic properties.
7. Know the limits of memory and determine if they can be expanded.
8. Understand how information is stored and how it is organized.
9. Define "schema." How are schemata used?
10. Discuss how and why memories change over time.
11. Understand and use techniques for improving your memory.
12. Describe and explain the brain structures and regions that are the bases for memory.

Multiple-Choice Questions: Recognizing What You Have Learned

These questions ask only that you recognize what you have learned. When you recognize a correct answer, you have accessed that information in memory. A knowledge of facts serves as a framework for later analysis and problem solving.

1. The entry points for raw information from the senses are called:

    a.   information registers   c.   sensory registers
    b.   processing registers   d.   sensory gates

2. The selection of some incoming information for further processing is called:

    a.   selectivity   c.   sensory selection
    b.   selective attention   d.   registering

3. Short-term memory is also called:

    a.   working memory   c.   registered memory
    b.   temporary memory   d.   coding

4. The grouping of information into meaningful units for easier handling by short-term memory is called:

    a.   bunching   c.   chunking
    b.   grouping   d.   massing

5. _____ theory holds that passage of time itself causes forgetting.

    a.   Non-use   c.   Interference
    b.   Decay   d.   Inhibition

6. Other information gets in the way of new or old information. This is the basis of _____ theory of forgetting.

    a.   interference   c.   blocking
    b.   decay   d.   schema

7. Retaining information in STM by repeating it over and over is known as:

    a.   elaborative rehearsal   c.   practicing
    b.   repetitive rehearsal   d.   rote rehearsal

8. Linking new information in STM to familiar material stored in LTM is called:

   a. elaborative rehearsal   c. the chain effect
   b. rote rehearsal   d. associative rehearsal

9. The portion of memory that is more or less permanent and corresponds to everything we "know" is called _____ memory.

   a. permanent   c. lifetime
   b. long-term   d. long-range

10. _____ memory is the portion of long-term memory that stores general facts and information.

    a. Abstract   c. Semantic
    b. Episodic   d. Somatic

11. _____ memory is the portion of long-term memory that stores more specific information that has personal meaning.

    a. Episodic   c. Episodal
    b. Semantic   d. Meaningful

12. The particular arrangement of verbal information, such as words in a sentence is called _____ structure.

    a. coding   c. elaborative
    b. deep   d. surface

13. The underlying meaning conveyed by verbal information is called _____ structure.

    a. profound   c. infra
    b. deep   d. buried

14. The process by which new information interferes with old information already in memory is called:

    a. novel interference   c. retroactive interference
    b. proactive interference   d. an obstruction

15. The process by which old material already in memory interferes with new information is called:

    a. retroactivity   c. proactivity
    b. proaction   d. proactive interference

16. A _____ is a set of beliefs or expectations about something that is based on past experience.

    a. concept   c. schema
    b. scheme   d. structure

17. A/an _____ memory is memory for information that either was unintentionally committed to memory or was unintentionally retrieved from memory.

    a. implicit   c. eidetic
    b. schematic   d. explicit

18. A/an _____ memory is memory for information that was intentionally committed to memory or intentionally retrieved from memory.

    a. repressed   c. implicit
    b. explicit   d. eidetic

19. The ability to reproduce unusually sharp and detailed images of something that has been seen is called:

    a. eidetic imagery   c. semantic recall
    b. flashbulb memory   d. a photographic mind

20. Someone with highly developed memory skills is called a:

    a. mnemonicalist   c. mnemorist
    b. memory artist   d. mnemonist

21. _____ are techniques that make material easier to remember.

    a. QSRR's   c. Mnemonics
    b. Schemata   d. Eidetics

Answers for this section:

1. c (231)	7. d (240)	13. b (245)	19. a (256)
2. b (232)	8. a (241)	14. c (246)	20. d (256)
3. a (234)	9. b (243)	15. d (246)	21. c (257)
4. c (237)	10. c (243)	16. c (250)	
5. b (239)	11. a (243)	17. a (254)	
6. a (239)	12. d (245)	18. b (254)	

Understanding the Facts

Now that you have found that you can recognize facts from Memory, the next step is to determine if you understand the meaning of newly-learned information. These multiple-choice questions require a higher level of thinking. They will help you establish more solid connections and provide practice in dealing with higher level concepts.

22. Which sensory registers have been most extensively studied?

   a.   visual and olfactory   c.   cutaneous and gustatory
   b.   visual and vestibular   d.   visual and auditory

23. Sensory registers have virtually unlimited capacity,

   a.   so they are similar to long-term memory
   b.   but information disappears from them rapidly
   c.   so they hold more information than short-term-memory
   d.   and the information remains for several minutes

24. Visual information is erased from the sensory registers:

   a.   in about a half of a second
   b.   in the same amount of time that audio information is erased
   c.   in about a quarter of a second
   d.   more slowly than it is erased from the auditory registers

25. Visual information is called a/an:

   a.   image   c.   scheme
   b.   echo   d.   icon

26. Auditory information is called a/an:

a. tone   c. repercussion
b. repeat   d. echo

27. The process of selective looking, listening, smelling, tasting, and feeling is called:

a. attention   c. echoing
b. selectivity   d. noticing

28. Short-term memory is sometimes referred to as:

a. preconsciousness c. temporary registers
b. the short register d. consciousness

29. Short-term memory is also sometimes called _____.

a. a primary memory c. a secondary memory
b. our working memory d. our registers

30. Early research by Miller and Sperling, (1956, 1960) suggested that STM can hold about _____ bits of information at the same time.

a. 5 to 10   c. 15
b. 25   d. 2

31. Recent research has indicated that STM can hold:

a. as much information as can be repeated or rehearsed in 5 to 10 seconds
b. 10 to 20 bits of information
c. little more information than the sensory registers
d. as much information as can be repeated or rehearsed in 1.5 to 2 seconds

32. Simon (1974) found that as the size of any individual chunk increases, the number of chunks that can be held in STM:

a. increases   c. remains the same
b. declines   d. cannot be determined

33. Research on the capacity of short-term memory:

    a. supports the 5-to-10 item limit
    b. supports the two-second limit
    c. finds no difference between the two-second limit and the 5-to-10 item limit
    d. finds that STM is limitless under certain conditions

34. Chunking works not only with numbers, but also with:

    a. unconscious wishes   c. eidetic images
    b. nonsense syllables   d. words and sentences

35. Which of the following statements about coding in STM is **true**?

    a. Capacity is greater with phonological coding than it is with visual coding.
    b. All material in STM is stored phonologically.
    c. Capacity is greater with visual coding than it is with phonological coding.
    d. Most people rely on shapes rather than sounds to retain STM information.

36. Which of the following statements about decay theory is **true**?

    a. Decay appears to be partly responsible for forgetting in STM.
    b. Decay theory has been discredited.
    c. Most of the evidence supporting decay theory comes from surveys.
    d. There is more empirical evidence favoring decay theory than for interference theory.

37. If you want to hold onto information for just a minute or two, the most effective device is:

    a. eidetic imaging   c. semantic practice
    b. elaborative rehearsal   d. rote rehearsal

38. Laboratory experiments have shown that repeating an item more often:

    a. is an effective way to improve recall
    b. is the most effective way to improve recall
    c. does not always improve recall
    d. interferes with recall

39. To be sure that information in STM will be remembered for a long time, most researchers believe that _____ is/are necessary.

   a. distractor studies
   b. elaborative rehearsal
   c. collaborative rehearsal
   d. rote rehearsal

40. Relating new information to something we already know is called:

   a. elaborative relativity
   b. rote rehearsal
   c. elaborative rehearsal
   d. retrograde rehearsal

41. Events that occur just before a person gets knocked unconscious are in STM. Rehearsal is stopped. These events are completely forgotten. This condition is called:

   a. antrograde amnesia
   b. motivated forgetting
   c. hysterical amnesia
   d. retrograde amnesia

42. In which part of the memory system do dreams take place? In:

   a. STM
   b. both STM and LTM
   c. sensory registers only
   d. sensory registers and STM

43. Statistical concepts and formulas are examples of:

   a. episodic memory
   b. mnemonic devices
   c. concepts stored in STM
   d. semantic memory

44. While semantic memory is like an encyclopedia or dictionary, episodic memory is like a _____.

   a. directory
   b. diary
   c. list
   d. set of categories

45. Diary is to episodic memory as:

   a. card catalog is to library
   b. dictionary is to encyclopedia
   c. encyclopedia is to thesaurus
   d. encyclopedia is to semantic memory

46. We can quickly retrieve isolated facts from LTM:

    a. because of organization
    b. only if we have above average intelligence
    c. because we have eidetic imagery
    d. when we use phonological coding

47. Successful retrieval of information from LTM is greatly enhanced by:

    a. rote rehearsal in STM
    b. separating semantic from episodic memories before processing
    c. careful organizing and cross-referencing of information as it goes into LTM
    d. eliminating retroactive interference

48. Most information in LTM seems to be coded in terms of:

    a. meaning   c. verbal images
    b. nonverbal images   d. episodic structures

49. For information to transfer from STM to LTM it must be:

    a. alphabetized   c. structured
    b. analyzed   d. rehearsed

50. Which of the following statements about coding in LTM is **true**?

    a. We most often use verbatim storage in LTM.
    b. Even simple sentences are usually coded in terms of their meaning.
    c. Only abstract concepts are coded in terms of their meaning.
    d. Storage in LTM is most often coded by surface structure.

51. Elaborative rehearsal is superior to rote rehearsal for transferring information to LTM because:

    a. elaborative rehearsal takes longer than rote rehearsal
    b. elaborate rehearsal deals only with surface structure
    c. the meaning of the information is extracted, then linked to existing information
    d. with elaborative rehearsal there is no need to link new information with existing information

52. Which of the following statements is **true**?

    a. We tend to remember semantic material better than episodic.
    b. We tend to remember episodic material better than semantic.
    c. Remembrance of semantic and episodic material is equal.
    d. Episodic memories are remembered better if we code the surface structure.

53. We tend to remember semantic material better than episodic because:

    a. episodic material cannot be elaboratively rehearsed
    b. episodic material has no meaning for us
    c. episodic material cannot be related to material already in LTM
    d. we code fewer cross-references for episodic material

54. Learn A, learn B, forget A is the definition for:

    a. decay of old material   c. proactive interference
    b. retroactive interference   d. elaborative inhibition

55. Learn A, learn B, forget B is the definition for:

    a. proactive interference   c. retroactive interference
    b. retrograde amnesia   d. reconstruction

56. Memories can be transformed into something at least partly different or to fit a person's current or desired view. This is called:

    a. elaborated recall   c. reconstructive memory
    b. episodic novelty   d. schematic linking

57. When an experience doesn't fit our view of the world or ourselves, we unconsciously adjust it or "forget" it entirely. Freud called this phenomenon:

    a. reconstruction   c. elaboration
    b. suppression   d. repression

58. Extreme repression can cause:

    a. hysterical amnesia   c. depression
    b. retrograde amnesia   d. antrograde amnesia

59. The way in which people use past reactions and experiences to organize perceptions of an episode in the present is called:

a. expectation theory   c. schema theory
b. elaboration theory   d. episodic reconstruction

60. _____ are powerful factors in retrieval from long-term memory.

a. Hints   c. Signals
b. Cues   d. Clues

61. When memories are called up spontaneously without any effort on our part, they are called _____ memories.

a. implicit   c. automatic
b. explicit   d. reconstructed

62. _____ enable(s) a person to see the features of an image in minute detail.

a. Eidetic imagery   c. Mnemonic devices
b. Implicit imagery   d. Elaborative rehearsal

63. "Thirty days hath September, April, June . . ." is an example of:

a. explicit memory   c. a mnemonic device
b. eidetic imagery   d. SQ3R

64. A well-known and effective system for studying is:

a. SR3Q   c. MMPI
b. TAT   d. SQ3R

65. Even though most memories are stored widely throughout the brain, which of the following brain structures is essential for the formation of memories? The:

a. hypothalamus   c. thalamus
b. hippocampus   d. reticular formation

Answers for this section:

22. d (231)   31. d (236)   40. c (241)   49. d (245)   58. a (249)
23. b (231)   32. b (237)   41. d (242)   50. b (245)   59. c (250)
24. c (232)   33. b (236)   42. a (242)   51. c (245)   60. b (251)
25. d (231)   34. d (238)   43. d (243)   52. a (245)   61. a (253)
26. d (232)   35. c (239)   44. b (244)   53. d (245)   62. a (256)
27. a (232)   36. a (239)   45. d (243)   54. b (246)   63. c (257)
28. d (234)   37. d (240)   46. a (244)   55. a (246)   64. d (259)
29. b (239)   38. c (241)   47. c (244)   56. c (247)   65. b (261)
30. a (234)   39. b (241)   48. a (245)   57. d (249)

Applying the Facts

The learning of facts and concepts is of little value unless it can be applied and employed to solve problems. The next group of multiple-choice questions reflects applications of your learning.

66. You are on your way to the shopping mall. Your sound system is turned on and you are thinking about the many chores you have planned for the day. You park your car, go in the mall, complete your shopping, return to the parking lot . . . and have no idea where your car is parked. The **best** explanation for this lapse of memory is:

   a.   retroactive interference
   b.   you did not pay attention to the location when you parked
   c.   proactive interference
   d.   you used only rote rehearsal to remember the location

67. You are at a large gathering of friends, concentrating on a conversation even though there is considerable noise because of many people talking. In spite of the confusion, you hear your name spoken from the other side of the room. You immediately refocus your attention in that direction. Cherry (1966) called this behavior:

   a.   the cocktail party phenomenon
   b.   the filter phenomenon
   c.   attention in the sensory registers
   d.   meaningful perception

68. You have a telephone credit card, but you do not like to use it in a public place for fear that someone will get the numbers and charge calls to you. The credit card has 14 digits. The findings of which of the following researchers might give you some confidence to use your card even if people are within hearing range?

   a. Baddeley, Schweickert and Boruff
   b. Herman Ebbinghaus
   c. Miller and Sperling
   d. Tulving and Patkau

69. Someone, wants to give you $500.00. You would rather have the money in 100's, 50's, 20's, 10's, and 5's than have 500 one-dollar bills (or $500.00 in pennies!). This situation is analogous to which of the following memory concepts?

   a. rehearsal   c. eidetics
   b. mnemonics   d. chunking

70. In spite of the fact that you see and handle pennies often, you would most probably fail to draw an accurate reproduction. Which of the following statements **best** explains your vain attempt?

   a. You do not have enough artistic talent.
   b. Mere repetition without intent to learn does not seem to enhance memory.
   c. You used only rote rehearsal to learn the characteristics of a penny.
   d. You did not use eidetic imagery to recall the characteristics.

71. George needed a plumber. He looked up the plumber's phone number in the directory. By the time he got to the telephone to dial it, he had forgotten the number. Which of the following is the **best** explanation for George's forgetfulness? He:

   a. did not use elaborative rehearsal to hold the number in STM until he got to the telephone
   b. did not rehearse the number into long-term memory
   c. was the victim of retroactive interference
   d. did not use rote rehearsal to hold the number in STM until he got to the telephone

72. Sue was in an automobile accident. She was not seriously injured, but was knocked unconscious. She is very worried because she cannot remember events that occurred just before the accident. Sue was a victim of:

   a. hysterical amnesia   c. retrograde amnesia
   b. antrograde amnesia   d. repression

73. You had a particularly interesting dream last night and you want to remember it. Which of the following techniques would be **most** helpful in reaching your goal?

   a. use elaborative rehearsal immediately upon awakening
   b. use rote rehearsal immediately upon awakening
   c. create a mnemonic device for recalling the dream
   d. try to dream the same dream tonight

74. If your professor would like the class to have higher grades on the next test, which of the following should he/she do long before the test date?

   a. Announce that there will be a 2-day review before test day.
   b. Tell the class what "kind" of a test it will be: recall, multiple choice, etc.
   c. Tell the class to have a party the night before the test for relaxation.
   d. Tell the class that the test will be very difficult in order to motivate students to study.

75. Is it possible that Senator Ted Kennedy's memory problems concerning the Chappaquiddick incident were caused by _____ ?

   a. retrograde amnesia   c. antrograde amnesia
   b. suppression   d. hysterical amnesia

76. Perhaps you remember Sue, who had open-heart surgery from the chapter on sensation and perception. She was overwhelmed by memories when she smelled a certain perfume used during her recovery. Now that you know something about memory, the **best** explanation for this phenomenon is:

   a. explicit memory   c. implicit memory
   b. spontaneous recovery   d. flashbulb memory

77. Phil's father was in the hospital in a coma. The condition was terminal. The patient was very wealthy. Phil and his brother were in his room one night discussing how wonderful it was going to be when they inherited all that money. The next day, the patient came out of the coma, called an attorney, and removed his sons from the will, leaving to them only what was required by law. Then, the patient died. This is a true story. Although your text does not discuss comas, it does point out that _____ is not completely blocked by anesthesia.

   a. implicit memory   c. reconstructive memory
   b. explicit memory   d. reasoning ability

Answers for this section:

66. b (232)   71. d (240)   76. c (253)
67. a (234)   72. c (242)   77. a (255)
68. c (236)   73. a (242)
69. d (237)   74. b (245)
70. b (240)   75. d (242)

Fill-in-the-Blank Questions: Recalling What You Have Learned

By now, there should be a considerable amount of new information about Memory in long-term memory. The following questions of recall rather than recognition will show if you are becoming more comfortable with the material.

Remembering the Facts

1.   Entry points for raw information from the senses are called _____ _____.

2.   The selection of some incoming information for further processing is called _____.

3.   Short-term memory is also called _____ memory.

4.   Consciousness is another term for _____ _____ memory.

5.   The grouping of information into meaningful units for easier handling by short-term memory is called _____.

6.   _____ theory holds that the passage of time itself causes forgetting.

7.   Other information gets in the way of old or new information according to _____ theory.

8.   Retaining information in STM by repeating it over and over is called _____ rehearsal.

9.   The linking of new information in STM to familiar material stored in LTM is called _____ rehearsal.

10.   The portion of memory that is more or less permanent and that corresponds to everything we "know" is called _____ memory.

11.   _____ memory is the portion of long-term memory that stores general facts and information.

12.   The portion of long-term memory that stores more specific information that has personal meaning is called _____ memory.

13.   The particular arrangement of verbal information, such as words in a sentence is called _____ structure.

14.   _____ structure is the underlying meaning conveyed by verbal information.

15.   The process by which old material already in memory interferes with new information is called _____ interference.

16.   _____ interference is the process by which new information interferes with old information already in memory.

17.   A set of beliefs or expectations about something that is based on past experience is called a/an _____.

18.   Memories that were either unintentionally committed to memory or unintentionally retrieved from memory are called _____ memories.

19.   Memory for information that was intentionally committed to memory or intentionally retrieved from memory is called _____ memory.

20.   _____ _____ is the ability to reproduce unusually sharp and detailed images of something that has been seen.

21.   A person with highly developed memory skills is called a/an _____.

22.   Techniques that make material easier to remember are called _____.

23.   A time-honored technique for effective studying is _____.

24.   A brain structure that is crucial for the formation of memories is the _____.

Answers for this section:

1.	sensory registers (231)	13.	surface (245)
2.	attention (231)	14.	deep (245)
3.	working (234)	15.	proactive (246)
4.	short-term (234)	16.	retroactive (246)
5.	chunking (237)	17.	schema (250)
6.	decay (239)	18.	implicit (254)
7.	interference (239)	19.	explicit (254)
8.	rote (240)	20.	eidetic imagery (256)
9.	elaborative (241)	21.	mnemonist (256)
10.	long-term (243)	22.	mnemonics (257)
11.	semantic (243)	23.	SQ3R (259)
12.	episodic (243)	24.	hippocampus (260)

Understanding and Applying the Facts

As you previously did with recognition-type questions, you will now move to a higher level of recall. The following questions will determine if you understand the facts.

25. Information will be lost from the sensory registers and will not be processed into STM unless you _____ _____.

26. Information from the _____ _____ disappears quite rapidly.

27. A visual image is called a/an _____ and an auditory image is called a/an _____.

28. According to Miller (1956) and Sperling (1960), STM can hold only _____ bits of information at the same time.

29. Baddeley, Schweikert, and Boruff have evidence that STM can hold as much information as can be repeated or rehearsed in _____ seconds.

30. At best, the capacity of STM is _____.

31. One reason you can remember a 10-digit telephone number is because you have learned to _____ it.

32. It appears that the capacity of STM is greater with _____ coding than it is with _____ coding.

33. If you need to hold onto information for only a minute or two, _____ rehearsal is most effective. However, if you want to be able to retrieve information from LTM, you should use _____ rehearsal.

34. Retrograde amnesia occurs because events just before the shock remained at the _____ _____ _____ level.

35. _____ rehearsal is necessary if you want to remember something more or less permanently.

36. Memory for the terminology and concepts in this psychology course is an example of _____ memory.

37. You had a dog when you were 5 years old, but he ran away and you never saw him again. You remember his name, what he looked like, and the fun you had with him. This is an example of _____ memory.

38. You probably do not remember what you had for dinner last Tuesday night because that is _____ memory and you most likely did not relate it to anything in LTM.

39. One month ago, your girlfriend cooked a special dinner for you. She was in a serious automobile accident the next day and you have not had the opportunity to see much of her since then. You remember exactly what you had for dinner that night. This is an example of _____ memory and you remember the details because the event had _____ for you.

40. _____ theory does not seem very likely to explain loss of memory from LTM.

41. _____ theory is a better explanation for loss of memory from LTM.

42. If you learn something in your 8:00 a.m. class and then you learn something in your 9:00 a.m. class, you may have difficulty remembering the information from the 8:00 a.m. class. This is an example of _____ interference.

43. Sometimes eyewitness accounts are not accurate. The witness believes the truth is being told. Lying is not a factor. This situation can be explained by _____ memory.

44. In _____ amnesia, there is no apparent organic reason for memory failure.

45. Meaning influences the amount of attention we pay to particular events, but another factor that influences our attention is the _____.

46. _____ seem to help people streamline their retrieval processes.

47. Bob met a girl who used the same perfume his mother used. His mother had died 5 years ago. A flood of memories returned to Bob about his mother that he had long ago "forgotten." The explanation for Bob's memories is called _____ memory.

48. Anesthesia blocks _____ memory.

49. Eidetic imagery is more common in _____.

50. The Russian newspaper reporter Shereshevskii was a famous _____.

51. _____ _____ _____ is a mnemonic device for remembering the colors of the visual spectrum.

52. The third R in SQ3R refers to _____.

53. Some of the learning that takes place in classical conditioning is apparently stored in the _____.

Answers for this section:

25.	pay attention (232)	40.	decay (246)
26.	sensory registers (232)	41.	interference (246)
27.	icon, echo (231, 232)	42.	retroactive (246)
28.	5 to 10 (236)	43.	reconstructive (247)
29.	1.5 to 2 (236)	44.	hysterical (249)
30.	limited (234)	45.	schema (250)
31.	chunk (237)	46.	schemata (250)
32.	visual, phonological (239)	47.	implicit (253)
33.	rote, elaborative (241)	48.	explicit (255)
34.	short-term memory (242)	49.	children (256)
35.	elaborative (241)	50.	mnemonist (256)
36.	semantic (243)	51.	Roy G. Biv (257)
37.	episodic (243)	52.	review (259)
38.	episodic (243)	53.	cerebellum (260)
39.	episodic, meaning (245)		

Testing Yourself For Mastery

      The following terms and concepts are found in boldface or italics in the chapter. The time has come to determine if you can define and discuss your new learning in your own words, then check your work against the text.

attention

sensory registers

short-term memory

chunking

decay theory

interference theory

rote rehearsal

elaborative rehearsal

retrograde amnesia

long-term memory

semantic memory

episodic memory

reconstructive memory

surface structure

deep structure

retroactive interference

proactive interference

schema

implicit memory

explicit memory

eidetic memory

mnemonics

mnemonist

SQ3R

Integrating Your Newly Learned Information

Now that you have recognized, recalled, and given definition to Memory, you are ready to try to integrate your knowledge in a definitive discussion through short-answer questions.

1. Explain the function of the sensory registers, short-term memory, and long-term memory. (230-243)

2. List and discuss the characteristics of short-term memory. (234-239)

3. Explain why chunking makes short-term memory more efficient. (237)

4. Explain the difference between rote rehearsal and elaborative rehearsal and discuss why rote rehearsal is ineffective for retrieval in long-term memory. (240)

5. Why do we tend to remember semantic material better than episodic material? (245)

6. Why does reconstructive memory occur? (247)

7. How do schemata serve memory? (250)

8. Discuss some of the factors that influence long-term memory. (251, 252)

9. How do implicit and explicit memory work together to make retrieval from LTM more effective? (253, 255)

10. How does a person go about becoming a mnemonist? (256, 257)

Applications

You have worked through a section of recognition-type questions to determine if you can apply information to real-life situations. It's time to try to respond to some applications. Some are based upon those questions. Answers to this section will not be given. Your questions concerning these applications will serve as a basis for classroom discussion and ideas for class projects throughout the course.

1. Your friend has a habit of "losing" her car in shopping mall lots and parking structures. What could you tell your friend that might be of help in breaking this habit?

2. The next time you are at a noisy gathering with one of your good friends, move some distance away and speak your friend's name. Describe what happened. See if you can get the *cocktail party phenomenon* to work.

3. Pete was taken to the Detroit Institute of Arts, as a child, to see the famous Diego Rivera fresco depicting the Ford Motor Company assembly line. Later in life he returned to see it again and was deeply impressed. He repeated the artist's name 15 times, but when he tried to recall the name he could not do it. Then he heard about elaborative rehearsal. He thought of his friend, Dennis who drove a Buick Riviera to San Diego to visit his mother. From that time on, whenever he wanted to recall the artist's name, all he had to do was think of Dennis. He never again failed to recall Diego Rivera. Think of an item of information you need to remember and devise a similar elaborative plan.

4. You have responded to a recognition-type question about Sue, who was in an automobile accident and was worried because she could not remember what happened just before the accident. You are Sue's friend and do not like her to believe that something is wrong with her. What can you tell her that will help her to understand that she has nothing to worry about?

5. Now that you know that dreams take place in short-term memory, be prepared to write down the content of your next dream as soon as you awaken. Use elaborative rehearsal, then see if you can remember the content one month later.

6. Try to think of one or two ways in which knowledge of schema theory could help you in your daily activities or improve a family or social relationship.

7. Why do stage actors often have "prompters?" Be sure to use the concepts from your knowledge of memory in your answer.

8. The next time you misplace something, use the concept of implicit memory to help you to locate it.

9. You responded to a recognition-type question about how Phil and his brother were taken out of their father's will. Since you now know something about implicit memory, what should you do if you are within hearing range of a person who is in a coma, unconscious, or under anesthesia?

10. What would your life be like if you had permanent eidetic imagery?

11. Develop a mnemonic device for remembering the parts of a neuron.

Return to Chapter Summary

Now that you have concluded these exercises, you should go back and reread the chapter summary in your textbook. It provides you with a framework that integrates all of this newly-learned information. By reviewing the chapter summary, you will strengthen the many connections between the various new pieces of information.

COGNITION AND MENTAL ABILITIES

7

Chapter Objectives

After you have read and studied this chapter, you should be able to:

1. Differentiate among and give definition to the building blocks of thought: language, images, and concepts.
2. Explain the functions of phonemes, morphemes, and the two parts of grammar.
3. Understand the nature of problem solving and be aware of the obstacles in solving problems.
4. Define and explain the solution strategies for solving problems.
5. Explain the difference between convergent and divergent thinking and how divergent thinking relates to creativity.
6. Consider the models that have been developed to aid in decision making and employ them in your own decisions when you can.
7. Understand the various ways in which intelligence has been defined and compare the newer theories with traditional approaches to measuring intelligence.
8. Tell the difference between individual, group, culture-fair, and performance tests, and how the Binet and Wechsler instruments differ.
9. Recognize the qualities of a "good test" and explain how reliability and validity are determined.
10. Understand why IQ tests have been criticized.
11. Explain the relative contributions of heredity and environment to intelligence.

12. Know that there are extremes in measured intelligence and determine how these extremes are assessed.
13. Consider the nature of creativity and its relationship to intelligence.

Multiple-Choice Questions: Recognizing What You Have Learned

These questions ask only that you recognize what you have learned. When you recognize a correct answer, you have accessed that information in memory. A knowledge of facts serves as a framework for later analysis and problem solving.

Remembering the Facts

This group of multiple-choice questions requires that you simply recognize facts from your textbook.

1. The process of thinking is called:

   a. linguistics　　　　　　c. semantics
   b. processing　　　　　　d. cognition

2. The basic sounds that make up any language are called:

   a. phonemes　　　　　　c. semantics
   b. cognates　　　　　　d. morphemes

3. The smallest meaningful units of speech are called:

   a. phonetics　　　　　　c. phonemes
   b. morphemes　　　　　　d. syntax

4. The language rules that determine the meaning and form of words and sentences are known as:

   a. roles　　　　　　　　c. syntax
   b. semantics　　　　　　d. grammar

5. The criteria for meaning in a language is termed:

   a. syntax　　　　　　　c. semantics
   b. morphemes　　　　　　d. rules of thought

6. Rules for the structure of word forms and sentences are called:

    a.   syntax   c.   semantics
    b.   phonemes   d.   algorithms

7. A mental representation of a sensory experience is called a/an:

    a.   concept   c.   icon
    b.   prototype   d.   image

8. A mental category for classifying objects, people, or experiences is termed a:

    a.   schema   c.   cognitive structure
    b.   concept   d.   mental structure

9. A mental model containing the most typical features of a concept is called a _____ by Rosch.

    a.   cognitive structure   c.   prototype
    b.   category   d.   representation

10. A problem-solving strategy based on successive elimination of incorrect solutions until the correct one is found is termed:

    a.   insight   c.   successive approximations
    b.   trial and error   d.   hill climbing

11. A correct solution to a problem is guaranteed by this step by step method:

    a.   heuristic   c.   insight
    b.   hill-climbing   d.   algorithm

12. _____ are rules of thumb that help in simplifying and solving problems, but they do not guarantee a solution.

    a.   Heuristics   c.   Insights
    b.   Subgoals   d.   Algorithms

13. Each step in this problem-solving strategy moves you progressively closer to the final goal:

    a.   successive approximations   c.   information retrieval
    b.   self-pacing   d.   hill-climbing

14. Which of the following is **not** a heuristic strategy?

   a. subgoals   c. trial and error
   b. hill-climbing   d. working backward

15. Another heuristic strategy is:

   a. working backward   c. functional set
   b. planning forward   d. obstacle removal

16. The tendency to perceive and approach problems in certain ways is referred to as:

   a. functional set   c. set
   b. rigidity   d. functional fixedness

17. Interference with the problem-solving process due to the tendency to perceive only a limited number of uses for an object is called:

   a. set   c. inflexibility
   b. functional fixedness   d. functional set

18. When principles or concepts are drawn, diagrammed, or charted so that they can be better understood the strategy is called:

   a. visualizing   c. converging
   b. imaging   d. invention

19. Thinking that is original, inventive, and flexible is called _____.

   a. creative   c. original
   b. convergent   d. divergent

20. Thinking that is directed toward one correct solution to a problem is called _____ thinking.

   a. divergent   c. concrete
   b. convergent   d. structured

21. _____ is a problem-solving strategy in which an individual or group collects ideas and evaluates them after all ideas have been collected.

   a. Brainstorming   c. Groupthink
   b. Barnstorming   d. Group dynamics

22. A/an _____ heuristic is one by which a judgement is based on information that is most easily retrieved from memory.

    a. functional   c. availability
    b. representative   d. tool

23. A/an _____ heuristic is one by which a new situation is judged on the basis of its resemblance to a stereotypical model.

    a. representative   c. availability
    b. structured   d. functional

24. Triarchic theory of intelligence was developed by:

    a. Sternberg   c. Binet
    b. Guilford   d. Wechsler

25. According to Sternberg, the ability to acquire new knowledge and to solve problems effectively is called _____ intelligence.

    a. contextual   c. componential
    b. performance   d. experiential

26. In Sternberg's approach, the ability to adjust to new tasks and to adapt creatively is called _____ intelligence.

    a. divergent   c. componential
    b. contextual   d. experiential

27. The ability to select environments in which one is able to function effectively is called _____ intelligence by Sternberg.

    a. experiential   c. contextual
    b. componential   d. adaptational

28. Terman's version of the intelligence test developed by Binet and Simon is called the:

    a. Terman-Binet Scale   c. Stanford-Binet Intelligence Scale
    b. Terman-Stanford Scale   d. TSBI

29. The numerical value given to intelligence that is determined from scores on an intelligence test is called a/an:

   a. intelligence rating   c. ability score
   b. intelligence quotient   d. performance rating

30. An intelligence test developed especially for school-aged children that measures verbal and performance abilities and yields an overall IQ is called the:

   a. WISC-III   c. WAIS-III
   b. WISC-II   d. Stanford-Binet-III R

31. An individual intelligence test developed especially for adults, measuring both verbal and performance abilities and yielding an overall IQ score is called the:

   a. Sternberg Triarchic Scale
   b. Spearman Scale
   c. Stanford-Binet Intelligence Scale
   d. WAIS-R

32. Written intelligence tests administered to many people at one time are called _____ tests.

   a. aggregate   c. performance
   b. group   d. triarchic

33. Intelligence tests that do not involve language are called _____ tests.

   a. performance   c. abstract
   b. culture-fair   d. culture-free

34. Which of the following developed a culture-fair test of intelligence?

   a. Sternberg   c. Cattell
   b. Wechsler   d. Thurstone

35. The ability of a test to produce consistent and stable scores is called:

   a. reliability   c. dependability
   b. coefficiency   d. validity

36. The ability of a test to measure what is has been designed to measure is termed:

   a.   correctness   c.   reliability
   b.   validity   d.   trustworthiness

37. When a test has an adequate sample of the skills or knowledge it is supposed to measure, it has:

   a.   content validity   c.   been standardized
   b.   reliability   d.   cultural fairness

38. When test scores are compared to independent measures of that which the test is designed to measure, there is an attempt to determine:

   a.   content validity   c.   test-retest reliability
   b.   criterion-related validity d.   face validity

39. A condition of significantly subaverage intelligence combined with deficiencies in adaptive behavior is called:

   a.   mental deficiency   c.   mental weakness
   b.   low mentality   d.   mental retardation

40. _____ refers to superior IQ combined with demonstrated or potential abilities.

   a.   Potential ability   c.   Above average intelligence
   b.   Giftedness   d.   Brilliance

41. _____ is the ability to produce novel and unique socially valued ideas or objects.

   a.   Genius   c.   Inventiveness
   b.   Originality   d.   Creativity

Answers for this section:

1.	d (268)	12.	a (274)	23.	a (281)	34.	c (289)
2.	a (268)	13.	d (274)	24.	a (284)	35.	a (290)
3.	b (268)	14.	c (274, 275)	25.	c (284)	36.	b (290)
4.	d (269)	15.	a (275)	26.	d (284)	37.	a (290)
5.	c (269)	16.	c (275)	27.	c (284)	38.	b (291)
6.	a (269)	17.	b (276)	28.	c (287)	39.	d (298)
7.	d (270)	18.	a (277)	29.	b (287)	40.	b (300)
8.	b (270)	19.	d (278)	30.	a (288)	41.	d (301)
9.	c (270)	20.	b (279)	31.	d (287)		
10.	b (273)	21.	a (281)	32.	b (289)		
11.	d (274)	22.	c (281)	33.	a (289)		

Understanding the Facts

Now that you have found that you can recognize facts from Cognition and Mental Abilities, the next step is to determine if you understand the meaning of newly-learned information. These multiple-choice questions require a higher level of thinking. They will help you establish more solid connections and provide practice in dealing with higher level concepts.

42.   Which of the following statements about phonemes is true?

   a.   Phonemes play an important role in helping us think.
   b.   There are about 55 phonemes in the English language.
   c.   By themselves, phonemes are meaningless.
   d.   Phonemes exist only in English and continental languages.

43.   When phonemes are grouped together to form words, prefixes, and suffixes they:

   a.   still do not play a significant role in thinking
   b.   form large units of speech
   c.   represent complex ideas
   d.   are called morphemes

44.   The task of semantics is to:

   a.   assign meaning to morphemes
   b.   assign meaning to phonemes
   c.   clarify syntactical rules
   d.   make grammar more understandable

45. "The duck put on his best ice cream cone and rode his suitcase to the chess board." This sentence is correct for _____ and incorrect for _____.

a. semantics, syntax
b. syntax, grammar
c. syntax, semantics
d. prefixes, suffixes

46. Putting a stimulus into a category and listing its characteristics that differentiate it from every other stimulus in the category is one way of defining a/an:

a. image
b. concept
c. precept
d. prototype

47. We would need a different name for every individual object if we could not:

a. understand grammar
b. form images
c. form concepts
d. manipulate images

48. Without the ability to _____ experience, every new experience would be a surprise.

a. categorize
b. imagine
c. learn from
d. conceptualize

49. Which of the following statements about concepts is **true**?

a. Concepts are simple and clear-cut.
b. Concepts overlap one another and are often poorly defined.
c. Concepts are unambiguous.
d. Prototypes are of no help in forming accurate concepts.

50. If we found a cat with no tail and no whiskers that did not "meow" we would most probably recognize it as a cat because:

a. our prototype is a perfect representation
b. we thought about our prototypical cat
c. this example is not a "fuzzy" concept
d. there is no ambiguity in the situation

51. The first step in solving a problem is called:

a. analysis
b. problem representation
c. functional structuring
d. conceptualizing the problem

52. Which of the following is a negative aspect of using trial and error as a strategy to solve a problem?

   a. The strategy is too difficult for most people.
   b. Trial and error is too time consuming.
   c. The strategy can only be used in mathematics.
   d. It takes too long to learn how to do it.

53. A problem-solving strategy that is useful when a solution must be found quickly is:

   a. an algorithm   c. the identification of subgoals
   b. a heuristic   d. information retrieval

54. Mathematical formulas that guarantee a correct solution if applied properly are examples of which of the following problem-solving strategies?

   a. the algorithm   c. a heuristic
   b. means-end analysis   d. end goal

55. _____ is a useful strategy for answering questions on a multiple-choice test.

   a. Trial and error   c. Hill-climbing
   b. An algorithm   d. Means-end analysis

56. Which of the following statements about sets is **true**?

   a. If properly used, sets can solve any problem.
   b. They can either help or hinder problem solving.
   c. Education tends to ignore the learning of sets.
   d. A strong set is the best guarantee for problem solution.

57. _____ is a set that can seriously hinder problem solving.

   a. Functional fixedness   c. Functional autonomy
   b. Working backward   d. Visualizing

58. If the assumption that a good solution to a problem exists and that assumption turns out to be true, using _____ is an effective strategy.

   a. creativity   c. the tactic of elimination
   b. an algorithm   d. visualizing

59. Problems that have no single correct solution and that require a flexible approach necessitates the use of:

    a. visualizing
    b. convergent thinking
    c. functional thinking
    d. divergent thinking

60. Decision making differs from other kinds of problem solving because:

    a. there are no criteria on which to base a selection
    b. the criteria for making a choice are not complex
    c. all the possible solutions are known
    d. there is no way to proceed logically toward a solution

61. To proceed into the decision making process logically, a person would use some kind of:

    a. compensatory model
    b. creativity
    c. divergent thinking
    d. noncompensatory model

62. When a decision is based upon information that matches a stereotyped model _____ is being used.

    a. the heuristic of availability
    b. discrimination
    c. the heuristic of representativeness
    d. generalization

63. In the absence of full and accurate information, decisions are often based on whatever information is most easily retrieved from memory and this constitutes use of:

    a. compensatory choice
    b. the availability heuristic
    c. the heuristic of representativeness
    d. noncompensatory choice

64. When laypersons define intelligence they stress _____.

    a. motivation
    b. verbal ability
    c. social competence
    d. problem-solving ability

65. Theorists who study intelligence have been classified as "lumpers" or "splitters." Which of the following researchers qualifies as a "lumper?"

   a.   Charles Spearman   c.   J.P. Guilford
   b.   L.L. Thurstone   d.   David Wechsler

66. Which of the following researchers performed so poorly on standard tests of intelligence that he became a professor at Yale and proposed his own theory of intelligence?

   a.   Charles Spearman   c.   J.P. Guilford
   b.   R.B. Cattell   d.   Robert Sternberg

67. R.B. Cattell's term for abilities such as reasoning and verbal numerical skills is _____ intelligence.

   a.   crystallized   c.   fluid
   b.   experiential   d.   triarchic

68. R.B. Cattell's term for skills such as spatial and visual imagery, noticing visual details, and rote memory is _____ intelligence.

   a.   creative   c.   crystallized
   b.   liquid   d.   fluid

69. The theory of intelligence that is closest to the informal view held by laypersons is that of:

   a.   R.B. Cattell   c.   J.P. Guilford
   b.   Robert Sternberg   d.   L.M. Terman

70. The term "intelligence quotient" was introduced:

   a.   in 1900
   b.   in 1930
   c.   by L.M. Terman
   d.   in opposition to the work of David Wechsler

71. Which of the following statements about the Stanford-Binet test is **true**?

   a.   It can be administered to a large group if necessary.
   b.   It is given individually.
   c.   Any certified teacher can administer the test.
   d.   It takes 2 hours to administer it to young children.

72. The individual test most often given to adults is the:

   a. WISC-III   c. SCAT
   b. Stanford-Binet   d. WAIS-R

73. Wechsler's chief innovation was in:

   a. validity   c. reliability
   b. scoring   d. increased sophistication

74. Which of the following is **not** a true difference between the Stanford-Binet and the Wechsler tests?

   a. The Binet reports intelligence in terms of an IQ, the Wechsler does not.
   b. The Wechsler test has both a verbal and a performance IQ. The Stanford-Binet does not.
   c. A person can earn extra points on the Wechsler, but not on the Stanford-Binet.
   d. Both speed and accuracy effect the Wechsler score, but not the Stanford-Binet.

75. The SCAT, CTMM, SAT, ACTP, and GRE are all examples of:

   a. culture fair tests
   b. individual tests of intelligence
   c. group tests
   d. test that have been demonstrated to lack validity

76. Which of the following is a disadvantage of group tests?

   a. Examiner bias is eliminated.
   b. Group tests can be scored quickly.
   c. More useful norms can be established.
   d. Emotionally disturbed children do better on individual tests.

77. _____ tests minimize or eliminate the use of words, therefore they may be more _____ than early tests of intelligence.

   a. Performance, culture-fair
   b. Groups, valid
   c. Individual, reliable
   d. Foreign, culture-fair

78. One of the earliest performance tests was the:

a. Koh blocks   c. Seguin Form Board
b. Bender-Gestalt   d. CTMM

79. One of the most effective tests for very young children is the:

a. Bagley Scale of Infant Development
b. Bayley Scale of Infant Development
c. Porteus Maze
d. Progressive Matrices

80. Among other important qualities, culture-fair tests:

a. emphasize skills and value
b. try to minimize skills and values
c. can be used with infants
d. emphasize the use of language

81. Which of the following is necessary to make a test "good?"

a. the ease in which it is administered
b. readability
c. validity and reliability
d. whether or not it is culture-fair

82. If a test contains an adequate sample of the skills or knowledge that it is supposed to measure, the test is said to have:

a. criterion-related validity   c. a high reliability coefficient
b. content validity   d. face validity

83. One reason why minority children might perform more poorly on IQ tests than middle-class whites is because they:

a. are more driven to achieve
b. do not care about adult approval
c. are too emotional
d. are more wary of adults

84. From Skeels 1930 research, which of the following practices does **not** appear to be a factor in IQ scores?

   a. playing with children
   b. rewarding children for achievements
   c. the encouragement of talking
   d. strict discipline

85. Nearly 70 percent of all people have IQ's between:

   a. 70 and 110   c. 65 and 125
   b. 100 and 140   d. 85 and 115

86. Persons who score below _____ on the Stanford-Binet test are considered to be profoundly retarded.

   a. 50   c. 19
   b. 60   d. 15

87. Which of the following statements about the causes of mental retardation is **true**?

   a. The cause of mild retardation is known.
   b. Biological complications account for most cases of mental retardation.
   c. PKU is caused by social, nutritional and other risk factors.
   d. In most cases the cause of retardation is not known.

88. The more severe forms of mental retardation appear to involve:

   a. psychosocial factors   c. psychosexual factors
   b. genetic or biological disorders   d. economic factors

89. The "fragile X" syndrome affects _____ males and _____ females.

   a. 1 in every 1,000, 1 in every 2,500
   b. black, white
   c. 1 in every 5,500, 1 in every 1,000
   d. 10 in every 1,000, 10 in every 2,500

90. Research on the gifted has revealed that:

    a.   gifted children contribute greatly to society when they become adults
    b.   high IQ scores by themselves do not predict success
    c.   gifted people are a distinct group superior to others in many areas
    d.   people gifted in one area are usually gifted in other areas

91. Research has indicated that below an IQ of _____, higher IQ scores are accompanied by higher creativity, but above this point there is little or no relationship between IQ and creativity. These findings are in support of _____ theory.

    a.   120, Getzle's and Jackson's
    b.   130, Sternberg's
    c.   140, effectiveness
    d.   110, threshold

Answers for this section:

42.	c (268)	55.	c (274)	68.	d (284)	81.	c (290)
43.	d (268)	56.	b (275)	69.	b (284)	82.	b (290)
44.	a (269)	57.	a (276)	70.	c (287)	83.	d (292)
45.	c (269)	58.	c (277)	71.	b (287)	84.	d (295)
46.	b (270)	59.	d (277)	72.	d (287)	85.	d (298)
47.	c (270)	60.	c (279)	73.	b (288)	86.	c (298)
48.	d (270)	61.	a (280)	74.	b (287, 288)	87.	d (299)
49.	b (270)	62.	c (281)	75.	c (289)	88.	b (299)
50.	b (270)	63.	b (281)	76.	d (289)	89.	a (300)
51.	b (272)	64.	c (282)	77.	a (289)	90.	b (301)
52.	b (273)	65.	a (282)	78.	c (289)	91.	d (302)
53.	d (273)	66.	d (284)	79.	b (289)		
54.	a (274)	67.	a (284)	80.	b (289)		

Applying the Facts

The learning of facts and concepts is of little value unless it can be applied and employed to solve problems. The next group of multiple-choice questions reflects applications of your learning.

92. When we think about the explosion of the spaceship Challenger, we "see" the lift-off, the fiery explosion, and the long, curving trail of smoke. In thinking about this momentous incident we are using a/an:

   a. concept   c. image
   b. eidetic   d. prototype

93. When you take a statistics course, you will find that there is a formula for calculating the standard deviation. Your professor asks you to calculate the standard deviation. Which of the following problem-solving strategies would you use?

   a. an algorithm   c. information retrieval
   b. trial and error   d. a heuristic

94. If you never used the heel of a shoe as a hammer, you might have been hampered by:

   a. too many sets   c. functional fixedness
   b. a set   d. functional rigidity

95. Writing a poem or a song requires:

   a. divergent thinking   c. high intelligence
   b. an algorithm   d. convergent thinking

96. You are trying to balance your budget. Each reduction of expenses brings you closer to your goal. This is an example of:

   a. trial and error   c. information retrieval
   b. hill-climbing   d. an algorithm

97. You are a clinical psychologist whose task it is to administer an intelligence test to a university professor who has recently arrived from Germany. He speaks and reads English. For this task you should use:

   a. a group test   c. a culture-fair test
   b. the WAIS-foreign   d. the WAIS-R

98. Jan is a graduate student taking testing practicum. She has a client whom she takes to a quiet, private room and spends 90 minutes giving a test. After the client leaves she must spend an hour or more scoring the test. Jan is most likely giving the:

   a. GRE
   b. WAIS-R
   c. Progressive Matrices
   d. MMPI

99. Your professor gives you a test on Monday, then surprises you by giving you the same test on Friday. It is **most** likely that your professor:

   a. wants to determine the test's reliability
   b. thought someone was cheating
   c. wants to determine the test's validity
   d. believed the grades were too low the first time

100. Your psychology professor told the class that the last test of the course would be on testing, measurement, and statistics. The test is distributed and when you look at it you see that it contains items from the entire course. The test:

   a. results will not be reliable
   b. does not have content validity
   c. is not culture fair
   d. discriminates against women

101. Which of the following is **most** analogous to an unreliable test?

   a. a yardstick with an extra 1/16 inch between each inch marker
   b. a yardstick with 1/16 inch taken out between each inch marker
   c. a ruler made of steel
   d. an elastic ruler

102. Jan is a graduate student taking testing practicum. She gives the WISC-III to an 8-year old child. The child scores 25. She determines from that score that the child:

   a. is severely retarded
   b. has average intelligence
   c. is profoundly retarded
   d. is mildly retarded

Answers for this section:

92. c (270)   95. a (278)   98. b (287)   101. d (290)
93. a (274)   96. b (274)   99. a (290)   102. a (298)
94. c (276)   97. c (289)   100. b (290)

168

Fill-in-the-Blank Questions: Recalling What You Have Learned

By now, there should be a considerable amount of new information about Cognition and Mental Abilities in long-term memory. The following questions of recall rather than recognition will show if you are becoming more comfortable with the material.

Remembering the Facts

1. The process of thinking is called _____.

2. The basic sounds that make up any language are termed _____.

3. _____ are the smallest meaningful units of speech.

4. There are about _____ phonemes in the English language.

5. The criteria for meaning in a language is called _____.

6. Language rules that determine the meaning and form of words and sentences are known as _____.

7. Rules for the structure of words and sentences are called _____.

8. Rosch's _____ is a mental model containing the most typical features of a concept.

9. Problem _____ is the process of interpreting or defining a problem.

10. When we successively eliminate incorrect solutions to a problem until the correct one is found we are using a strategy called _____ _____ _____.

11. A problem-solving strategy that requires only the recovery of information from long-term memory is known as _____ _____.

12. The guarantee of a correct solution to a problem through a step-by-step method is the definition for a/an _____.

13. These strategies may help in simplifying and solving problems, but they do not guarantee a correct solution. They are called _____.

14. _____ _____ is a heuristic problem-solving strategy in which each step moves you progressively closer to a final goal.

15. Intermediate, more manageable goals used in one heuristic strategy to make it easier to reach a goal are called _____.

16. The tendency to perceive and approach problems in certain ways is known as a/an _____.

17. The tendency to perceive only a limited number of uses for an object, thus interfering with the process of problem solving is called _____ _____.

18. Thinking that meets the criteria of originality, inventiveness, and flexibility is called _____ thinking.

19. A problem-solving strategy in which possible solutions are evaluated according to appropriate criteria and discarded as they fail to contribute to a solution is called the _____ of _____.

20. When principles or concepts in a problem situation are drawn, diagrammed or charted so they can be better understood, the strategy is called _____.

21. Thinking that is directed toward one correct solution to a problem is called _____ thinking.

22. When an individual or group collects numerous ideas and evaluates them after all ideas have been collected, they have been _____.

23. A rational decision-making model in which choices are systematically evaluated on various criteria is called a/an _____ model.

24. The _____ model does not try to systematically weigh comparisons among alternatives.

25. The _____ heuristic is one by which a judgement is based on information that is most easily retrieved from memory.

26. A heuristic by which a new situation is judged on the basis of its resemblance to a stereotypical model is called _____.

27. Triarchic theory of intelligence comes from the work of _____.

28. The three aspects of Sternberg's triarchic theory are _____, _____, and _____.

29. The ability to select contexts in which you can excel and to shape the environment to fit your strengths is the _____ aspect of triarchic theory.

30. The ability to use insight and to adapt creatively in new situations is the _____ aspect of triarchic theory.

31. The ability to acquire new knowledge and to solve problems effectively is the _____ aspect of triarchic theory.

32. A numerical value given to intelligence is the _____ _____.

33. The _____ is an individual intelligence test developed especially for children.

34 The _____ is an intelligence test developed especially for adults.

35. Intelligence tests that do not involve language are called _____ tests.

36. Intelligence tests designed to eliminate cultural bias are called _____ - _____ tests.

37. The ability of a test to produce consistent and stable scores is called its _____.

38. _____ is the ability of a test to measure what it has been designed to measure.

39. If a test has an adequate sample of the skills or knowledge it is supposed to measure the test has _____ validity.

40. A condition of significantly subaverage intelligence combined with deficiencies in adaptive behavior is called _____ _____.

41. Persons with superior IQ's combined with ability in academic aptitude, creativity, or leadership are referred to as _____.

42. The ability to produce novel and unique socially valued ideas or objects is called _____.

Answers for this section:

1.	cognition (268)	23.	compensatory (280)
2.	phonemes (268)	24.	noncompensatory (280)
3.	morphemes (268)	25.	availability (281)
4.	45 (268)	26.	representativeness (281)
5.	semantics (269)	27.	Sternberg (284)
6.	grammar (269)	28.	componential, experiential, contextual (284)
7.	syntax (269)	29.	contextual (284)
8.	prototype (270)	30.	experiential (284)
9.	representation (272)	31.	componential (284)
10.	trial and error (273)	32.	intelligence quotient (IQ) (287)
11.	information retrieval (273)	33.	WISC III (288)
12.	algorithm (274)	34.	WAIS-R (287)
13.	heuristics (274)	35.	performance (289)
14.	hill-climbing (274)	36.	culture, fair (289)
15.	subgoals (274)	37.	reliability (290)
16.	set (275)	38.	validity (290)
17.	functional fixedness (276)	39.	content (290)
18.	divergent thinking (278)	40.	mental retardation (298)
19.	tactic, elimination (277)	41.	gifted (300)
20.	visualizing (277)	42.	creativity (301)
21.	convergent (278)		
22.	brainstorming (279)		

Understanding and Applying the Facts

As you previously did with recognition-type questions, you will now move to a higher level of recall. The following questions will determine if you understand the facts.

43. There are as many as _____ phonemes in some languages.

44. Phonemes seldom play an important role in helping us think because by themselves, phonemes are _____.

45. To put meaning into our language we must incorporate the use of _____.

46. In the sentence, "The dog black run to the window and barks at the cat yellow," the rules of _____ are being broken.

47. In the sentence, "The rat chased the computer over the tea kettle until the tree dissolved," the criteria of _____ are being violated.

48. _____ allow us to think in nonverbal ways.

49. Since concepts are not simple and clear-cut, we tend to construct a model or _____ of a representative stimulus in a category and then use those _____ in our thinking.

50. You recognize that a penguin is a bird even though it does not fly because you have constructed a _____ to help categorize it.

51. The first step in solving a problem is called _____ _____.

52. If your problem is to learn to drive an automobile, you certainly would not want to try to solve it by _____ _____ _____.

53. In statistics, to calculate the mean, you would add up all of the scores and divide that total by the number of scores. This is an example of solving a problem with a/an _____.

54. Part of problem solving is to decide which _____ is most appropriate for a given problem.

55. Jane needed to leave someone a note and she didn't have a pencil, so she used her eyeliner. Jane is **not** a victim of _____ _____.

56. Joe is a wood worker. He bought a plumber's plunger, painted the handle pink, and constructed the head of a flamingo for the top of the handle. Joe displayed _____ or _____ _____.

57. If you were to proceed into the decision making process in a logical way, systematically evaluating the choices on various criteria you would be employing the _____ model.

58. Aletta wanted to be the breeder of show dogs. She wanted a breed with "class" and one that was unusual. She also wanted a small animal, but one that would definitely be noticed. She used the _____ model to decide on the Bichon Frise.

59. Evan the Welshman is 84 years old. He retired from his job as minister of music for a large church, but he likes to play the organ occasionally. He is very much in demand and is offered more part-time jobs than he can handle. The people making the decisions to hire him are **not** using the heuristic of _____.

60. Jeannie is middle-aged and married. She wants a doctorate in psychology. Her grades are high, often a 4.00 for several semesters. She expends extreme effort in her studying. Her graduate entrance test scores were mediocre, but were acceptable at a university. Her husband is ill and out of work. Her son is very ill also. There are severe financial problems. But Jeannie continues in her quest, sometimes working around the clock. She would fit Sternberg's _____ aspect of intelligence.

61. If you were taking an individual intelligence test and were asked to put a jigsaw puzzle together, you were most likely taking the _____.

62. The WAIS-R consists of two parts. One is the verbal scale and the other is the _____ scale.

63. A test used to evaluate developmental abilities of children from two months to two and one half years is the _____ _____ of _____ _____.

64. There are some obvious problems with attempting to determine reliability using the test-retest method. A way to overcome those problems is to use _____ _____ of the test.

65. If you were to take a test for the HIV virus, you would want to be sure the test was both _____ and _____.

66. If a test measures "the thing it is supposed to measure," the test is _____.

67. All but _____ percent of the population falls between 70 and 130 for intelligence.

68. A genetically based disease in which the liver fails to produce an enzyme necessary for brain development is called _____.

69. The first researcher to study giftedness was _____. The studies were begun in the _____ (decade).

70. People who don't always look for the "right answer," but rather look for numerous possibilities and try to produce different solutions are called _____ thinkers. They are displaying _____ thinking.

71. Sara is a college professor with a sense of humor and an obvious tendency to be _____. Someone had put a metal file box in the faculty office with the label, "suggestion box." Sara constructed a paper head for the top of the box and a paper tongue sticking out of the box. Sara was also showing _____ thinking.

72. _____ theory says that for a person to be considered creative, he or she must first be slightly more intelligent than average, but beyond that point there is little relationship between IQ and creativity.

Answers for this section:

43. 85 (268)
44. meaningless (268)
45. morphemes (268)
46. syntax (269)
47. semantics (268)
48. images (270)
49. prototype, prototypes (270)
50. prototype (270)
51. problem representation (270)
52. trial and error (273)
53. algorithm (274)
54. heuristic (274)
55. functional fixedness (276)
56. creativity, divergent thinking (278)
57. compensatory (280)

58. compensatory (280)
59. representativeness (281)
60. contextual (284)
61. WAIS-R (288)
62. performance (287)
63. Bayley Scales, Infant Development (289)
64. alternate forms (290)
65. reliable and valid (290)
66. valid (290)
67. 5 (298)
68. phenylketonuria (PKU) (299)
69. Terman, 1920's (300)
70. creative, divergent (302)
71. creative, divergent (302)
72. threshold (302)

Testing Yourself For Mastery

The following terms and concepts are found in boldface or italics in the chapter. The time has come to determine if you can define and discuss your new learning in your own words, then check your work against the text.

cognition

phonemes

morphemes

grammar

semantics

syntax

image

concept

prototype

problem representation

trial and error

information retrieval

algorithms

heuristics

hill-climbing

subgoals

working backward

set

functional fixedness

tactic of elimination

visualizing

divergent thinking

convergent thinking

brainstorming

compensatory model

noncompensatory model

representativeness

availability

intelligence

triarchic theory

componential aspects of intelligence

experiential aspects of intelligence

contextual aspects of intelligence

intelligence test

intelligence quotient (IQ)

Wechsler Adult Intelligence Scale Revised (WAIS-R)

Wechsler Intelligence Scale for Children-Third Edition (WISC-III-R)

group tests

performance tests

culture-fair tests

reliability

validity

content validity

criterion related validity

mental retardation

giftedness

creativity

Integrating Your Newly Learned Information

Now that you have recognized, recalled, and given definition to Cognition and Mental Abilities, you are ready to try to integrate your knowledge in a definitive discussion through short-answer questions.

1.   Discuss the difference between phonemes and morphemes and explain the function of each. (268, 269)

2.   What are the two major components of grammar? Explain the functions of each. (269)

3.   Why is it necessary to construct prototypes in dealing with concepts? (270, 271)

4.   What are some of the obstacles to successful problem solving? Use specific terminology in your answer. (275, 276)

5.   Explain the difference between convergent and divergent thinking. (278)

6.   How does Sternberg's triarchic theory of intelligence differ from traditional views of intelligence and traditional methods of testing intelligence? (282, 284, 287)

7.   Describe how the Binet test and the Wechsler test are administered. (288, 289)

8.   List some group tests and discuss their advantages and disadvantages. (289)

9.   Why is there a need for performance and culture-fair tests? (289)

10.   Explain the difference between validity and reliability and tell how reliability is determined. (290)

Applications

You have worked through a section of recognition-type questions to determine if you can apply information to real-life situations. It is time to try to respond to some applications. Some are based upon those questions. Answers to this section will not be given. Your questions concerning these applications will serve as a basis for classroom discussion and ideas for class projects throughout the course.

1.   Construct at least two sentences that are syntactically correct, but which violate criteria for semantics. Verbalize those sentences to a (close) friend and take notice of the friend's reaction.

2.   Evan, the Welshman, was in an automobile accident. Three ribs were broken. Hospital personnel knew he was 84 years old. They paid no attention to his incoherent speech and disorientation three days after the accident, dismissing this behavior as the confusion of old age. A close friend knew that his mind did not reflect his years and discussed the problem with a nurse. As a result, tests were made. His brain was not getting enough oxygen because of breathing problems due to the broken ribs. He was put on oxygen and within hours was returned to his normal, brilliant self. What heuristic was being used by hospital personnel in making the treatment decisions before the friend intervened?

3. Make a list of some of the algorithms you know about and match them with a problem solved by each.

4. You have just swept up a pile of dust and dirt in your garage. You look around and find that you do not have a dust pan. What do you do now?

5. How many uses can you think of for a nylon stocking (or many of them)? How many uses can you think of for a plastic milk jug (or many of them)?

6. Mike rented a new luxury apartment. It had a lower level room intended for storage, but Mike decided to turn it into a study and office. There was only one problem: the main drain pipe went through one corner of the room. He thought of building a wall around it, but did not want the expense. He also knew he would have to tear the wall down if the pipe needed repair. Someone suggested that he hang a shower curtain around the pipe. He did not like the idea. Mike's creative powers solved the problem. What do you suppose he did to solve the problem of hiding the pipe without building anything in that corner?

7. Your friend heard the statement, "A test can be reliable without being valid, but a test cannot be valid without being reliable." Your friend does not understand that statement. Can you explain it?

8. Jim took the Miller Analogies Test to be admitted to graduate school. He scored 66. This a very respectable score and it would be accepted at some universities. He earned his master's degree. Ten years later he decided to pursue a doctorate. He had to take the Miller Analogies Test again. He scored 66. There are two major qualities that make a test "good." Which one of those qualities underlies this situation with Jim?

9. You own a river barge and need to hire someone who can pilot the craft up and down the river. You find someone who thinks he/she can do it. You are not sure this person is qualified so you give a "test" on the boat by accompanying your employee. But that is too time consuming. You want to devise a test that will tell you if a person is qualified for the job. What kind of validity will you need to determine and how would you go about determining it?

Return to Chapter Summary

Now that you have concluded these exercises, you should go back and reread the chapter summary in your textbook. It provides you with a framework that integrates all of this newly-learned information. By reviewing the chapter summary, you will strengthen the many connections between the various new pieces of information.

DEVELOPMENT ACROSS THE LIFE SPAN

8

Chapter Objectives

After you have read and studied this chapter, you should be able to:

1. Recognize the differences between and know the advantages and disadvantages of the methods for studying development.
2. Describe the prenatal environment.
3. Describe the physical development of the newborn baby and the perceptual abilities of infants.
4. Trace the physical and motor development from infancy through early childhood.
5. Explain the cognitive capabilities of the child from birth to age 15 using Piaget's theoretical approach and understand the criticisms of Piaget's theory.
6. Trace language development from infancy through age 5 or 6.
7. Differentiate between Skinner and Chomsky's theories of language development.
8. List the factors associated with the child's social development and explain how sex-role identity is formed.
9. Discuss the problems of adolescence and the transition to adulthood.
10. Explain the biological and cognitive changes in late adulthood.
11. Trace the Kübler-Ross five stage theory of death and dying and be aware of the criticisms of the Kübler-Ross approach.

Multiple-Choice Questions: Recognizing What You Have Learned

These questions ask only that you recognize what you have learned. When you recognize a correct answer, you have accessed that information in memory. A knowledge of facts serves as a framework for later analysis and problem solving.

Remembering the Facts

This group of multiple-choice questions requires that you simply recognize facts from your textbook.

1. The method of studying developmental changes by examining groups of subjects who are at different ages is called a _____ study.

    a.   developmental   c.   cross-sectional
    b.   longitudinal   d.   cross-segment

2. A group of people born during the same period in historical time is called:

    a.   a cohort   c.   a clique
    b.   a peer group   d.   an associates

3. The method of studying developmental changes by examining the same group of subjects two or more times as they get older is called a _____ study.

    a.   longitudinal   c.   cross-sectional
    b.   multiple-factor   d.   cross-developmental

4. A/an _____ study tries to reconstruct an individual's past.

    a.   cohort   c.   longitudinal
    b.   cross-sectional   d.   biographical

5. The developing human between two weeks and three months after conception is called a/an:

    a.   neonate   c.   fetus
    b.   placenta   d.   embryo

6. The reflex that causes a newborn baby to turn its head toward something touching its cheek and to grope around with its mouth is called the _____ reflex.

    a.   stepping   c.   rooting
    b.   Moro   d.   grasp

7. A reflex that causes newborn babies to close their fists around anything that is put in their hands is called the _____ reflex.

    a. Moro   c. clench
    b. grasp   d. grab

8. The age at which an average individual achieves some developmental milestone is referred to as:

    a. a development goal   c. a completeness standard
    b. the par criterion   d. a developmental norm

9. According to Piaget, a baby develops the concepts of object permanence and the ability to form mental representations during the:

    a. preoperational stage
    b. concrete-operational stage
    c. sensory-motor stage
    d. stage of formal-operational thought

10. The concept, acquired during infancy, that things continue to exist even when you cannot see them or touch them is called:

    a. tangibility   c. object permanence
    b. object continuity   d. perceptual fixity

11. A symbol used to think about or remember an object, person, or event is called a/an:

    a. image   c. icon
    b. mental representation d. cognitive representation

12. According to Piaget, a person who cannot see things from another person's point of view is:

    a. conceited   c. egocentric
    b. self-centered   d. selfish

13. Piaget found that children in the _____ stage are egocentric.

    a. preoperational   c. sensory-motor
    b. formal-operation   d. concrete-operational

14. A form of primitive bonding seen in some species of animals whereby the newborn has a tendency to follow the first moving thing is called _____.

    a. instinctive adherence   c. attachment
    b. imprinting   d. copying

15. An emotional bond that develops in the first year of life that causes babies to cling to their caregivers is called:

    a. attachment   c. imprinting
    b. socialization   d. dependence

16. A sense of independence and a desire not to be controlled by others is called:

    a. self-reliance   c. immunity
    b. autonomy   d. self-sufficiency

17. The process by which children learn the behaviors and attitudes appropriate to their family and culture is called:

    a. social cognition   c. cultural cognition
    b. compliance   d. socialization

18. When two children play side by side, but pay little attention to each other the activity is called:

    a. coextention   c. parallel play
    b. co-play   d. noninteractive play

19. A little girl's knowledge that she is a girl and a little boy's knowledge that he is a boy is called:

    a. gender identity   c. gender typing
    b. sex-typing   d. sex-difference

20. The fourth and final stage in Piaget's theory characterized by the transition from concrete to abstract thinking is termed:

    a. formal-operational stage
    b. formal cognition
    c. advanced operations
    d. cognitive abstraction

21. David Elkind used the term _____ for the adolescent delusion that he or she is constantly being observed by others.

    a. selective watching   c. imaginary onlookers
    b. imaginary audience   d. personal error

22. Erikson's term for the development of a stable sense of self necessary to make the transition from dependence on others to dependence on oneself is called:

    a. identity formation   c. self worth
    b. self identity   d. autonomy

23. A period of intense self-examination and decision making that is a part of the process of identity formation is called the:

    a. role crisis   c. identity crisis
    b. self-disclosure   d. adolescent crisis

24. According to Marcia, the status of adolescents who have achieved a stable sense of identity by passing through an identity crisis is called:

    a. crises resolution   c. accomplishment record
    b. identity achievement status   d. identity resolution

25. Marcia's _____ is the status of those who accept an identity provided by others without going through an identity crisis.

    a. imitation   c. closed status
    b. foreclosure rank   d. foreclosure status

26. _____ status is characteristic of an adolescent who is involved in an identity crisis, according to Marcia.

    a. Moratorium   c. Formation
    b. Foreclosure   d. Stress

27. _____ status describes adolescents who have failed to develop a clear sense of their own identity, according to Marcia.

    a. Moratorium   c. Identity formation
    b. Foreclosure   d. Identity diffusion

28. Agemates who provide a supportive social network for a person, especially an adolescent, is/are called:

    a. friends   c. the peer group
    b. "groupies"   d. social equals

29. Ginsberg terms the first stage of vocational choice the _____ period.

    a. "dream-job"   c. unrealistic
    b. fantasy   d. delusional

30. Ginsberg's second stage of vocational choice during which adolescents begin to match interests, abilities, and values with opportunities is called the _____ choice period.

    a. tentative   c. provisional
    b. experimental   d. temporary

31. Young adults who actively explore various kinds of work and make a commitment to a career are in the _____ choice period, according to Ginsberg.

    a. opportunistic   c. decisive
    b. explorative   d. realistic

32. A process, according the Levinson, whereby adults assess the past and formulate new goals for the future is called:

    a. midlife transition   c. middle-age crisis
    b. midlife crisis   d. midlife passage

33. _____ is a brain disorder that eventually results in a loss of all intellectual abilities.

    a. AIDS   c. Alzheimer's Disease
    b. Senility   d. Crone's Disease

Answers for this section:

1.	c (314)	10.	c (324)	19.	a (333)	28.	c (342)
2.	a (314)	11.	b (324)	20.	a (338)	29.	b (348)
3.	a (314)	12.	c (325)	21.	b (340)	30.	a (348)
4	d (314)	13.	a (325)	22.	a (341)	31.	d (348)
5.	d (315)	14.	b (330)	23.	c (341)	32.	a (351)
6.	c (316)	15.	a (330)	24.	b (341)	33.	c (354)
7.	b (316)	16.	b (331)	25.	d (342)		
8.	d (321)	17.	d (331)	26.	a (342)		
9.	c (324)	18.	c (332)	27.	d (342)		

Understanding the Facts

Now that you have found that you can recognize facts from Human Development Across the Life Span, the next step is to determine if you understand the meaning of newly-learned information. These multiple-choice questions require a higher level of thinking. They will help you establish more solid connections and provide practice in dealing with higher level concepts.

34. If a researcher interested in developmental changes starts with a group of 3-year-olds, then tests the same children again at age 6, the researcher is using:

    a. the cross-sectional method
    b. developmental norms
    c. the longitudinal method
    d. the habituation technique

35. Although it is not obvious to many people, development begins:

    a. when a child begins to walk
    b. at conception
    c. in the first few minutes after birth
    d. at birth

36. A _____ fetus roughly resembles a human being.

    a. two-month old   c. one-week old
    b. two-week old   d. three-month old

37.   A three-month old fetus is about _____ inch(es) in length.

a.   one   c.   2
b.   1/2   d.   6

38.   Syphilis, rubella, and AIDS can all be transmitted to an unborn child:

a.   through the mother's diet
b.   through the genes
c.   through the placenta
d.   by the father

39.   Neonates spend up to _____ hours a day sleeping.

a.   10 or 15   c.   5 or 10
b.   16 or 20   d.   8 or 12

40.   Neonates come equipped with _____ that are essential to life outside the uterus.

a.   reflexes   c.   insights
b.   beliefs   d.   perceptions

41.   A baby would not be able to nurse without:

a.   instincts   c.   bonding
b.   attachment   d.   reflexes

42.   Which of the following statements about reflexes is **true**?

a.   The grasp and stepping reflexes usually disappear after two or three months.
b.   Reflexes are the same as instincts.
c.   Very young babies' seemingly reflexive imitation of facial expressions is thought to be learned.
d.   The grasp reflex is still present at five months of age.

43.   At about six weeks of age, babies have a way of saying "thank you" to people who make them happy. They do this by:

a.   hugging   c.   smiling
b.   imitating   d.   laughing

44. Which of the following statements about a newborn's vision is **true**?

   a. They can adjust their eyes to distant objects or to very close ones.
   b. Newborns see most clearly when faces or objects are eight to ten inches away.
   c. Babies cannot see any colors for the first month.
   d. At two weeks they can distinguish blue and purple from gray.

45. One reason why babies show interest in pictures of a human face may be because:

   a. it is easier to focus on a human face than on other objects
   b. they prefer curved lines to patterns with straight lines
   c. the pictures remind them of their mothers
   d. the human face is not a complex pattern

46. Depth perception of infants is studied with a device called the:

   a. optical cliff   c. visual cliff
   b. Skinner Box   d. Fantz box

47. A baby's ears are in working order:

   a. immediately after birth   c. two weeks after birth
   b. one week after birth   d. before they are born

48. Which of the following statements about a child's physical development is **not** true?

   a. Physical growth is rapid during the second year.
   b. The average baby grows 10 inches in height and gains 15 pounds in weight during the first year.
   c. Adolescence brings rapid increases in height and weight.
   d. Babies and toddlers have heads that are very large relative to their bodies.

49. An infant's brain reaches three-quarters of its adult size by the age of
   _____.

   a. 6 months   c. 1 year
   b. 2 years   d. 18 months

50.　Which of the following statements about the maturation of girls and boys is **true**?

　　a.　A girl enters puberty one year before her male agemates.
　　b.　Girls have less fat in their bodies than boys do.
　　c.　A boy has achieved about half of his adult height by age two.
　　d.　A girl achieves less than half of her adult height by age two.

51.　According to established developmental norms, the average infant can stand up holding onto something at about:

　　a.　9 months　　　　　　　　　　c.　6 months
　　b.　8 months　　　　　　　　　　d.　1 year

52.　According to established developmental norms, the average infant crawls at about:

　　a.　9 months　　　　　　　　　　c.　5 months
　　b.　7 months　　　　　　　　　　d.　10 months

53.　Accurate reaching begins when a baby is about _____ months old.

　　a.　6　　　　　　　　　　　　　　c.　4
　　b.　9　　　　　　　　　　　　　　d.　12

54.　The grasping reflex, involving the whole hand, disappears and is replaced by the ability to pick up a small object with the thumb and forefinger:

　　a.　at 18 months　　　　　　　　c.　at 9 months
　　b.　by the end of the first year　　d.　at 2 years

55.　Through the years, research on the relationship between practice or training on the normal course of motor development has found that:

　　a.　exercise to enable a baby to walk earlier is beneficial for later development
　　b.　practice or training has relatively little effect on the normal course of motor development
　　c.　Hopi Indian babies, strapped to a stiff cradle board during the first year, were significantly behind the norms for walking
　　d.　in the Gesell and Thompson (1929) research, the untrained twin was behind the trained twin in walking by six months

56.　Piaget's approach was based on which of the following methodologies?

　　a.　experimentation　　　　　　　c.　naturalistic observation
　　b.　the clinical method　　　　　　d.　case studies

57. An important task of the sensory-motor stage is to:

a. learn to walk
b. develop the concept of object permanence
c. lose the grasp reflex
d. lose the suck reflex

58. "Out of sight, out of mind" is a cognitive characteristic of a _____ month old.

a. 3   c. 8
b. 12   d. 18

59. By the end of the sensory-motor stage, children have developed:

a. logic
b. ability to consider the past
c. a sense of self-recognition
d. the ability to put themselves in the place of others

60. In the stage of preoperational thought, children:

a. overcome egocentricity
b. learn to walk
c. can reason in the abstract
d. begin to use language for describing, remembering, and reasoning about the world

61. Children in the stage of preoperational thought:

a. cannot think symbolically
b. have difficulty putting themselves in someone else's place
c. focus on many aspects of a problem at one time
d. can consider both the past and the future

62. Children in the stage of concrete operations:

a. can solve problems dealing with abstract concepts
b. can formulate hypothesis and test them mentally
c. cannot infer what another person may be thinking
d. are able to use a logical approach to problem solving

63. Which of the following is the major cognitive ability of children in the stage of formal operations?

   a. the ability to use logic to solve problems
   b. the ability to think in the abstract
   c. the overcoming of egocentricity
   d. the external testing of ideas with logic

64. A child's language development begins with _____ at about _____ months of age.

   a. babbling, 2   c. intonation, 3
   b. cooing, 2   d. "dada", 12

65. Which of the following infant speech capabilities **first** enables adults to distinguish between a question and a statement?

   a. intonation at 4 to 6 months
   b. imitation of what others say
   c. intonation at 2 months
   d. the use of one-word sentences

66. Which of the following is the overwhelming verbal passion of a 2-year-old?

   a. use of the word "dada"
   b. the word, "no"
   c. naming things
   d. the use of short, but complete sentences

67. Two-and three-word sentences are begun:

   a. during the third year
   b. after the child outgrows egocentricity
   c. by age two
   d. at age four

68. The child's two-and three-word sentences noticeably omit:

   a. personal pronouns   c. two syllable words
   b. proper syntax   d. auxiliary verbs

69. The child's two-and three-word sentences also noticeably omit:

   a. questions
   b. wanting things
   c. prepositions and articles
   d. references to themselves

70. Children begin to fill in their sentences and use the past as well as the present tense:

   a. at 3 to 4 years of age   c. at 6 years
   b. when they enter school   d. at 18 months

71. By the age of 5 or 6 most children have a vocabulary of more than _____ words.

   a. 1,000   c. 3,000
   b. 2,500   d. 3,500

72. Which of the following theorists believes, as a result of research, that children are born with an internal device for processing adult speech?

   a. B.F. Skinner   c. Jean Piaget
   b. Benjamin Whorf   d. Noam Chomsky

73. At which age does an infant tend to react negatively if separated from its mother?

   a. between 8 and 15 months   c. at 6 months
   b. around 7 months   d. at 2 months

74. Attachment becomes especially intense at around:

   a. 15 months   c. 7 months
   b. 18 months   d. one year

75. "I want my mommy back" is an example of _____ and is characteristic of a _____ child.

   a. imprinting, 6-month-old
   b. object permanence, one-year-old
   c. person permanence, 9-month-old
   d. negativity, shy

76. Secure mother-child attachments are a sign of:

   a. the negativity that is to follow
   b. excess dependency
   c. a lack of independence
   d. a strengthening of the child's autonomy

77. An essential first step in the process of socialization is:

   a. attachment
   b. the two-year-old's propensity for being negative
   c. bonding
   d. early signs of autonomy

78. According to Baumrind (1972), the most successful parenting style is what she calls:

   a. authoritative   c. laissez-faire
   b. authoritarian   d. permissiveness

79. By the age of _____ children engage in cooperative games involving group imagination.

   a. 3 or 3 1/2   c. 18 months
   b. 2   d. 1 year

80. _____ children run the greatest risks in the process of building social relationships.

   a. Overly bright   c. Overly sensitive
   b. Neglected   d. Rejected

81. By the age of _____ most children know that gender is neither a matter of choice nor is it easily changed.

   a. 5   c. 6 or 7
   b. 3   d. 2

82. It appears that an important subtle source of sex-typed behavior has _____ as its source.

   a. expectations
   b. genetics
   c. instinct
   d. imagined biological differences

83. The most obvious, dramatic physical milestone for adolescence is:

   a. the growth spurt
   b. puberty
   c. menarche
   d. beard growth

84. The **first** sign of approaching sexual maturity in boys is:

   a. growth of the testes
   b. facial hair
   c. pubic hair
   d. deepening of the voice

85. One of the last noticeable changes of male maturation is:

   a. the growth spurt
   b. deepening of the voice
   c. appearance of pubic hair
   d. growth of the penis

86. In females, the first sign of approaching puberty is the:

   a. beginning of the growth spurt
   b. appearance of pubic hair
   c. end of the growth spurt
   d. appearance of acne

87. Which of the following statements about menarche is **not** true?

   a. The onset of menstruation does not necessarily mean that a girl can get pregnant.
   b. A girl is immediately capable of getting pregnant at the onset of menstruation.
   c. A girl can get pregnant during her first menstrual cycles.
   d. Female fertility increases gradually during the first year after menarche.

88. Reaching the stage of formal operations means that adolescents:

   a. automatically apply formal operational thinking to everyday problems
   b. have a deep understanding of the ambiguity of moral judgements
   c. can understand and manipulate abstract concepts
   d. reason on the formal-operational level on matters of high importance

89. According to David Elkind, the adolescent's propensity for self-consciousness and showing off comes from:

   a. their inability to cultivate a distinctive image
   b. lack of confidence is their new found mental abilities
   c. the fact that others share their mental processes
   d. their tendency to feel that they are constantly being watched

90. Which of the following is a dangerous side of the adolescents sense of self-importance?

   a. They become overly conscious of their state of health.
   b. It makes them feel that they are invulnerable.
   c. They are afraid to take risks.
   d. It makes them feel overly vulnerable.

91. Which of the following is **not** one of Marcia's four possible statuses of adolescent attempts to achieve a stable sense of identity?

   a. moratorium   c. maturity diffusion
   b. foreclosure   d. identity achievement

92. In which of the following of Marcia's four statuses of the identity crisis would an adolescent delay making important decisions?

   a. identity diffusion   c. foreclosure
   b. moratorium   d. identity achievement

93. In which of the following of Marcia's four statuses of the identity crisis would an adolescent settle on an identity that is provided for them by others?

   a. foreclosure   c. identity achievement
   b. moratorium   d. identity diffusion

94. The low point of parent-child relationship generally occurs:

    a. in early adolescence
    b. during toilet training
    c. in late adolescence
    d. during the transition from adolescence to early adulthood

95. Two mental disorders: _____ and _____ often make their first appearance in adolescence.

    a. phobias, obsession-compulsive reactions
    b. multiple personality, hysterical amnesia
    c. mania, antisocial personality
    d. schizophrenia, depression

96. Which of the following statements about adolescent suicide is **not** true?

    a. Suicide itself is more common in females than in males.
    b. The rate of suicide among adolescents and young adults in America has tripled since 1950.
    c. Suicide is the third leading cause of death in adolescence and young adults.
    d. In a given year, 11 youths out of 100,000 succeed in ending their lives.

97. For women, the low point in marriage is likely to come:

    a. during child-rearing years
    b. when children leave home
    c. in late middle age
    d. in early middle age

98. Almost _____ of today's marriages will eventually end in divorce.

    a. one-half   c. one-fifth
    b. one-third   d. two-thirds

99. Which of the following statements about widowhood is **not** true?

    a. Men are said to suffer more than women from the loss of a mate.
    b. Men are more likely to remarry.
    c. There are many more widowers than widows.
    d. In one study it was found that 5 percent of widowers 55 and older died in the first six months following their wife's death.

100. Which of the following statements about dual-career families is **not** true?

   a. Most women report increases in self-esteem when they are employed.
   b. Women who work outside of the home are as healthy as those who do not work.
   c. Women who work outside of the home are less likely to suffer from depression than those who do not work.
   d. There are no benefits for the children of women who work.

101. Which of the following statements is **not** true about sexuality in old age?

   a. Seventy percent of married 70-year-old men are sexually active.
   b. The aged have outlived their sexuality.
   c. Menopause does not put a halt to a woman's sexual interest.
   d. The majority of older adults can enjoy sex and have orgasms.

102. Data suggests that the problem of facing death is of greater concern for:

   a. young adults or those in middle age
   b. adolescents
   c. people over 65
   d. retired persons

103. According to Kübler-Ross, the **third** stage people pass through as they react to their own impending death is:

   a. acceptance   c. bargaining
   b. anger   d. depression

104. Although there have been criticisms of the Kübler-Ross' five-stage theory of dying, her model can increase our understanding of the needs of dying people if we:

   a. ignore the evidence against it
   b. do not apply it too rigidly
   c. do not attempt to apply it to ourselves
   d. encourage health care professionals to look for the expected stages

Answers for this section:

34.	c (314)	52.	d (323)	70.	a (328)	88.	c (338)
35.	b (315)	53.	c (323)	71.	b (328)	89.	d (340)
36.	d (315)	54.	b (323)	72.	d (329)	90.	b (340)
37.	a (315)	55.	b (323)	73.	a (330)	91.	c (341, 342)
38.	c (315)	56.	c (323)	74.	c (330)	92.	b (342)
39.	b (316)	57.	b (324)	75.	c (331)	93.	a (342)
40.	a (316)	58.	a (324)	76.	d (331)	94.	a (343)
41.	d (316)	59.	c (324)	77.	d (331)	95.	d (343)
42.	a (316)	60.	d (325)	78.	a (332)	96.	a (344)
43.	c (317)	61.	b (325)	79.	a (332)	97.	a (345)
44.	b (318)	62.	d (325)	80.	d (333)	98.	a (346)
45.	b (318)	63.	b (326)	81.	c (333)	99.	c (347)
46.	c (318)	64.	b (326)	82.	a (334)	100.	d (353)
47.	d (319)	65.	a (327)	83.	a (335)	101.	b (355)
48.	a (320)	66.	c (328)	84.	a (336)	102.	a (355)
49.	b (321)	67.	a (328)	85.	b (336)	103.	c (355)
50.	c (321)	68.	d (328)	86.	a (336)	104.	b (356)
51.	a (321)	69.	c (328)	87.	b (337)		

Applying the Facts

The learning of facts and concepts is of little value unless it can be applied and employed to solve problems. The next group of multiple-choice questions reflects applications of your learning.

105. Ben is a graduate student in developmental psychology. He is gathering data on neonates' visual abilities. His dissertation will be based upon some of this data, but he plans to study the same children when they are 2, 6, 8, and 10 months old and again when they are a year old. Ben is using a method called:

    a.   co-twin studies   c.   naturalistic observation
    b.   cross-sectional study   d.   longitudinal study

106. Barbara has had a drinking problem for years. Her baby was born with physical abnormalities and growth defects and was diagnosed as having *fetal alcohol syndrome*. Barbara either did not know or did not care that:

   a. her blood mingled with that of the unborn child
   b. she was setting the stage for the transmission of rubella
   c. her child will grow up to be alcoholic
   d. the toxic effects of alcohol were transmitted to her unborn baby through the placenta

107. Bobby wasn't quite sure he liked his baby brother. When Nicky came home from the hospital, Bobby stuck his tongue out at him. Nicky stuck his tongue out at Bobby, and their mother could not believe it. Which of the following is the **best** explanation of Nicky's startling behavior?

   a. It appears to be a kind of primitive reflex.
   b. A hospital nurse taught him how to do it through modeling.
   c. A hospital nurse taught him how to do it using operant conditioning.
   d. Imitation of facial expressions of adults is instinctive.

108. Allen was 11 months old. He was propelling himself about the kitchen in a walker. While his mother watched (amazed), he opened every cupboard door within his reach. Allen:

   a. had, at last, attained thumb and forefinger opposition
   b. had reactivated the lost grasp reflex
   c. was angry with his mother for beginning toilet training
   d. was looking for something to eat

109. Janie is 4 years old. Her father took her Christmas shopping and, by herself, Janie picked out a silk scarf for her mother. Janie illustrates which of the following areas of criticism of Piaget's theory?

   a. self-centeredness
   b. object permanence
   c. sequential development
   d. egocentricism

110. Virgina is 60-years-old. She was asked to participate in a cross-sectional study comparing 40-year-olds with 60-year-olds. The person conducting the study may be committing a methodological error because:

   a. of sex differences
   b. Virginia may not be able to remember much about her youth
   c. of cohort differences
   d. the biographical approach is not often accurate

111. Judy has just had her first menstrual period. She is 13. The contents of which of the following statements can be **most** helpful to Judy?

   a.   A girl cannot get pregnant during her first menstrual cycles.
   b.   Judy still looks like a child, therefore has nothing to worry about.
   c.   It is not unheard of for a girl to become pregnant during her first menstrual cycles.
   d.   The onset of menstruation does not necessarily mean that a girl can get pregnant.

112. Annie is 16 years old. She had been placed in an accelerated academic program in high school, but had to quit because she became pregnant. Although she is capable of thought characteristics of Piaget's stage of formal operations, Annie is the victim of an adolescent condition called _____ by David Elkind.

   a.   imaginary fable   c.   imaginary audience
   b.   personal fable   d.   egocentism

113. Jordan, age 17, and his friends went out one winter night against the advice of weather bulletins telling of slippery road conditions. The friends enjoy speeding to their destination. They turned onto an asphalt road that appeared wet, but it was covered with a thin layer of ice. The speeding car rolled over into a ravine. Jordan and all of his friends were killed. The source of this risk taking is _____ according the David Elkind.

   a.   identity confusion
   b.   being in a state of moratorium
   c.   the delusion of self-importance
   d.   the delusion of invulnerability

114. Allison just turned 21. She entered a community college after high school and worked part time, but quit school before the first term was over. She gets low paying jobs, but loses them after a few months. Her major interests are clothes and rock concerts. She spends everything she makes from part time jobs. Although she is a young adult, Allison **most** resembles an adolescent in which of Marcia's statuses of the identity crisis?

   a.   identity diffusion   c.   moratorium
   b.   foreclosure   d.   identity achievement

115. Tommy is 13. He likes to "hang out" with five particular boys in his school. Most of Tommy's free time is spent with them and he misses them if they are not around. Psychologists call this type of group:

a. peers   c. an assemblage
b. a cluster   d. a clique

Answers for this section:

105. d (314)	108. a (323)	111. c (337)	114. a (342)
106. d (315)	109. d (326)	112. b (340)	115. d (342)
107. a (316)	110. c (314)	113. d (340)	

Fill-in-the-Blank Questions: Recalling What You Have Learned

By now, there should be a considerable amount of new information about Human Development Across the Life Span in long-term memory. The following questions of recall rather than recognition will show if you are becoming more comfortable with the material.

Remembering the Facts

1. The study of changes that occur in people as they get older is called _____ psychology.

2. The method of studying developmental changes by examining groups of subjects who are of different ages is termed a/an _____ - _____ study.

3. A group of people born during the same period in historical time is called a _____.

4. Studying developmental changes by examining the same group of subjects two or more times as they get older is called the _____ method.

5. A method of studying developmental changes that tries to reconstruct an individual's past is called a/an _____ study.

6. Development from conception to birth is called _____ development.

7. The developing human between three months after conception and birth is called a/an _____.

8.   The _____ is an organ by which an embryo is attached to its mother's uterus and which nourishes it during prenatal development.

9.   A newborn baby is called a/an _____.

10. The _____ reflex causes a newborn baby, if touched on the cheek, to turn its head in that direction and grope around with its mouth.

11. A newborn baby will close its fist around anything that is put in its hands because of the _____ reflex.

12. Newborn babies will make little stepping motions if they are held upright with their feet touching the floor because of the _____ reflex.

13. The age at which an average individual achieves some developmental milestone is referred to as a/an _____ _____.

14. A baby develops the concept of object permanence and the ability to from mental representations during Piaget's _____ - _____ stage.

15. When things continue to exist even when they cannot be seen or touched is the concept of _____ _____.

16. An image or symbol used to think about or remember an object, person, or event is called a/an _____ _____.

17. According to Piaget, the second stage of cognitive development is the _____ stage during which thought is egocentric.

18. The third stage of cognitive development in Piaget's theory is the _____ - _____ stage and includes children age 7-11.

19. Children are _____ if they cannot see things from another's point of view.

20. _____ is a form of primitive bonding seen in some species of animals.

21. An emotional bond that develops in the first year of life and that makes human babies cling to their caregivers is called _____.

22. A sense of independence and a desire not to be controlled by others is termed _____.

23. _____ is the process by which children learn the behaviors and attitudes appropriate to their families and their culture.

24. When two children play side by side at the same activities, paying little or no attention to each other, their behavior is called _____ _____.

25. A little girl's knowledge that she is a girl, and little boy's knowledge that he is a boy is called _____ _____.

26. Behavior that is typical of females or of males is called _____ - _____ behavior.

27. The rapid increase in height and weight that begins around 10 1/2 in girls and 12 1/2 in boys is called the _____ _____.

28. The onset of sexual maturation is called _____.

29. _____ is the term for the first menstrual period.

30. Adolescents have a delusion that they are constantly being watched by others. David Elkind calls this a/an _____ _____.

31. David Elkind's term for the adolescent delusion that they are unique, important, and invulnerable is the _____ _____.

32. Adolescents who accept an identity provided by others are in _____ status, according the Marcia.

33. Adolescents who have failed to develop a clear sense of their own identity are in _____ _____ status, according to Marcia.

34. Adolescents who have achieved a stable sense of identity by passing through an identity crisis are in _____ _____ status, according to Marcia.

35. _____, according to Marcia, is the status of an adolescent who is actively involved in an identity crisis.

36. _____ _____ is Erikson's term for the development of a stable sense of self necessary to make the transition from dependence on others to dependence on oneself.

37. The part of the process of identity formation which is a period of intense self-examination and decision making is called the _____ _____.

38. Agemates who provide a supportive social network for a person, especially an adolescent is called the _____ _____.

39. The first stage of vocational choice, during which children choose exciting careers without regard to practical considerations is called the _____ period by Ginsberg.

40. When adolescents begin to match interests, abilities, and values with opportunities, they are in the _____ _____ period of vocational choice, according the Ginsberg.

41. When young adults actively explore various kinds of work and make a commitment to a career they are in the _____ period of vocational choice.

42. A process whereby adults assess the past and formulate new goals for the future is termed _____ _____ by Levinson.

43. _____ is the time in a woman's life when menstruation ceases.

44. A brain disorder that eventually results in a loss of all intellectual abilities is

_____ _____.

45. _____ described a sequence of five stages through which people pass as they react to their own impending death.

Answers for this section:

1.	developmental (314)	24.	parallel play (332)
2.	cross-sectional (314)	25.	gender identity (333)
3.	cohort (314)	26.	sex-typed (335)
4.	longitudinal (314)	27.	growth spurt (335)
5.	biographical (314)	28.	puberty (336)
6.	prenatal (315)	29.	menarche (336)
7.	embryo (315)	30.	imaginary audience (340)
8.	placenta (315)	31.	personal fable (340)
9.	neonate (316)	32.	foreclosure (342)
10.	rooting (316)	33.	identity diffusion (342)
11.	grasp (316)	34.	identity achievement (341)
12.	stepping (316)	35.	moratorium (342)
13.	developmental norm (321)	36.	identity formation (341)
14.	sensory-motor (324)	37.	identity crisis (341)
15.	object permanence (324)	38.	peer group (342)
16.	mental representation (324)	39.	fantasy (328)
17.	preoperational (324)	40.	tentative choice (348)
18.	concrete-operational (325)	41.	realistic (348)
19.	egocentric (325)	42.	midlife transition (351)
20.	imprinting (330)	43.	menopause (353)
21.	attachment (330)	44.	Alzheimer's disease (354)
22.	autonomy (331)	45.	Kübler-Ross (355)
23.	socialization (331)		

Understanding and Applying the Facts

As you previously did with recognition-type questions, you will now move to a higher level of recall. The following questions will determine if you understand the facts.

46. The _____, _____, and _____ reflexes enable a baby to nurse.

47. The imitation of facial expressions by very young babies appears to be a kind of _____ _____.

48. Newborns see most clearly when faces or objects are _____ inches away from them.

49. By the time babies are _____ months old they can recognize a line drawing of a human face.

50.   Little George at 6 months refused to crawl across the _____
_____, a device designed to test babies for depth perception.

51.   By age one year, Michael could not sit up. Michael was far beyond the range of
the _____ _____ for sitting up and needed an immediate
medical evaluation.

52.   When little Allen began to try to pull buttons off of pillows it was obvious that he
had lost his _____ _____.

53.   Jean Piaget was trained as a _____.

54.   Jean Piaget saw development as a way of _____ to the environment.

55.   Piaget believed that children in the _____ stage have difficulty
distinguishing between things as they appear to be and the way they really are.

56.   According to Piaget, children can first apply logic to concrete problems in the
stage of _____ _____ which occurs from _____ years
of age.

57.   According to Piaget, children between 11 and 15 years enter the stage of
_____ _____ and can then think in _____ terms.

58.   Marvin's (1975) research showed that 4-year-olds choose gifts for their mothers on
the basis of what their mothers would like rather than what they would like.
This illustrates a major criticism of Piaget's theory. That criticism is that the
preoperational child is not necessarily _____.

59.   Three-year-olds characteristically leave _____ and _____ out of
their sentences.

60.   The transition from "Johnny goes walk" to "Johnny goes for a walk" is
accomplished at about _____ years of age.

61.   The researcher who believes that children have an internal device for processing
the adult speech that they hear around them is _____.

62.   _____ would be happy to hear that babies raised in institutions babble like
other children, but possibly because they are not reinforced by _____ like
children raised in families, they are behind in language development. That
example is a vote for his viewpoint.

63. Tommy placed a soccer ball in front of a newly hatched duckling on his farm. The duckling followed the ball when Tommy rolled it. This is an example of _____.

64. If you have a young baby and would like to leave your child with a sitter and go out for a little diversion, you should do that before the baby is _____ months old, because before that age your baby is not capable of _____ _____ and will not be disturbed by your absence.

65. _____ and _____ are two sides of the same coin. If a child feels secure in the relationship with its caregiver, the child feels free to explore a new environment knowing that the caregiver will return.

66. Dick and Jane provide firm discipline, structure, and guidance with their children, but they do not over-control. They listen to their children and explain their decisions, but they, not the children, make and enforce the rules. Their style of parenting is _____, according to _____.

67. Tom and Jody insist on unquestioning obedience on the part of their children. Their parenting style is called _____ by _____.

68. _____ and _____ are most likely to have children who are self-reliant and socially responsible.

69. Becky and Beth each have a child close to 2-years-old. They get together occasionally and allow the children to play together. They notice that the children play with the toys they give them, but pay little or no attention to each other. The children are engaged in _____ _____.

70. Sally's classmates rarely notice her. She is shy and quiet and does not have friends at school. But Sally plays the violin and has quite a following because of her recitals and she is active in her Sunday school. As far as school is concerned, Sally would classify as a _____ child.

71. Efforts are being made to help Roger, but not much progress is being made. He is aggressive and his classmates actively dislike him. Roger would classify as a _____ child.

72. Describing a newborn daughter as "delicate and beautiful" and a newborn son as "strong and well-coordinated" may well be the beginnings of later _____ _____ behavior.

73. The growth spurt begins with a lengthening of _____, _____, _____, and _____.

74. The last noticeable changes of male maturation is _____ of the _____.

75. Larry is 16-years-old. He contracted childhood diabetes when he was 12. His parents must continue to monitor his diet and insulin injections even though he is cognitively capable of meeting the crucial requirements himself. According to David Elkind, Larry has a delusion called the _____ _____.

76. G. Stanley Hall coined the term "_____ and _____" to describe the period of adolescence.

77. Peter's father is an Episcopal priest and is dean of a cathedral. Peter's father has always wanted him to follow in his footsteps. Peter, at 16, has plans to enter college, then the seminary. On the surface, Peter appears to be in the _____ status in quest of identity formation.

78. Mark went through high school in a blaze of personal glory. A handsome athlete, his grades were above average, but his athletic skills and musical talent were most noticeable. His parents wanted him to be a dentist, but the demands of the pre-dental curriculum were too much for him. At the beginning of his sophomore year, he changed his major to literature education. He has now been a secondary teacher for 25 years. When he was a late adolescent, Mark would have been classified as an example of Marcia's _____ _____ status.

79. When adolescents put off making decisions, but continue to explore various alternatives and choices, they are in _____ status, according to Marcia.

80. _____ disagrees with Erikson that a person cannot form a close bond of intimacy without a firm sense of identity, but the evidence is on Erikson's side because teen marriages are more likely to end in divorce.

81. Jake is a college freshman taking required courses before deciding upon a major. He is concerned about his future and spends considerable time with his academic advisor. His advisor suggested that he see the campus counselor to explore career opportunities to fit his interests and abilities. Jake appears to be in Ginsberg's _____ _____ period of career choice decision making.

82. Alzheimer's disease is the cause of what formerly was called _____ when it appears in older people.

83. The second stage of Kübler-Ross dying process is _____.

Answers for this section:

46.	rooting, sucking, swallowing (316)	65.	autonomy, attachment (331)
47.	primitive reflex (316)	66.	authoritative, Baumrind (332)
48.	8 to 10 (318)	67.	authoritarian, Baumrind (332)
49.	2 or 3 (318)	68.	Dick, Jane (332)
50.	visual cliff (318)	69.	parallel play (332)
51.	developmental norm (321)	70.	neglected (333)
52.	grasping reflex (321, 322)	71	rejected (333)
53.	biologist (323)	72.	sex-typed (335)
54.	adapting (323)	73.	hands, feet, arms, legs (335)
55.	preoperational (325)	74.	deepening, voice (336)
56.	concrete operations, 7-11 (325)	75.	personal fable (340)
57.	formal operations, abstract (326)	76.	storm, stress (340, 341)
58.	egocentric (326)	77.	foreclosure (342)
59.	prepositions, articles (328)	78.	identity achievement (341)
60.	3 to 4 (328)	79.	moratorium (342)
61.	Noam Chomsky (329)	80.	Carol Gilligan (345)
62.	Skinner, smiles (328, 329)	81.	realistic choice (348)
63.	imprinting (330)	82.	senility (354)
64.	9, person permanence (330, 331)	83.	anger (355)

Testing Yourself For Mastery

The following terms and concepts are found in boldface or italics in the chapter. The time has come to determine if you can define and discuss your new learning in your own words, then check your work against the text.

developmental psychology

cross-sectional study

cohort

longitudinal study

biographical study

prenatal development

embryo

fetus

placenta

neonate

rooting reflex

grasp reflex

stepping reflex

developmental norm

sensory-motor stage

object permanence

mental representation

preoperational stage

egocentric thought

concrete-operational stage

imprinting

attachment

autonomy

socialization

parallel play

gender identity

sex-typed behavior

growth spurt

puberty

menarche

formal-operational thought

imaginary audience

personal fable

identity formation

identity crisis

identity achievement status

foreclosure status

moratorium status

identity diffusion status

peer group

fantasy period

tentative choice period

midlife transition

menopause

Alzheimer's disease

Integrating Your Newly Learned Information

Now that you have recognized, recalled, and given definition to Human Development Across the Life Span, you are ready to try to integrate your knowledge in a definitive discussion through short-answer questions.

1. Explain the difference between the cross-sectional method and the longitudinal method for studying development. (314)

2. List some of the disastrous effects for an unborn child of the mother's poor diet, drinking, smoking, sex practices, and exposure to disease and explain how those effects are implemented. (315, 316)

3. Explain the role of reflexes in the infant's early life, name them, and describe their functions. (316)

4. List two characteristics each of children in the sensory motor, preoperational, concrete-operational, and formal-operational stages. (323, 326)

5. What is attachment and how does it contribute to a child's sense of autonomy? (330, 331)

6. What are the visible signs of puberty in both males and females and at what age do they occur? (336, 337)

7. What is Elkind's explanation for the adolescent's risk-taking behavior? (340)

8. List some of the more important factors in career choice. (347, 348)

9. List some of the physical and cognitive changes in adulthood and old age and discuss positive methods of dealing with them. (351-354)

10. Discuss a criticism of Kübler-Ross' five stages of the dying process and explain how her theory can be of value if handled properly. (355, 356)

Applications

You have worked through a section of recognition-type questions to determine if you can apply information to real-life situations. It is time to try to respond to some applications. Some are based upon those questions. Answers to this section will not be given. Your questions concerning these applications will serve as a basis for classroom discussion and ideas for class projects throughout the course.

1. Barbara has a drinking problem. She is pregnant. Fortunately she has regular check-ups by her physician. What are some of the aspects of this drinking problem as it regards her unborn child and what kind of action should her physician take?

2. Eileen's friend has a child who walked at 9 months of age. Eileen's child is 13 months old and is not walking yet. Does she have any cause for alarm? Why or why not?

3. When Allen was 12 months old he found a pin on the floor and picked it up. His mother caught him just before he put it in his mouth. After she checked the entire area for more dangerous objects she smiled, for she knew that Allen had achieved a new level of capability. What is that new capability?

4. Jan, a graduate student, was giving some Piagetian type tests to a small group of children age 6 to 11 years old. She formed a small piece of clay into a ball, divided it into two equal pieces, and asked the 6-year-old if the two pieces of clay were the same size. The child responded, "yes." Jan then flattened one ball into a "pancake" and asked the child if the two pieces of clay were the same size. The child replied, "no." Then, Jan did the same thing with the clay for a 9-year-old. The 9-year-old's reply was, "Boy, are you dumb, of course they are both the same size!" According the Piaget's theory which stage of cognitive development was each child in?

5. If you try to teach fractions to a 6-year-old and present such symbols as $1/2 + 1/4$ you will most likely find that the child will not comprehend what you are doing. But if you show the child a pie, cut it in half, then cut the half in half the child might be better able to understand the concept of fractions. This is an application of what theory of cognitive development? Why can't the 6-year-old grasp the idea behind $1/2 + 1/4$?

6. Your younger sister has just had her first menstrual period. She has always turned to you to help in important matters. You know she will be relying on you again at this milestone in her life. Using what you have learned in this chapter, prepare yourself for the type of support you are going to give her.

7. Allison, who just turned 21, has done nothing to plan for her future. She lives at home with her mother, works part time, dates her boyfriend, and spends all the money she makes on clothes. Without knowing anything about her background, analyze her behavior in terms of the findings of Erikson and Marcia and project into the future as to what some of her next problems might be.

8.   Roger's father died when he was 3-years-old. His mother went to work to support him and his two sisters. Roger is now 43. His sisters are self-supporting, but Roger, a veteran of the Vietnam war lives with his mother. He and his mother claim that he has his own "business," but he does not make enough money to be financially independent. Utilizing what you know from your study of childhood, adolescence, and adulthood, think of some of the factors that might have led to this situation.

9.   Your grandfather is dying. He just came home from the doctor and gave you the news. You have just finished studying the theory of Elisabeth Kübler-Ross. You love your grandfather. Bearing in mind the criticisms of her approach is there something in her views that can be of help to you, to your grandfather and to your family?

Return to Chapter Summary

Now that you have concluded these exercises, you should go back and reread the chapter summary in your textbook. It provides you with a framework that integrates all of this newly-learned information. By reviewing the chapter summary, you will strengthen the many connections between the various new pieces of information.

MOTIVATION AND EMOTION

9

Chapter Objectives

After you have read and studied this chapter, you should be able to:

1. Define motive and emotion and explain the roles of stimulus, behavior, and goals in motivation.
2. Identify the primary drives and their physiological bases.
3. Describe how hunger is controlled in the brain. Explain how external cues and experience influence hunger.
4. Explain how the thirst regulators in the body work.
5. List the biological factors involved in the sex drive. Discuss psychological influences on sexual motivation. List the causes of sexual dysfunction.
6. List the characteristics of the following stimulus motives: activity, exploration, curiosity, manipulation, and contact.
7. Define aggression. Discuss three theories of aggressive behavior.
8. Explain why the need for achievement is so strong in some people.
9. Distinguish between the motives for power and achievement. Give an example.
10. Explain how the affiliation motives are aroused.
11. Identify the five categories in Maslow's hierarchy of motives.
12. Describe and give an example of each of the three basic categories of emotions.
13. Summarize the Yerkes-Dodson law.
14. Explain how Plutchik categorized emotions.

15. Describe and differentiate among the James-Lange, Cannon-Bard, cognitive, and Izard's theories of emotion.
16. List three reasons why people may not be able or willing to report their emotions.
17. Identify several kinds of nonverbal communications. Give one example of each kind.

Multiple-Choice Questions: Recognizing What You Have Learned

These questions ask only that you recognize what you have learned. When you recognize a correct answer, you have accessed that information in memory. A knowledge of facts serves as a framework for later analysis and problem solving.

Remembering the Facts

This group of multiple-choice questions requires that you simply recognize facts from your textbook.

1. A specific need, desire or want that energizes and directs goal-oriented behavior is called a/an:

   a. drive   c. emotion
   b. motive   d. instinct

2. A feeling that energizes and directs behavior is called a/an:

   a. affect   c. sensation
   b. motive   d. emotion

3. An inborn, inflexible, goal-directed behavior that is characteristic of an entire species is known as a/an:

   a. instinct   c. imprint
   b. reflex   d. impulse

4. A/an _____ is a state of tension or arousal due to a biological deficit.

   a. need   c. drive
   b. emotion   d. incentive

221

5. An external stimulus that prompts goal-directed behavior is termed a/an:

   a. drive   c. homeostatic mechanism
   b. incentive   d. learned instinct

6. _____ is a state of stability in which an organism functions effectively.

   a. Homeostasis   c. Equalization
   b. Balance   d. Equilibrium

7. "Motivated behavior moves the organism toward a reduction of arousal" is the definition for _____ theory.

   a. goal attainment   c. need satiation
   b. need fulfillment   d. drive reduction

8. A physiologically based unlearned motive is called a/an:

   a. primary drive   c. primary motive
   b. crucial need   d. instinctive drive

9. _____ is a hormone that is a primary determinant of the sex drive in both men and women.

   a. Epinephrine   c. Testosterone
   b. Estrogen   d. Parathormone

10. Substances that enhance the sexual readiness of the opposite sex in some animals are called:

    a. sex hormones   c. pheronemes
    b. pheromones   d. androgens

11. A/an _____ is an unlearned motive that depends more on external stimuli than on internal physiological states.

    a. stimulus motive   c. instinct
    b. drive   d. arousal motive

12. A learned motive that is associated with relationships among people is called a/an:

    a. instinct   c. social motive
    b. group motive   d. communal drive

13. _____ is psychology's term for behavior aimed at doing harm to others.

   a. Belligerence   c. Resistance
   b. Violence   d. Aggression

14. The need to excel and to overcome obstacles is called a/an:

   a. homeostatic motive   c. achievement motive
   b. incentive   d. power motive

15. The need to win recognition or to influence or control other people or groups is termed:

   a. the authority motive c. an achievement motive
   b. the power motive   d. forcefulness

16. The need to be with others is called:

   a. the affiliation motive c. cooperation
   b. friendship   d. the unity motive

17. _____ states that there is an optimal level of arousal for the best performance on any task.

   a. Maslow's hierarchy   c. Cannon-Bard theory
   b. James-Lange theory   d. The Yerkes-Dodson law

18. _____ states that physical reactions precede experienced emotions.

   a. Cognitive theory   c. Cannon-Bard theory
   b. James-Lange theory   d. The Yerkes-Dodson law

19. The experience of emotion occurs simultaneously with biological changes according to:

   a. Izard's theory   c. Cannon-Bard theory
   b. Maslow's hierarchy   d. James-Lange theory

20. Emotional experience depends on one's perception or judgement of the situation one is in according to:

   a. cognitive theory   c. Abraham Maslow
   b. C.E. Izard   d. Cannon-Bard theory

Answers for this section:

1.	b (364)	6.	a (366)	11.	a (376)	16.	a (384)
2.	d (364)	7.	d (365)	12.	c (378)	17.	d (388)
3.	a (365)	8.	a (366)	13.	d (378)	18.	b (391)
4.	c (365)	9.	c (374)	14.	c (381)	19.	c (392)
5.	b (366)	10.	b (374)	15.	b (382)	20.	a (392)

Understanding the Facts

Now that you have found that you can recognize facts from Motivation and Emotion, the next step is to determine if you understand the meaning of newly-learned information. These multiple-choice questions require a higher level of thinking. They will help you establish more solid connections and provide practice in dealing with higher level concepts.

21. Which of the following statements relating to instincts is **not** true?

    a. Instincts describe behavior, but do not explain it.
    b. Much of human behavior is rigid, inflexible, unchanging, and specie specific.
    c. Most significant human behavior is not inborn, but is learned.
    d. After World War I, psychologists started looking for better explanations than instincts for human behavior.

22. When we are too hot we perspire. When we are too cold we shiver. These behaviors are examples of our body striving for:

    a. homeostasis   c. equilibrium
    b. perfection   d. balance

23. The view of motivation that holds that bodily needs create a state of tension or arousal is called _____ theory.

    a. instinct   c. primary
    b. homeostatic   d. drive reduction

24. A state of psychological tension or arousal is called a/an:

    a. instinct   c. drive
    b. need   d. incentive

25. Hunger, thirst, and sex which are common to every animal including humans are called:

   a. instincts
   b. primary drives
   c. primary needs
   d. primitive drives

26. Centers in the brain that are especially important for controlling hunger are located in the:

   a. thalamus
   b. limbic system
   c. reticular area
   d. hypothalamus

27. The _____ center stimulates eating, while the _____ center reduces the feeling of hunger.

   a. satiety, hunger
   b. hunger, satiety
   c. drive, satiety
   d. need, drive

28. Which of the following statements about hunger is **not** true?

   a. The role of the amygdala in hunger has been precisely defined.
   b. Both the hunger center and the satiety centers are located in the hypothalamus.
   c. If neurons in the hunger center are stimulated, the neurons in the satiety center will fire less often.
   d. If the neurons in the satiety center are stimulated, the neurons in the hunger center will fire less often.

29. The brain monitors the level of glucose in the blood. When the glucose level falls, neurons in the hunger center:

   a. become satiated
   b. are inhibited
   c. are stimulated
   d. signal the amygdala

30. Which of the following are most likely to become grossly overweight?

   a. skunks
   b. raccoons
   c. squirrels
   d. house cats

31. Looking at the clock and knowing that it is dinner time can cause a person to experience hunger. In this case, hunger stems from:

    a.   a biological need for food
    b.   an external cue
    c.   a cultural cue
    d.   inhibition of the satiety center

32. Rodin (1985) found that the sight, smell, or thought of food causes an increase in:

    a.   thyroxin production   c.   pheromones
    b.   glucose levels   d.   insulin production

33. Since the body has a normal tendency to maintain weight at all costs, one way to lose weight is to:

    a.   increase the body's metabolism
    b.   decrease the body's metabolism
    c.   punish yourself for overeating
    d.   maintain metabolism at its current level

34. Which of the following is **especially** important in reducing weight?

    a.   moderate reduction of calories
    b.   reduction of unsaturated fat consumption
    c.   reduction of saturated fat consumption
    d.   increasing water consumption

35. When the level of sodium in the blood reaches a certain point, a thirst center in the _____ is stimulated and the thirst drive is activated.

    a.   amygdala   c.   pancreas
    b.   hypothalamus   d.   kidneys

36. Which of the following statements about the sex drive is **true**?

    a.   Despite low testosterone levels, some people maintain an active interest in sex.
    b.   Sex is vital to the survival of the individual.
    c.   Testosterone is the major biological influence on the sex drive, but only in males.
    d.   There is no evidence that humans secrete pheromones.

37. Men and women tend to be sexually aroused in different ways. While men are more aroused by _____ women respond more to _____.

    a.   touch, visual
    b.   fantasies, pheromones
    c.   visual cues, touch
    d.   copulins, visual cues

38. Activity, curiosity, exploration, manipulation, and contact are termed:

    a.   primary drives   c.   social motives
    b.   stimulus motives   d.   social needs

39. The function of stimulus motives is:

    a.   dealing with environmental information
    b.   survival
    c.   to counteract primary drives
    d.   to enhance the sex drive

40. Which of the following statements of the need for activity is **true**?

    a.   There is a "separate" activity motive.
    b.   The need for activity is largely learned.
    c.   A person's temperament is not a factor in the degree of activity.
    d.   It is unclear whether the need for activity is a separate motive or the result of other motives.

41. Exploration and curiosity appear to be activated by:

    a.   familiar sights and places
    b.   the new and unknown
    c.   the spinal cord
    d.   complexity

42. Manipulation is a motive that appears to be limited to:

    a.   young children   c.   primates
    b.   dogs   d.   females

43. Which of the following is a characteristic of primates that is a factor in the manipulation motive?

   a.   agility of fingers and toes
   b.   superior intelligence
   c.   ability to walk upright
   d.   binocular vision

44. In the Harlow and Zimmerman experiment with baby monkeys, babies:

   a.   went to the wire "mother" who provided food and warmth
   b.   clung to the terry cloth "mother" who provided no food
   c.   were afraid of the wire "mothers"
   d.   were afraid of the terry cloth "mothers"

45. An important element of aggression is:

   a.   it's universality
   b.   it's instinctiveness
   c.   the degree of harm
   d.   intent

46. According to Lorenz (1968), aggression is widespread because:

   a.   we learn it early in childhood
   b.   it is an instinct triggered by pain and frustration
   c.   it is characteristic of the adolescent period
   d.   it is an instinct triggered by boredom

47. According to Bandura (1973), frustration:

   a.   generates aggression in people who have learned to be aggressive
   b.   always results in aggression
   c.   rarely results in aggression
   d.   is an innate drive

48. An important way to learn aggression is:

   a.   through classical conditioning
   b.   to combine it with a high frustration tolerance
   c.   to observe aggressive models
   d.   to read about it

49. When nonangry people are encouraged to express their aggression they tend to:

    a. withdraw   c. fantasize
    b. become more aggressive   d. become less aggressive

50. Today the view of human aggression, based on evidence, is that:

    a. it is an innate response to pain or frustration
    b. it is instinctive
    c. aggression continues to build up until it is released
    d. it is largely a learned response

51. An important method for experimentally measuring the achievement motive is use of the:

    a. Thematic Apperception Test   c. MPPI
    b. Rorschach Test   d. Bender-Gestalt Test

52. Which of the following is **not** a characteristic of people who are high in the need for achievement? They:

    a. are self-confident
    b. tend to have psychophysiological disorders
    c. tend to be hypochondriacal
    d. are relatively resistant to outside social pressures

53. What did Theodore Roosevelt, Franklin Roosevelt, Harry Truman, Woodrow Wilson, John Kennedy, and Lyndon Johnson have in common other than the fact that they were all Democrats?

    a. They were the lowest scorers on power motives.
    b. They were the highest scorers on power motives.
    c. Their high scores on power drives were second only to the scores of Jimmy Carter.
    d. They all scored high on the affiliation motive.

54. Which of the following U.S. presidents scored relatively low in power motivation?

    a. Jimmy Carter   c. Harry Truman
    b. Woodrow Wilson   d. Richard Nixon

55. Which of the following tends to be highly positively correlated with a president's high score on the power motive?

   a.   a period of peace   c.   economic recession
   b.   war   d.   economic recovery

56. The affiliation motive is aroused when:

   a.   people feel lonely   c.   people are not afraid
   b.   anxiety level is low   d.   people feel threatened

57. Schachter's (1959) experiments with the affiliation motive suggested that people affiliate in an effort to:

   a.   be praised for achievement
   b.   interpret unfamiliar situations
   c.   get feedback in familiar situations
   d.   attain power

58. According to Stanley Schachter, "misery loves _____ company."

   a.   miserable   c.   a variety of
   b.   cheerful   d.   lively

59. According to Rofe, Hoffman, and Lewin (1985), patients with major illnesses preferred:

   a.   to be with other seriously ill patients
   b.   to talk about their illnesses
   c.   to be with healthy people
   d.   to be alone

60. Abraham Maslow believed that the most highly evolved motive in the hierarchy is:

   a.   self-esteem   c.   achievement
   b.   self-actualization   d.   belonging

61. One of the criticisms of Maslow's theory is:

   a.   he did not use the experimental method
   b.   his correlations were not significant
   c.   the sample was biased
   d.   there was observer bias

62. It is useful to classify emotions as to whether they cause us to:

    a. turn to or away from objects
    b. have high or low anxiety
    c. experience anger or fear
    d. experience frustration or aggression

63. According to the Yerkes-Dodson law, extremely high levels of emotion:

    a. makes completion of complex tasks a more enjoyable experience
    b. enhances accurate performance on a complex task
    c. results in higher quality performance than when there is no arousal
    d. interferes with performance on a complex task

64. According to Plutchik's (1980) eight basic categories of emotions, anticipation and joy combine to become:

    a. love   c. ecstasy
    b. optimism   d. exaltation

65. Although Plutchik's model contains only eight categories of emotion, it accounts for a large number of different emotions because:

    a. within each category emotions vary in volume
    b. within each category emotions vary in meaning
    c. other emotions can be added as they are discovered
    d. within each category emotions vary in intensity

66. Which of the following is a criticism of the James-Lange theory of emotion?

    a. There is evidence that bodily changes do not cause specific emotions.
    b. The insistence that emotions and bodily responses occur simultaneously.
    c. There is no evidence of a connection between bodily responses and emotion.
    d. The theory does not take the sympathetic nervous system into account.

67. Which of the following factors did the Cannon-Bard theory add to our understanding of emotion?

    a. He found eight basic categories of emotions.
    b. Feelings are the result of cognitions.
    c. Emotions can be experienced without intervention of cognition.
    d. What we perceive plays an important role in emotional experience.

68. Zajonc's (1980) research turned up opposition to the cognitive theory of emotion. It was found that:

    a.   feelings are not always the result of cognitions
    b.   cognition comes before emotion
    c.   response to emotional situations are delayed
    d.   cognition occurs at the same time as emotion

69. The work of C.E. Izard (1971) showed that James-Lange theory was essentially right. Emotional experience does arise from bodily reactions, however Izard's theory stresses _____ as crucial to emotional experience, while the James-Lange theory emphasizes _____.

    a.   the parasympathetic nervous system, the sympathetic nervous system
    b.   visceral reaction, the face and body posture
    c.   innate responses, learning
    d.   face and body posture, visceral reactions

70. The most obvious emotional indicators are:

    a.   the eyes   c.   facial expressions
    b.   body postures   d.   hand movements

71. In the Thompson and Meltzer (1964) study on faking certain emotions by using facial expressions, most subjects found _____ difficult to express convincingly.

    a.   determination   c.   love
    b.   fear   d.   suffering

72. Facial expressions, body language, distance, explicit acts, and gestures:

    a.   are not useful as emotional indicators
    b.   are all nonverbal emotional indicators
    c.   usually show the opposite of what a person is feeling
    d.   are infallible clues to a person's feelings

73. Which of the following statements about nonverbal communication is **true**?

    a.   Women are better than men at understanding nonverbal cues.
    b.   Men are better than women at understanding nonverbal cues.
    c.   Sensitivity to nonverbal cues is highest in young children.
    d.   Sensitivity to nonverbal cues decreases with age.

74.   Research on gender differences and emotion has found that:

   a.   Men are likely to turn anger inward toward themselves.
   b.   Women are more likely to interpret the cause of anger to something in the
          environment.
   c.   Men tend to interpret the cause of anger to something in the environment.
   d.   Both men and women are equally likely to become depressed.

Answers for this section:

21.	b (365)	36.	a (374)	51.	a (381)	66.	a (392)
22.	a (366)	37.	c (375)	52.	c (382)	67.	d (392)
23.	d (366)	38.	b (376)	53.	b (383)	68.	a (394)
24.	c (366)	39.	a (376)	54.	d (383)	69.	d (395)
25.	b (366)	40.	d (376)	55.	b (384)	70.	c (397)
26.	d (367)	41.	b (376)	56.	d (384)	71.	d (399)
27.	b (367)	42.	c (377)	57.	b (385)	72.	b (399)
28.	a (367)	43.	a (377)	58.	a (385)	73.	a (400)
29.	c (367)	44.	b (378)	59.	c (385)	74.	c (400, 401)
30.	d (368)	45.	d (378)	60.	b (386)		
31.	b (368)	46.	b (380)	61.	c (386)		
32.	d (368)	47.	a (380)	62.	a (388)		
33.	a (370)	48.	c (380)	63.	d (388)		
34.	c (370)	49.	b (380)	64.	b (389)		
35.	b (372)	50.	d (381)	65.	d (391)		

Applying the Facts

     The learning of facts and concepts is of little value unless it can be applied and
employed to solve problems. The next group of multiple-choice questions reflects
application of your learning.

75.   Ducks and geese fly to warm climates in the winter. This is an example of:

   a.   learned behavior   c.   incentive
   b.   instinct   d.   homeostasis

76. Hilde, the Wiemaraner, had 7 puppies. A friend picked up one of the puppies and carried it out of the room. Hilde did not appear to notice. She laid down to feed the puppies, looked at them, then jumped up and scouted the area. A puppy was missing! Which of the following motivators is the **most** likely explanation for Hilde's behavior?

    a. primary drive   c. homeostasis
    b. curiosity   d. instinct

77. Margie is 65-years-old. She is obese. Her weight is now a life-threatening situation. Throughout her life she tried diets. Her weight would decline, then she would put the weight back on. She has given up dieting. This sequence happens because:

    a. when calories are reduced, metabolism is lowered, so fewer calories are needed to maintain weight
    b. Margie did not exercise enough
    c. Margie's fat cells did not shrink
    d. the diet caused an increase in metabolism which caused fat cells to send out signals to eat more

78. Saundra is 65-years-old. She never had to work. She wants to travel all the time. Her husband will not travel with her as often as she likes, so she takes trips alone if she cannot find a companion. She has a collection of photographs of state capitol buildings among many other souvenirs of her travels. Of the following which motive is **most** likely to be an explanation for her behavior?

    a. contact   c. achievement
    b. curiosity   d. affiliation

79. Anne's friend was confronted with a serious crisis situation. She gave her friend as much support as possible. One day Anne presented her friend with a gift; a small piece of polished marble with a depression in it. She instructed Anne to hold it in her hand occasionally and press the indentation with her thumb. It is likely that Anne was helping her friend to fulfill the motive of:

    a. achievement   c. manipulation
    b. affiliation   d. activity

80. You open the door to the dentist's waiting room. You are there because you are going to have a tooth capped. You are scared. You begin pacing the floor. Then you notice a young man with his feet propped up on a table reading a magazine. You think up a reason to talk to him. Your motive is **most** likely?

a. contact   c. belonging
b. affiliation   d. curiosity

81. In the past several years there has been an increase in the number of support groups for people with specific problems; most anything from divorce to the Persian Gulf War. Which of the following researchers has the best explanation for support groups?

a. Abraham Maslow   c. Robert Plutchik
b. Stanley Milgrim   d. Stanley Schachter

82. Jane went to the grocery store, then to pick up her cat at the veterinarian. When she went to pay the doctor she realized that she had left her purse at the grocery store. She calmly got back in her car, drove to the store, retrieved her purse, and started back to get the cat. But she could not drive. She was perspiring and shaking and felt nauseated. This example most closely resembles which theory of emotion?

a. James-Lange   c. cognitive theory
b. Cannon-Bard   d. Izard's theory

83. Andrew was writing a book on a deadline when news of the stockmarket crash of October, 1987 was announced. His anxiety level had been appropriate for writing the book, but he found that after the news of the plunge of the value of his securities, his writing was not as effective as it had been. Ideas and the words to express them would not come. Andrew's plight is a reaffirmation of:

a. Plutchik's categorization of emotions
b. the Cannon-Bard theory of emotion
c. the Yerkes-Dodson law
d. Izard's law of arousal

84. Hal likes to play poker. He wins more than he loses. It is very possible that Hal is a serious student of:

a. C.E. Izard   c. verbal communication
b. nonverbal communication   d. Sigmund Freud

Answers for this section:

75.	b (365)	80.	b (384)
76.	d (365)	81.	d (385)
77.	a (370)	82.	a (391)
78.	b (376)	83.	c (388)
79.	c (377)	84.	b (396)

Fill-in-the-Blank Questions: Recalling What You Have Learned

By now, there should be a considerable amount of new information about Motivation and Emotion in long-term memory. The following questions of recall rather than recognition will show if you are becoming more comfortable with the material.

Remembering the Facts

1.   A specific need, desire, or want that energizes and directs behavior is called a/an _____.

2.   A feeling that energizes and directs behavior is called a/an _____.

3.   A/an _____ is inborn, inflexible, goal-directed behavior that is characteristic of a specie.

4.   A state of tension or arousal due to biological needs is called a/an _____.

5.   Motivated behavior that moves the organism toward arousal reduction is the definition of _____ - _____ theory.

6.   _____ is a state of balance and equilibrium in which the organism functions effectively.

7.   An external stimulus that prompts goal-directed behavior is called a/an _____.

8.   A physiologically based unlearned motive is called a/an _____ _____.

9.   _____ is a simple sugar that is the main source of body energy.

10.   _____ is a hormone that is the primary determinant of the sex drive in both men and women.

11. Substances secreted by some animals that enhance the sexual readiness of the opposite sex are called _____.

12. A _____ motive is unlearned and depends more on external stimuli than on internal physiological states.

13. Behavior aimed at doing harm to others is termed _____.

14. The need to excel and to overcome obstacles is called the _____ motive.

15. The need to win recognition or to influence or control other people or groups is called the _____ motive.

16. _____ is the need to be with others.

17. The _____-_____ _____ states that there is an optimal level of arousal for the best performance on any task.

18. Physical reactions precede experienced emotions according to the _____ _____ theory.

19. The _____ _____ theory states that the experience of emotion and biological changes occur simultaneously.

20. Emotional experience depends on the person's perception or judgement of the situation the person is in according the _____ theory of emotion.

Answers for this section:

1. motive (364)
2. emotion (364)
3. instinct (365)
4. drive (365)
5. drive-reduction (365)
6. homeostasis (366)
7. incentive (366)
8. primary drive (366)
9. glucose (367)
10. testosterone (374)
11. pheromones (374)
12. stimulus (376)
13. aggression (378)
14. achievement (381)
15. power (382)
16. affiliation (384)
17. Yerkes-Dodson law (388)
18. James-Lange (391)
19. Cannon-Bard (392)
20. cognitive (392)

Understanding and Applying the Facts

As you previously did with recognition-type questions, you will now move to a higher level of recall. The following questions will determine if you understand the facts.

21. Most significant human behavior is _____ as a result of experience.

22. Lafitte, the poodle, was a diabetic. When his insulin level went too high something had to be done to restore his body's _____.

23. The two centers in the brain that are especially important for controlling hunger are the hunger center which stimulates eating and the _____ center which reduces hunger. Both centers are located in the _____.

24. When the level of _____ falls, neurons in the hunger center are stimulated.

25. Hunger does not always stem from a biological need for food. _____, _____ like looking at the clock can trigger the desire to eat.

26. Roden (1985) found that the mere sight, smell, or thought of food cause an increase in _____ production.

27. Just before you sat down to eat dinner you had a call informing you that a close friend had died. You are no longer hungry. Your motivation is affected by _____.

28. Your family has an exchange student from Germany living with you. Your family always eats dinner at 5:30 p.m. You are having trouble with Hans. He does not get hungry until 8:30. This illustrates _____ _____ in the hunger motive.

29. Margie is 65-years-old and dangerously obese. Diets do not good. If she loses a little weight her _____ _____ shrink, but do not disappear and they send out urgent signals for her to eat more.

30. In attempting to lose weight, it is especially important to reduce consumption of _____ _____.

31. Basic hunger and thirst are both _____ drives.

32. While hunger and thirst are vital to the survival of the _____, sex is vital only to the survival of the _____.

33. Despite low _____ levels some people maintain an active interest in sex.

34. In both humans and other animals, the sex drive is affected by _____ and the _____ _____.

35. Human sexual motivation is much more dependent upon _____ and _____ , especially in the early stages of excitement and arousal.

36. Sex is a _____ biological drive, but environmental _____ that lead to arousal are determined largely by _____.

37. Danny draws "doodles" on paper napkins when he is waiting for his food in a restaurant. This behavior may be the need for _____ and is classified as a _____ motive.

38. Frostie, the Bichon, wandered into every room at the grooming shop the first time he went there for a bath. Perhaps Frostie had a need for _____ and _____ , and his behavior is an example of a _____ motive.

39. Anne gave her friend a small piece of polished marble and told her to hold it in her hand occasionally and press the indentation. Anne's friend was experiencing a crisis. This _____ of the piece of marble could be an example of the need to be _____.

40. Harriet is 80-years-old. She has many friends and attends social functions often. She is known as "Harriet the hugger." She is indiscriminate with her hugging. She apparently has a need for _____ which is a _____ motive.

41. According to Lorenz, (1968) aggression is widespread because it is part of an _____ that is triggered by _____ and _____.

42. When nonangry people are encouraged to express aggression, they are either unaffected or become (more, less) aggressive.

43. One important way to learn aggression is to _____ aggressive models.

44. Helmreich and Spence (1978) found that there are three interrelated aspects of achievement-oriented behavior: _____ _____, _____, and _____.

45. Democratic presidents appear to be the highest scorers on power motives. These high power motives appear to correlate positively with _____.

46. The _____ motive is aroused when people feel threatened.

47. Martha's husband died recently. She attends meetings a grief group at her church. Martha appears to lend support to the research of _____ who concluded that "misery loves _____ company."

48. Rofe (1984), said that Schachter created ambiguous situations and that people behave differently in less ambiguous situations. In less ambiguous situations, people prefer to _____ _____.

49. The most highly evolved motive, according the Abraham Maslow is _____ _____.

50. While Andrew was writing his book, the news came of the stock market crash of October, 1987. When he found his arousal level too high to write, he went to his yard to rake leaves. According to the _____ _____ law his arousal level was not too high to be an effective leaf raker.

51. You are walking in the forest. You hear a strange sound and turn to see a coiled rattlesnake. You jump out of the way and run. Then you begin to perspire, your stomach hurts, and the hair on your arms stand up. You have illustrated the _____ _____ theory of emotion.

52. The _____ _____ theory would disagree with the reason for actions you took because of the snake. What you _____ plays the important role in emotional experience.

53. The _____ theory of emotion would say that you sized up the _____ with the snake before you reacted.

54. Zajonc rejects the idea that feelings must always be the result of _____.

55. _____ claims that emotions can be experienced without the intervention of cognition.

56. If you were engaged in the art of picking pockets you would, of necessity, have to become a serious student of _____ communication.

57. If you want to know how people are feeling, look at their _____.

58. One nonverbal means of communication that may not have a high level of accuracy is _____ _____.

59. In every culture there appears to be a _____ that is generally thought appropriate for normal conversation.

60. Explicit _____ and _____ are two more examples of nonverbal clues to emotion.

61. Women are consistently better than men at understanding _____ clues.

62. Sensitivity to nonverbal clues _____ with age and the vicarious response of _____ helps us to read people's emotions.

63. Jack tends to interpret the cause of his anger to something in the environment, therefore enters into violent behavior occasionally. His wife, Mary, sees herself as the source of the problem and turns her anger inward and therefore tends to be _____.

Answers for this section:

21.	learned (365)	43.	observe (380)
22.	homeostasis (366)	44.	work orientation, mastery,
23.	satiety, hypothalamus (367)		competitiveness (382)
24.	glucose (367)	45.	war (384)
25.	external cues (368)	46.	affiliation (384)
26.	insulin (368)	47.	Schachter, miserable (385)
27.	emotions (368)	48.	be alone (385)
28.	cultural differences (368)	49.	self-actualization (386)
29.	fat cells (370)	50.	Yerkes-Dodson (388)
30.	saturated fats (370)	51.	James-Lange (391)
31.	primary (366)	52.	Cannon-Bard, perceive (392)
32.	individual , species (373)	53.	cognitive, situation (392)
33.	testosterone (374)	54.	cognition (394)
34.	hormones, nervous system (374)	55.	C.E. Izard (394)
35.	experience, learning (374)	56.	nonverbal (395)
36.	primary, cues, learning (374)	57.	faces (397)
37.	activity, stimulus (376)	58.	body language (399)
38.	exploration, curiosity, stimulus (376)	59.	distance (399)
		60.	acts, gestures (399)
39.	manipulation, soothed (377)	61.	nonverbal (400)
40.	contact, stimulus (378)	62.	increases, empathy (400)
41.	instinct, pain, frustration (380)	63.	depressed (401)
42.	more (380)		

Testing Yourself For Mastery

The following terms and concepts are found in boldface or italics in the chapter. The time has come to determine if you can define and discuss your new learning in your own words, then check your work against the text.

motive

emotion

instinct

drive

drive reduction theory

homeostasis

incentive

primary drive

glucose

testosterone

pheromones

stimulus motives

exploration

curiosity

manipulation

contact

social motive

aggression

achievement motive

power motive

affiliative motive

Yerkes-Dodson law

James-Lange theory of emotion

Cannon-Bard theory of emotion

cognitive theory of emotion

Izard's theory of emotion

nonverbal communication

empathy

Integrating Your Newly Learned Information

Now that you have recognized, recalled, and given definition to Motivation and Emotion, you are ready to try to integrate your knowledge in a definitive discussion through short-answer questions.

1.   Explain why the concept of instinct has lost favor as a way to understand and explain the dynamics of human behavior. (365)

2.   Briefly describe drive reduction theory and identify the reasons why it does not explain all motivated behavior. (365, 366)

3.   Explain the physiological reasons why weight reduction is so difficult for people. (370)

4.   How does learning and experience interact with biological factors in the sex drive? (373-376)

5.   List some psychological influences on sexual motivation. (374-376)

6.   List the stimulus motives and give an example of each. (376-378)

7.   List the social motives and give an example of each. (378-385)

8.   Is aggression learned or innate? Explain. (378-381)

9.   List Maslow's Hierarchy of Motives and present at least one criticism of Maslow's work. (385-387)

10.   Choose two theories of emotion and explain how they differ. (391-395)

Applications

You have worked through a section of recognition-type questions to determine if you can apply information to real-life situations. It is time to try to respond to some applications. Some are based upon those questions. Answers to this section will not be given. Your questions concerning these applications will serve as a basis for classroom discussion and ideas for class projects throughout the course.

1.   Since you are attending college, it is obvious that you are motivated to do so. Explain your motivation to attend college on the basis of drive reduction theory. After you have done that, explain your college attendance on the basis of stimulus motives and social motives. Which explanation was the easiest to do?

2.   Find someone you know who is overweight (this person will not be difficult to find). Observe the behavior as closely as you can. Taking into account what you know about the person and what you have learned in this chapter, try to determine why this person is overweight. If you had the chance, what could you tell this person about losing weight or the chances of losing weight?

3. If you were to travel to a foreign country, what kind of problems, generated by a cultural difference, might you have to solve in reducing your hunger drive?

4. Frostie, the Bichon, went for "day care" at the home of his master's friend. As soon as he was released from his lead in the house he disappeared. He was found wandering from room to room. Choose either instinct or stimulus motives and explain this behavior. Defend your choice of the view for your explanation.

5. Ralph is majoring in business. He is a member of the football team, president of his fraternity, and serves on two student-faculty committees. Which one of the social motives currently appears to be the most prominent in Ralph's life?

6. You come into the classroom to take an exam. Most of the students who arrived early are flipping through the text and looking at their notes. It is obvious that anxiety prevails. But you have studied sufficiently and you know something your classmates do not know. You put your books under your seat, get out your pencil, stretch your muscles, and take a few deep breaths. What do you know that makes your behavior different and more efficient than the other students in the class?

7. The next time you experience a fearful situation try to analyze what happened and determine which theory of emotion best explains your experience.

8. The next time a stranger stands close to you (other than on a crowded elevator), try to determine what kind of an emotion you felt and explain that emotion by what you have learned in this chapter.

Return to Chapter Summary

Now that you have concluded these exercises, you should go back and reread the chapter summary in your textbook. It provides you with a framework that integrates all of this newly-learned information. By reviewing the chapter summary, you will strengthen the many connections between the various new pieces of information.

PERSONALITY 10

Chapter Objectives

After you have read and studied this chapter, you should be able to:

1. Define personality.
2. Summarize the interaction of Freud's id, ego, and superego.
3. Identify Freud's five stages of psychosexual development.
4. Differentiate between the theories of Jung, Adler, and Horney.
5. Identify Erik Erikson's eight stages of personality development.
6. Contrast Carl Rogers' humanistic theory with Freudian theory.
7. Explain the contributions of William James and William Sheldon to the study of personality.
8. Explain trait theory.
9. Explain Mischel's situationism and the concept of interactionism.
10. Compare the behaviorist approach and social learning theory to early views of personality.
11. Describe the four basic tools psychologists use to measure personality.
12. List two objective tests and their uses. List the advantages and disadvantages of objective tests.
13. Discuss the advantages of projective tests. Explain how the Rorschach Test and the Thematic Apperception Test are administered.
14. Define locus of control. Discuss the attitudes of externally and internally oriented people and the effect these attitudes may have on their lives.

Multiple-Choice Questions: Recognizing What You Have Learned

These questions ask only that you recognize what you have learned. When you recognize a correct answer, you have accessed that information in memory. A knowledge of facts serves as a framework for later analysis and problem solving.

Remembering the Facts

This group of multiple-choice questions requires that you simply recognize facts from your textbook.

1. All of the ideas, thoughts and feelings of which we are not and cannot normally become aware are called _____ in Freudian theory.

    a. the conscience
    b. the unconscious
    c. consciousness
    d. repressions

2. In Freudian theory, the instincts that lead toward aggression, destruction, and death are called:

    a. death drives
    b. violent desires
    c. negative instincts
    d. death instincts

3. In Freudian theory, _____ is/are involved in the survival of the individual and the species.

    a. libido
    b. ego instincts
    c. the life instincts
    d. id instincts

4. The collection of unconscious urges and desires that continually seek expression are termed _____ by Freud.

    a. id
    b. libido
    c. primary processes
    d. life instincts

5. The way in which the id seeks immediate gratification of an instinct is termed _____ by Freud.

    a. the pleasure principle
    b. compulsion
    c. reality
    d. primary process thinking

6. The id achieves partial satisfaction of an instinct through dreams and daydreams. Freud termed this phenomenon:

   a. primary illusion   c. primary process thinking
   b. primary fantasizing   d. fantasizing

7. In Freudian theory, the _____ mediates between reality, conscience and instinctual needs.

   a. superego   c. libido
   b. ego   d. id

8. A characteristic of the ego that enables us to satisfy instincts safely and effectively is called, by Freud:

   a. the reality principle   c. consciousness
   b. primary process   d. the pleasure principle

9. The process by which the ego uses intelligent reasoning to find safe and effective ways to gratify id instincts is called _____ by Freud.

   a. rationalism   c. secondary process thinking
   b. logical process   d. ego function

10. The internalized parental standards that lead to conscience is termed _____ by Freud.

   a. superself   c. moral guardian
   b. superid   d. superego

11. According to Freud the part of the ego that consists of standards of what one would like to be is the:

   a. superego   c. ideal self
   b. ego ideal   d. personal conscience

12. The energy generated by the sexual instinct is Freud's term for _____ .

   a. life   c. sexual
   b. libido   d. psychosexual

13. According to Freud, a partial or complete halt at some point in a person's psychosexual development is called:

   a. an arrest
   b. discontinuity

   c. culmination
   d. fixation

14. In which of Freud's psychosexual stages do the infant's erotic feelings center on the mouth, lips, and tongue?

   a. oral
   b. anal

   c. phallic
   d. latency

15. Which of the following is the second psychosexual stage in Freud's theory of personality development?

   a. anal
   b. phallic

   c. oral
   d. genital

16. In the _____ stage of Freud's theory of personality development, erotic feelings center on the genitals.

   a. anal
   b. oral

   c. latency
   d. phallic

17. Freud termed a child's attachment to the parent of the opposite sex and jealousy toward the parent of the same sex:

   a. the latency period
   b. the Oedipus complex

   c. fixation
   d. a conflict complex

18. Normal sexual development occurs during _____ in Freud's theory of personality development.

   a. latency
   b. the anal stage

   c. the genital stage
   d. dream analysis

19. According to Carl Jung, the individual's repressed thoughts, forgotten experiences, and underdeveloped ideas are housed in the:

   a. id
   b. personal unconscious

   c. collective unconscious
   d. archetypes

20. According to Freud, in the _____ period the child appears to have no interest in the opposite sex.

    a. phallic   c. archetypal
    b. oral   d. latency

21. In Jung's theory, the level of unconsciousness that is inherited and common to all members of a species is called:

    a. collective history   c. the universal unconscious
    b. the collective unconscious d. selective unconscious

22. Jung termed the thought forms common to all human beings:

    a. personas   c. animas
    b. archetypes   d. archeforms

23. The mask we put on to represent ourselves to others is called the _____ by Jung.

    a. persona   c. personal shield
    b. humana   d. disguise

24. The feminine side of the masculine personality is termed _____ by Jung.

    a. femina   c. anima
    b. animus   d. androgyny

25. The masculine side of the feminine personality is termed _____ by Jung.

    a. mascula   c. homme
    b. anima   d. animus

26. According to Jung, a person who usually focuses on social life and the external world instead of internal experience is called a/an:

    a. ambivert   c. introvert
    b. extrovert   d. humanist

27. According to Jung, a person who usually focuses on inner thoughts and feelings is called a/an:

   a. extrovert   c. ambivert
   b. isolate   d. introvert

28. A person's efforts to overcome imagined or real personal weaknesses is termed _____ by Alfred Adler.

   a. compensation   c. retaliation
   b. striving   d. counteraction

29. In Adler's theory, motivating goals that people establish to guide their behavior even though such goals may not be attainable are called:

   a. life styles   c. fictional finalisms
   b. archetypes   d. functional sets

30. In Adler's theory, an individual's development of a particular set of meanings and beliefs is called:

   a. style of life   c. philosophical style
   b. purpose of life   d. mystical imagery

31. According to Karen Horney, a feeling similar to fear but without an identifiable source is termed:

   a. apprehension   c. anxiety
   b. worry   d. mental anguish

32. Irrational strategies for coping with emotional problems and minimizing anxiety are termed _____ by Horney.

   a. neurotic trends   c. aggressive acts
   b. adjustment trends d. defense mechanisms

33. In Horney's theory, a person whose relations with others is marked by deference and submission is called a _____ type.

   a. consenting   c. conforming
   b. submissive   d. compliant

34. In Horney's theory, a person who customarily relates to others aggressively is called a/an _____ type.

   a. violent   c. aggressive
   b. frustrated   d. belligerent

35. The drive of every organism to fulfill its biological potential is called the _____ tendency by Carl Rogers.

   a. actualizing   c. self-actualizing
   b. functioning   d. self

36. According to Rogers, the drive to fulfill the images we have formed of ourselves is called the _____ tendency.

   a. actualizing   c. superiority
   b. functioning   d. self-actualizing

37. A/an _____ person is an individual whose self-concept closely resemble(s) his/her inborn potentials.

   a. actualized   c. self-actualized
   b. fully functioning   d. mature

38. Enduring dispositions within the individual that cause the person to think, feel, and act in characteristic ways are called:

   a. personality traits   c. personal dispositions
   b. personal traits   d. individual characteristics

39. A statistical technique used by Cattell to identify a set of basic personality traits is called:

   a. correlation   c. factor analysis
   b. cannonical correlation d. analysis of variance

40. _____ is the theory that views behavior solely as a response to external stimuli.

   a. Interactionism   c. Behaviorism
   b. Externalism   d. Situationism

41. According to Bandura, the expectancy that one's efforts will be successful is termed:

a. self-realization   c. self-actualization
b. self-efficacy   d. self-accomplishment

42. The most widely used objective personality test is the:

a. Sixteen PF   c. MMPI
b. H-T-P   d. TAT

43. A projective test composed of ambiguous inkblots is called the:

a. Rorschach   c. MMPI
b. TAT   d. Bender-Gestalt

Answers for this section:

1. b (409)	12. b (411)	23. a (414)	34. c (417)
2. d (409)	13. d (411)	24. c (414)	35. a (421)
3. c (409)	14. a (411)	25. d (414)	36. d (421)
4. a (409)	15. a (411)	26. b (414)	37. b (421)
5. a (409)	16. d (411)	27. d (414)	38. a (422)
6. c (409)	17. b (411)	28. a (415)	39. c (423)
7. b (409)	18. c (412)	29. c (416)	40. d (425)
8. a (409)	19. b (414)	30. a (416)	41. b (429)
9. c (409)	20. d (412)	31. c (416)	42. c (437)
10. d (410)	21. b (414)	32. a (417)	43. a (438)
11. b (410)	22. b (414)	33. d (417)	

Understanding the Facts

Now that you have found that you can recognize facts from Personality, the next step is to determine if you understand the meaning of newly-learned information. These multiple-choice questions require a higher level of thinking. They will help you establish more solid connections and provide practice in dealing with higher level concepts.

44. The id operates according to:

    a.   primary process   c.   the reality principle
    b.   the pleasure principle   d.   laws of logic

45. Another term for the superego is:

    a.   wish fulfillment   c.   conscience
    b.   conscious   d.   ego ideal

46. If a child is deprived of pleasure or allowed too much gratification from the part of the body that dominates a certain psychosexual stage:

    a.   some sexual energy may remain permanently tied to that body part
    b.   libido will be lost
    c.   the child will not be capable of fixating
    d.   the ego ideal will not develop properly

47. Most children eventually resolve the Oedipus complex by:

    a.   identifying with the parent of the opposite sex
    b.   the age of 14
    c.   developing a collective unconscious
    d.   identifying with the parent of the same sex

48. Which of the following statements about Jung's subcategories of the introvert-extrovert categorization is **true**?

    a.   Rational people regulate their actions through sensation.
    b.   Most people exhibit all four psychological functions: thinking, feeling, sensing and intuiting.
    c.   Irrational people are primarily extroverts.
    d.   The feeling person has a balanced sense of values.

49. While Freud might say that the "master motive" of man is sex and aggression, Adler might say that our master motive is:

    a.   overcoming inferiority, striving for superiority
    b.   balancing opposites within us
    c.   overcoming neurotic trends
    d.   meeting life's crisis periods

50. The first and extremely crucial of Erickson's "eight ages of man" is:

   a. initiative versus guilt
   b. autonomy versus shame and doubt
   c. industry versus inferiority
   d. trust versus mistrust

51. Theoretically a person at the onset of old age will not come to terms with the approach of death unless that person:

   a. did not have a crisis at each stage
   b. had a crisis at each stage
   c. has resolved the crisis of all the earlier stages
   d. omitted the stage of autonomy versus shame and doubt

52. Which of the following is **not** necessarily a characteristic of *fully functioning persons*, according to Carl Rogers? They:

   a. have extremely high intelligence
   b. are self-directed
   c. decide for themselves what they wish to become
   d. are open to experience

53. According to Rogers, people become constricted, rigid, and defensive when they:

   a. are fixated at the oral stage
   b. cannot resolve the generativity crisis
   c. have lost sight of their inborn potential
   d. have not developed basic trust

54. Which of the following descriptions is characteristic of a mesomorph?

   a. sturdy, upright body, strong bones and muscles
   b. small-boned fragile body
   c. round, soft body
   d. thin, but with large abdomen

55. Traits that are so general that they influence every act a person performs are called:

   a. central traits   c. archetypes
   b. primary traits   d. cardinal traits

56. Which of the following statements is **not** true of Gordon Allport's view of personality?

    a.   He agreed with the idea of dividing people into various types.
    b.   Traits literally exist in the nervous system.
    c.   Each individual personality has a unique constellation of traits.
    d.   Traits guide consistent behavior across a wide variety of situations.

57. Raymond Cattell concluded that:

    a.   factor analysis tells us nothing about personality
    b.   just 24 traits account for the complexity of human personality
    c.   just 16 traits account for the complexity of human personality
    d.   there is no need to add more traits to the original list

58. Which of the following statements about the view of Walter Mischel is **not** true?

    a.   Observers often read consistency into the behavior of others when there is none.
    b.   We tend to ignore behaviors that do not match our pre-existing image of that person.
    c.   Some behaviors appear to be highly consistent in a variety of situations.
    d.   Approaches that rely on internal dispositions are adequate in explaining personality.

59. Which of the following theorists found that there is always an interaction between the person, the situation, and feedback obtained from a person's behavior in a situation?

    a.   Skinner   c.   Bandura
    b.   Cattell   d.   Allport

60. Which of the following theorists concentrates on finding the observable links between behavior and the conditions that cause or control it?

    a.   Skinner   c.   Cattell
    b.   Rotter   d.   Freud

61. Bandura calls interactions between personalities and their environment:

    a.   efficient determination   c.   reciprocal determination
    b.   loci of control   d.   performance standards

62. A test of personality that does not depend on the skills of an interviewer or observer interpretive abilities is the:

a. Rorschach   c. TAT
b. MMPI   d. SCAT

63. Projective tests of personality are based upon:

a. conscious determinants of personality
b. clusters of central traits
c. unconscious determinants of personality
d. factor analysis

64. Which of the following is **not** an advantage of projective tests of personality?

a. They do not have to be administered by a professional.
b. They are flexible.
c. They can be administered in a relaxed atmosphere.
d. They often hide the true purpose of the test.

65. Which of the following is **not** a factor in the controversy surrounding the Rorschach and the TAT?

a. Often they are not administered according to standard procedure.
b. They are seldom scored objectively.
c. Often the final interpretation of results differs from one examiner to another.
d. They are frequently administered by a layperson.

Answers for this section:

44.	b (409)	55.	d (422)
45.	c (410)	56.	a (423)
46.	a (411)	57.	c (423)
47.	d (412)	58.	d (425)
48.	b (414)	59.	c (431)
49.	a (415)	60.	a (427)
50.	d (418)	61.	c (430)
51.	c (419)	62.	b (436)
52.	a (421)	63.	c (438)
53.	c (421)	64.	a (438)
54.	a (422)	65.	d (440)

Applying the Facts

The learning of facts and concepts is of little value unless it can be applied and employed to solve problems. The next group of multiple-choice questions reflects applications of your learning.

66. Jim is 16 years old. Very often he fantasizes about good-looking girls. According to Freud, Jim is engaged in:

    a. planning for the future
    b. primary-process thinking
    c. resolving the Oedipus complex
    d. secondary-process thinking

67. While Alex was sitting in class one day he was thinking about how hungry he was. The lecture would continue for another hour. He left class early, went to the student center, and ate lunch. He "gave in" to the:

    a. ego   c. id
    b. superego   d. reality principle

68. If your professor suddenly approaches your desk, picks up a sheet of your notes, tears the sheet into small pieces and eats them, something is very wrong with the development of your professor's:

    a. ego   c. id
    b. collective unconscious   d. primary-process thinking

69. Perhaps each of the Freudian structures of personality has a theme song. The id sings, "I want!" the ego sings, "I will!" and the superego sings,

    a. "I should!"
    b. "Thou shalt not!"
    c. "I will see!"
    d. "I can try!"

70. I do whatever is pleasurable. I want something all the time. I am amoral. I have no conscience. I have no self-restraint. I am: a/an

    a. human infant   c. adolescent
    b. young adult   d. toddler

71. Albert has recurring dreams about Indians. In his dreams he is one of them and engages in their ceremonial rights. There has been a progression from childhood to adulthood. Carl Jung would say the source of his dreams is:

    a. his extroversion   c. the collective unconscious
    b. the preconscious   d. the animus

72. Bob was stricken with polio when he was 12. He had always had an interest in sports, but could pursue these activities no longer. He was not a good student in his early years, but pursued a college education, eventually earning a Ph.D in literature. He became the head of the English Department at a major university. Bob is a good illustration of:

    a. Sheldon and body type
    b. Jung and introversion
    c. Horney and insecurity
    d. Adler and compensation

73. Grace is involved in an unhappy marriage. Her husband is hostile and finds fault with everything she does. She gives in to everything her husband requests and will not retaliate against his actions that lower her self-esteem. Inspite of this treatment, she will not consider leaving him. She is afraid to be alone and wants the financial security. Karen Horney would say that Grace is:

    a. the detached type
    b. a compliant type
    c. lacking autonomy
    d. not a fully functioning person

74. Evan, the Welshman, at age 84 is faced with dying from an aortic aneurysm or having the surgery to repair it along with the risks. He told his doctor that he has had a long, happy, and productive life and that he should, perhaps, refuse the surgery and allow the inevitable to happen when it will. Erikson would describe Evan as having:

    a. stagnation   c. integrity
    b. a neurotic trend   d. ectomorphic thoughts

75. Michael has always been a hard worker. He was always doing small jobs to earn money when he was in early adolescence. He learned by his many mistakes through the years and saw to it that he did not make "big" mistakes. He studied diligently in college to earn good grades so that he could qualify for dental school. Rotter would say that Michael:

    a.   has an internal locus of control
    b.   has been reinforced by the environment
    c.   has many cardinal traits
    d.   is typical of cerebrotonic mesomorphs

Answers for this section:

66.	b (409)	71.	c (414)
67.	c (409)	72.	d (415)
68.	a (409)	73.	b (417)
69.	b (410)	74.	c (419)
70.	a (410)	75.	a (426)

Fill-in-the-Blank Questions: Recalling What You Have Learned

By now, there should be a considerable amount of new information about Personality in long-term memory. The following questions of recall rather than recognition will show if you are becoming more comfortable with the material.

Remembering the Facts

1. A person's unique pattern of thoughts, feelings, and behaviors that persist over time is termed _____.

2. All of the ideas, thoughts, and feelings of which we are not aware is termed the _____ by Freud.

3. Freud's theory of personality **and** his form of therapy are termed _____.

4. In Freudian theory the collection of unconscious urges and desires that constantly seek expression is called the _____.

5. The _____ principle in Freudian theory is the way in which the id seeks immediate gratification.

6. Freud called the process by which the id achieves immediate partial satisfaction through dreams and daydreams _____ _____ thinking.

7. According to Freud, the part of the personality that mediates between environmental demands, conscience, and instinctual needs is the _____.

8. Using intelligent reasoning to find safe and effective ways to gratify id instincts is called _____ _____ thinking by Freud.

9. The social and parental standards the individual has internalized is called the _____ by Freud.

10. _____ is Freud's term for the energy generated by the sexual instinct.

11. A partial or complete halt at some point in a person's psychosexual development is termed _____ by Freud.

12. Erotic feelings center on the genitals during Freud's _____ stage of psychosexual development.

13. In Jung's theory, the level of the unconscious that is inherited and common to all members of the species is the _____ _____.

14. Thought forms, common to all human beings are called _____ in Jung's theory.

15. Jung's term for the masculine side of feminine personality is _____.

16. Adler calls the person's effort to overcome imagined or real weaknesses _____.

17. Motivating goals that people establish to guide their behavior even though the goals may not be attainable are called _____ _____ by Adler.

18. Adler considers the _____ _____ _____ to be each individual's development of a particular set of meanings and beliefs.

19. Horney's _____ _____ are irrational strategies for coping with emotional problems and minimizing anxiety.

20. _____ versus _____ is the fourth stage in Erikson's "Eight Ages of Man."

21. _____ personality theories emphasize the fundamental goodness of people and their striving toward higher levels of functioning.

22. The acceptance and love for another person regardless of that person's behavior is called _____ _____ _____ by Carl Rogers.

23. According to Rogers, individuals whose self concepts closely resemble their inborn capacities or potential are called _____ _____ persons.

24. The personality theory that proposes a relationship between a person's body type and behavior is called _____ theory by _____.

25. Enduring dispositions that cause a person to think, feel, and act in characteristics ways are known as personality _____.

26. _____ _____ is a statistical technique used to identify a set of basic personality traits.

27. The theory that views behavior solely as a response to external stimuli is known as _____.

28. _____, in Bandura's view, are what a person anticipates in a situation or as a result of behaving in a certain way.

29. An expectancy about whether reinforcements are under internal or external control is called _____ of _____ by Rotter.

30. People rate the adequacy of their own behavior in a variety of situations through _____ _____, according to Bandura.

31. The expectancy that one's efforts will be successful is termed _____ - _____ by Bandura.

32. Bandura proposed that the person influences the environment and is in turn influenced by the environment. He termed the process _____ _____.

33. According to Mischel, there are cognitive processes that influence behavior in different situations. These are called _____ _____.

34. Personality tests that are administered and scored in a standard way are called _____ tests.

35. The most widely used objective personality test is the _____ _____ _____ _____.

36. _____ tests consist of ambiguous or unstructured material that do not limit the response to be given.

37. Two major projective tests of personality are the _____ and the _____ _____ _____.

Answers for this section:

1. personality (408)
2. unconscious (409)
3. psychoanalysis (409)
4. id (409)
5. pleasure (409)
6. primary process (409)
7. ego (409)
8. secondary process (409)
9. superego (410)
10. libido (411)
11. fixation (411)
12. phallic (411)
13. collective unconscious (414)
14. archetypes (414)
15. animus (414)
16. compensation (415)
17. fictional finalisms (416)
18. style of life (416)
19. neurotic trends (417)
20. industry, inferiority (419)

21. humanistic (420)
22. unconditional positive regard (421)
23. fully functioning (421)
24. constitutional, Sheldon (422)
25. traits (422)
26. factor analysis (423)
27. situationism (425)
28. expectancies (426)
29. locus, control (426)
30. performance standards (429)
31. self-efficacy (429)
32. reciprocal determination (430)
33. person variables (431)
34. objective (436)
35. Minnesota Multiphasic Personality Inventory (MMPI) (437)
36. projective (438)
37. Rorschach, Thematic Apperception Test (TAT) (438, 439)

Understanding and Applying the Facts

As you previously did with recognition-type questions, you will now move to a higher level of recall. The following questions will determine if you understand the facts.

38. Jack was angry with his friend Tom because Tom had not reported a significant amount of his income to the IRS for years. Jack liked to think about turning Tom's name into the IRS and then imagined what the law would do to Tom. According to Freud, Jack was engaging in _____ _____ _____.

39. Freud's term "superego" could also be called _____ or _____ _____.

40. Becky is 4 1/2-years-old. She has temper tantrums and on one occasion, tried to drown her cousin in a swimming pool. Although Becky should, by now, be showing signs of it, she has not, as yet, developed a _____.

41. Melanie at 32 is flirtatious and promiscuous. Freud would say that she is fixated at the _____ stage of psychosexual development.

42. Men who take great pride in their sexual prowess and treat women with contempt are fixated at the _____ stage, according to Freud.

43. The latency period occurs (just before, after) the phallic stage.

44. Perhaps Carl Jung's most original concept was that of the _____ _____.

45. Overemphasis on the public self or _____ is, for Jung, an important source of maladjustment.

46. Jung believed that everyone possesses some aspects of both _____ and _____, but one is usually dominant.

47. Jung proposed that there are four psychological functions within the two general attitude types of introversion and extroversion. They are _____, _____, _____, and _____.

48. Freud emphasized sexual instincts while Jung stressed _____ and _____ qualities in human personality.

49. Alfred Adler believed that an individual's life style develops by age _____ or _____.

50. Freud's vision of the selfish person locked into conflict with society is countered by Adler's view that people are striving for _____.

51. Horney proposed three general strategies that help people cope with emotional problems and ensure safety, perhaps at the expense of personal independence. Those orientations are moving _____ people, moving _____ people, and moving _____ people.

52. According the Erikson, one response to _____ - _____ is the practice of abiding compulsively to fixed routines.

53. During middle adulthood the challenge is, according to Erikson, to become
_____.

54. Janie's mother, in an effort to stop Janie from wetting the bed, often told her that,
"Mommy won't love you anymore unless you stop." Janie's mother's remark is an
example of _____ _____ _____ according to Rogers.

55. Sheldon believed that personality type is caused by _____
_____.

56. According to Sheldon, chubby endomorphs are likely to be high in _____.

57. Ben is extremely parsimonious when it comes to money. He won't even buy
things he needs for himself, although he can afford most anything. This
characteristic prevails in most of his behavior. This characteristic would be
termed a _____ trait.

58. People who waste their money on lotteries would most likely have an
_____ locus of control according to Rotter.

59. Skinnerian theory agrees that early development is important for explaining
patterns of adult behavior, but he would rely on _____ _____
that a person experiences early in life.

60. Even mental patients who have remained socially unresponsive for years have
been known to interact with the environment to obtain _____.

61. Because the behavior of an interviewer can make a difference, interviews are
often _____.

62. Because the use of observation for personality assessment has some disadvantages,
most observations are now _____.

63. The MMPI was originally developed to diagnose _____ _____.

64. Walter is being given a test as part of his psychiatric assessment. He is asked to
look at pictures of human figures and make up a story for each picture. The test is
called the _____ _____ test.

Answers for this section:

38.   primary process thinking (409)
39.   conscience, moral guardian (410)
40.   superego (410)
41.   phallic (411)
42.   phallic (411)
43.   after (412)
44.   collective unconscious (414)
45.   persona (414)
46.   introversion, extroversion (414)
47.   thinking, feeling, sensing intuiting (414)
48.   rational, spiritual (415)
49.   4, 5 (416)
50.   perfection (416)
51.   toward, away from, against (417)

52.   self-doubt (418)
53.   generative (419)
54.   conditional positive regard (421)
55.   body type (422)
56.   viscerotonia (422)
57.   cardinal (422)
58.   external (426)
59.   reinforcement contingencies (428)
60.   tokens (429)
61.   unreliable (435)
62.   quantified (436)
63.   psychiatric disorders (437)
64.   Thematic Apperception (439)

Testing Yourself For Mastery

The following terms and concepts are found in boldface or italics in the chapter. The time has come to determine if you can define and discuss your new learning in your own words, then check your work against the text.

unconscious

psychoanalysis

death instincts

life instincts

id

pleasure principle

primary-process thinking

ego

reality principle

secondary-process thinking

superego

ego ideal

libido

fixation

oral stage

anal stage

phallic stage

Oedipus complex

latency period

genital stage

personal unconscious

collective unconscious

archetypes

persona

anima

animus

extrovert

introvert

rational people

irrational people

compensation

inferiority complex

fictional finalism

style of life

anxiety

neurotic trends

compliant type

aggressive type

detached type

eight ages of man

humanistic personality theory

self

actualizing tendency

self-actualizing tendency

fully functioning person

unconditional positive regard

conditional positive regard

constitutional theory

somatotypes

personality traits

factor analysis

situationism

expectancies

locus of control

reinforcement contingencies

token economies

social learning theory

performance standards

self-efficacy

reciprocal determinism

person variables

objective tests

Sixteen Personality Factor Questionnaire (16PF)

Minnesota Multiphasic Personality Inventory (MMPI)

projective tests

Rorschach test

Thematic Apperception Test (TAT)

Integrating Your Newly Learned Information

Now that you have recognized, recalled, and given definition to Personality, you are ready to try to integrate your knowledge in a definitive discussion through short-answer questions.

1. Explain the role of the Freudian structures; id, ego, and superego and tell how they interact to produce a unique individual. (409, 410)

2. List the three stages of psychosexual development in Freudian theory and include the focus of the child's erotic feeling for each. (410, 412)

3. Briefly contrast the theories of Freud, Jung, and Adler focusing on two or three major differences. (408-416)

4. What was Horney's basic disagreement with Freud? (416)

5.	On what factor in personality development did Erikson agree with Freud? What important factor did Erikson add to the influence of libidinal needs on personality? (417)

6.	Historically there has been considerable disagreement between Carl Rogers and B.F. Skinner over personality development. Explain at least two points on which they would disagree. (420, 421 & 426-428))

7.	How do Mischel, Bandura, and Rotter challenge traditional views of personality? (425, 426)

8.	List the ways in which personality is assessed. (434-439)

9.	Explain the difference between objective and projective tests of personality and give an example of each. (436-440)

10.	Indicate at least two criticisms of the Rorchach and the TAT. (440)

Applications

You have worked through a section of recognition-type questions to determine if you can apply information to real-life situations. It is time to try to respond to some applications. Some are based upon those questions. Answers to this section will not be given. Your questions concerning these applications will serve as a basis for classroom discussion and ideas for class projects throughout the course.

1. Beth and Phil have a 19-month-old son. It is time to begin toilet training. Beth has had a course in psychology and knows enough to realize that this period in the baby's life could be fraught with problems that could effect his future. What personality theorist would present warnings about the process of toilet training and what are the dangers?

2. Sabrina and her mother never got along very well. Their relationship was always in a state of conflict. Sabrina worshipped her father and identified with him, taking on not only his values and attitudes, but many of his skills and interests. Sabrina is highly intelligent, talented, and creative, and although she became a college professor, she did nothing to bring out her full potential. At one time she drank heavily and used drugs. She has had both homosexual and heterosexual encounters, but was never able to enter into a long-term, stable relationship with another person. Which personality theorist has the most obvious explanation for Sabrina's development and what is that explanation?

3. Suzie is 6 years old. She has just entered the first grade at school and is enthusiastic. When she comes home from school she likes to "help" her mother. Sometimes her mother becomes a little exasperated with Suzie's energy combined with lack of skill in the kitchen, but she allows her to "make her mess." What is Suzie's crisis period? Is her mother doing anything to assist Suzie in meeting her crisis, and why is this important?

4. Mary is a counselor at a small two-year college. One day a student came into her office and cried for 15 minutes. The student continued doing this every day for a week. Mary asked no questions and did not work while the student was there. She only made her feel comfortable and welcome and handed her a Kleenex occasionally. The following week, the student came back, all smiles, and thanked Mary for her help. Although you did not study therapy in this chapter, you might be able to figure out which personality theorist was guiding Mary's helpful behavior.

5.	There was a professor at an unidentified university who caused considerable trouble for himself in gathering data for a research project. Students were asked to be photographed without their clothes on (privately, of course). He apparently collected a significant number of photographs before someone complained too strongly. Who was the professor and what theory emerged from his research?

6.	Allison, who at 21, has not made any progress toward a career choice, spends all she makes at part-time jobs, lives for today, and feels that she is a victim of bad luck. Her parents were divorced and she had a temporary illness that kept her from functioning for a few weeks. Because of the financial problems resulting from the divorce, Allison could not have some of the things and experiences her classmates had in high school. Analyze Allison's behavior in terms of Rotter's view of personality.

Return to Chapter Summary

Now that you have concluded these exercises, you should go back and reread the chapter summary in your textbook. It provides you with a framework that integrates all of this newly-learned information. By reviewing the chapter summary, you will strengthen the many connections between the various new pieces of information.

STRESS AND ADJUSTMENT

11

Chapter Objectives

After you have read and studied this chapter, you should be able to:

1. Define adjustment and stress. Identify sources of stress.
2. Describe the nature of pressure, frustration, conflict, and anxiety, and identify situations that produce each one.
3. Identify the five basic sources of frustration.
4. Give examples of each of the following: approach/approach conflict; avoidance/avoidance conflict; approach/avoidance conflict; double approach/avoidance conflict.
5. Distinguish between direct coping and defensive coping.
6. Identify and characterize the three ways that people cope directly.
7. Describe all of the defense mechanisms.
8. Discuss the psychological and physiological effects of stress on people.
9. Identify five sources of extreme stress.
10. Discuss the opposing views of what characterizes a well-adjusted individual.

Multiple-Choice Questions: Recognizing What You Have Learned

These questions ask only that you recognize what you have learned. When you recognize a correct answer, you have accessed that information in memory. A knowledge of facts serves as a framework for later analysis and problem solving.

Remembering the Facts

This group of multiple-choice questions requires that you simply recognize facts from your textbook.

1. Any attempt to cope with stress is called:

   a. adaptation
   b. adjustment
   c. pressure
   d. frustration

2. An adjustment demand that creates a state of tension or threat and requires change or adaptation is called:

   a. frustration
   b. pressure
   c. stress
   d. conflict

3. The feeling that one must speed up, intensify, or change behavior or live up to a higher standard of performance is called:

   a. compression
   b. compulsion
   c. anxiety
   d. pressure

4. When a person is prevented from reaching a goal, that person experiences:

   a. frustration
   b. conflict
   c. anxiety
   d. pressure

5. The simultaneous existence of incompatible goals, needs, demands, or opportunities is termed:

   a. opposition
   b. pressure
   c. conflict
   d. frustration

6. Simultaneous attraction of two appealing, but incompatible possibilities is called a/an _____ conflict.

   a. avoidance/avoidance
   b. approach/approach
   c. approach/avoidance
   d. double-avoidance

7. Facing a choice between two undesirable possibilities is called a/an
_____ conflict.

a. avoidance/avoidance   c. serious
b. approach/approach   d. approach/avoidance

8. Being simultaneously attracted to and repelled by the same thing is called:

a. vacillation   c. a double-avoidance conflict
b. repulsion   d. an approach/avoidance conflict

9. Acknowledging a stressful situation directly and attempting to find a solution or attain a goal is termed:

a. defensive coping   c. confrontation
b. opposition   d. vacillation

10. Deciding on a more realistic solution or goal when an ideal solution or goal is not practical is called:

a. compensation   c. substitution
b. compromise   d. confrontation

11. Avoiding a situation when other forms of coping are not practical is called:

a. withdrawal   c. regression
b. retreat   d. separation

12. Self-deceptive techniques for reducing stress are called:

a. coping mechanisms   c. defense mechanisms
b. direct coping   d. unconscious coping

13. The refusal to acknowledge a painful or threatening reality is called:

a. negation   c. repudiation
b. denial   d. dissent

14. _____ is the act of excluding uncomfortable thoughts, feelings, and desires from consciousness.

a. Repression   c. Projection
b. Suppression   d. Regression

15. Attributing one's own repressed motives, feelings, or wishes to others is called:

    a. rejection   c. projection
    b. reaction formation   d. denial

16. The taking on of the characteristics of someone else to avoid feeling incompetent is called:

    a. internalization   c. displacement
    b. identification   d. projection

17. Reverting to childlike behaviors and defenses is termed:

    a. regression   c. retrocession
    b. repression   d. withdrawal

18. _____ is a process of thinking abstractly about stressful problems as a way of detaching oneself from them.

    a. Displacement   c. Reaction formation
    b. Cognitizing   d. Intellectualization

19. _____ is the expression of exaggerated ideas and emotions that are the opposite of one's repressed beliefs or feelings.

    a. Displacement   c. Reaction formation
    b. Projection   d. Oppositioning

20. Shifting repressed motives and emotions from an original object to a substitute object is called:

    a. sublimation   c. substitution
    b. displacement   d. projection

21. _____ is the redirecting of repressed motives and feelings into more socially acceptable channels.

    a. Displacement   c. Sublimation
    b. Projection   d. Exaltation

Answers for this section:

1.	b (448)	7.	a (455)	13.	b (460)	19.	c (463)
2.	c (449)	8.	d (455)	14.	a (461)	20.	b (464)
3.	d (452)	9.	c (458)	15.	c (461)	21.	c (464)
4.	a (452)	10.	b (459)	16.	b (462)		
5.	c (454)	11.	a (459)	17.	a (462)		
6.	b (454)	12.	c (460)	18.	d (463)		

Understanding the Facts

Now that you have found that you can recognize facts from Stress and Adjustment, the next step is to determine if you understand the meaning of newly-learned information. These multiple-choice questions require a higher level of thinking. They will help you establish more solid connections and provide practice in dealing with higher level concepts.

22. Perhaps one of the **most** important factors contributing to stress is:

   a. not getting what you want   c. change
   b. lack of change   d. predictability

23. _____, although not dramatic, are a major source of stress because they have a cumulative effect.

   a. Pressures   c. Conflicts
   b. Hassles   d. External events

24. Internal pressure can be destructive if:

   a. the competition is too strong
   b. there is too much change
   c. we do not repress the unconscious desire
   d. our aims are impossible to achieve

25. Failure is a frequent source of frustration. The aspect of failure that is the most difficult to cope with is:

   a. guilt   c. remorse
   b. anxiety   d. change

26. Which of the following would be the **most** common source of frustration for low-income families?

a. delays   c. lack of resources
b. failure   d. discrimination

27. When conflict arises, it is inevitable that we:

a. will avoid the central issue
b. must make a choice
c. will use defense mechanisms
d. will repress our thoughts

28. Which of the following theorists described conflict in terms of two opposite tendencies?

a. Sigmund Freud   c. Karen Horney
b. Albert Bandura   d. Kurt Lewin

29. Whatever we do in a conflict situation, we are going to:

a. experience frustration   c. lower anxiety
b. resolve the conflict   d. eliminate stress

30. When faced with an avoidance/avoidance conflict, people usually try to:

a. resolve it   c. escape
b. rationalize   d. deny it

31. Another common behavior when faced with an avoidance/avoidance conflict is:

a. violence   c. apathy
b. anxiety   d. hesitation

32. Which of the following statements about an approach/avoidance conflict is **true**?

a. The approach tendency usually increases in strength faster than does the avoidance tendency.
b. Both approach and avoidance tendencies increase at the same rate.
c. The desire to avoid a goal weakens as the goal is approached.
d. The avoidance tendency usually increases in strength faster than does the approach tendency.

33. Aaron Beck (1967, 1976) found that self-defeating thoughts and the resulting self-imposed stress is a leading cause of:

a. schizophrenia   c. depression
b. ulcers   d. phobias

34. Kobasa's (1979) research showed that stress-resistant people had in common a trait called:

a. hardiness   c. empathy
b. sturdiness   d. durability

35. Any action we take to change an uncomfortable situation is called:

a. regulating   c. direct coping
b. defensive coping   d. adapting

36. Defensive coping is a form of:

a. lying   c. self-punishment
b. instability   d. self-deception

37. Confrontation, compromise, and withdrawal are all examples of:

a. vacillating   c. denial
b. direct coping   d. defensive coping

38. Controlled anger might be a healthy way to cope in a direct manner. It would most likely be used in:

a. confrontation   c. compromise
b. withdrawal   d. resistance

39. If we are emotionally mature, we know that we cannot have everything we want so we:

a. withdraw   c. compromise
b. regress   d. use denial

40. When our adversary is more powerful than we are, many times it is a healthy and realistic adjustment to:

a. substitute   c. compromise
b. withdraw   d. confront

41. Freud would say that direct coping is _____ while defensive coping is
_____.

    a.   conscious, unconscious   c.   positive, negative
    b.   healthy, unhealthy   d.   unconscious, conscience

42. Wolff and his colleagues who interviewed parents of children who were dying of
    leukemia found that parents who used denial:

    a.   had excess stomach acid
    b.   were putting on an act for their family
    c.   did not have the physiological symptoms of stress found in those who had
         accepted their children's illness
    d.   did not believe that their children would recover

43. The most common mechanism for blocking out painful memories and feelings is:

    a.   repression   c.   regression
    b.   projection   d.   suppression

44. In its most extreme form, repression becomes:

    a.   painful   c.   projection
    b.   amnesia   d.   intolerable

45. Which of the following defense mechanisms form the bases for other defensive
    ways of coping?

    a.   projection and rationalization
    b.   reaction formation and identification
    c.   regression and displacement
    d.   denial and repression

46. Which of the following statements about projection is **true**?

    a.   It is the attribution of one's own unacceptable feelings to others.
    b.   Projection is a method of direct coping.
    c.   It locates the source of conflict inside ourselves.
    d.   It is the same as reaction formation.

47. Identification is the reverse of:

    a.   reaction formation   c.   projection
    b.   displacement   d.   intellectualization

48. Bruno Bettleheim, once a prisoner in a Nazi concentration camp, found that one way to survive the feelings of utter helplessness was to:

   a. use regression
   b. use denial
   c. identify with the other prisoners
   d. identify with the aggressor

49. An adult having a temper tantrum is a good example of:

   a. repression   c. regression
   b. sublimation   d. reaction formation

50. We can detach ourselves from our problems by analyzing them and talking about them in an "academic" way, thus leaving the emotion out of them. This is a defense mechanism called:

   a. rationalization   c. sublimation
   b. displacement   d. intellectualization

51. When we display to the world the opposite of the way we feel and do it with exaggeration, we are using the defense mechanism of:

   a. projection   c. displacement
   b. reaction formation   d. sublimation

52. If someone frustrates us and we "take it out" on someone else, we are using the defense mechanism of:

   a. reaction formation   c. regression
   b. projection   d. displacement

53. Which of the following defense mechanisms is not only necessary, but desirable according to Sigmund Freud?

   a. sublimation   c. displacement
   b. identification   d. projection

54. In which stage of Hans Selye's General Adaptation Syndrome do respiration and heart rate quicken and muscles tense along with other physiological changes?

   a. resistance   c. alarm reaction
   b. exhaustion   d. stage 3

55. Some people lose touch with reality and show signs of emotional disorder or mental illness during the _____ stage of Selye's General Adaptation Syndrome.

a. exhaustion   c. resistance
b. alarm reaction   d. opposition

56. Marmot and Syme's (1976) study on coronary heart disease found that:

a. Japanese living in Japan were more likely to have CHD than Japanese Americans
b. CHD is almost non-existent in Japan
c. Japanese American's were more likely to have CHD than Japanese living in Japan
d. London bus drivers were less likely to have CHD than conductors

57. Research on the connection between stress and a variety of serious diseases indicates that:

a. stress directly causes specific diseases
b. the relationship between stress and physical illness is weak
c. opportunity to control the source of stress is not a factor
d. stress weakens the body's immune system

58. Which of the following statements about the stress of unemployment is **not** true?

a. Death rates go up during times of unemployment.
b. Good change does not cause stress.
c. Psychiatric symptoms get worse during periods of unemployment.
d. Psychiatric symptoms get worse during short, rapid upturns in the economy.

59. Which of the following defense mechanisms are **most** used in responding to the stress of divorce and separation?

a. regression and reaction formation
b. rationalization and displacement
c. repression and identification
d. denial and projection

60. In World War II about _____ percent of combat soldiers were discharged for psychiatric reasons.

a. 5   c. 6
b. 2   d. 8

61. The need to describe experiences over and over again is particularly characteristic of which of the following sources of extreme stress?

   a. combat
   b. divorce and separation
   c. natural and man-made catastrophes
   d. unemployment

62. Which of the following criteria for evaluating adjustment was **not** proposed by Morris (1990)?

   a. Does the person meet the adjustive demand or postpone resolving the problem?
   b. Is the person flexible, spontaneous and creative?
   c. Does the person's actions meet his or her own needs?
   d. Is the person's action compatible with the well-being of others?

Answers for this section:

22.	c (450)	33.	c (457)	44.	b (461)	55.	a (465)
23.	b (452)	34.	a (457)	45.	d (461)	56.	c (466)
24.	d (452)	35.	c (458)	46.	a (461)	57.	d (467)
25.	a (454)	36.	d (458)	47.	c (462)	58.	b (469)
26.	c (454)	37.	b (458, 459)	48.	d (462)	59.	d (469)
27.	b (454)	38.	a (459)	49.	c (462)	60.	a (470)
28.	d (454)	39.	c (459)	50.	d (463)	61.	c (471)
29.	a (454)	40.	b (459)	51.	b (463)	62.	b (473)
30.	c (455)	41.	a (460)	52.	d (464)		
31.	d (455)	42.	c (461)	53.	a (464)		
32.	d (455, 456)	43.	a (461)	54.	c (465)		

Applying the Facts

The learning of facts and concepts is of little value unless it can be applied and employed to solve problems. The next group of multiple-choice questions reflects applications of your learning.

63. Mollie cannot decide between two prom dresses. They are both the same price and she knows she would look great in either one. Mollie has a/an:

   a. major frustration   c. approach/avoidance conflict
   b. approach/approach conflict   d. adjustment demand

64. When Jack gets into a traffic jam he honks his horn and lowers the window so he can gesture and yell at other motorists. Jack is attempting to solve his problem by _____ and his problem is _____.

    a. regression, anxiety
    b. confrontation, frustration
    c. projection, guilt
    d. reaction formation, frustration

65. Amy is in college, but she is having financial problems along with many difficulties at home that center around her mother's serious illness and the need to assist her with the care of a younger brother. Amy has decided to quit college temporarily, get a part-time job, and hope that the situation will improve. Amy is using _____ to cope with her problems.

    a. confrontation   c. intellectualization
    b. denial   d. withdrawal

66. Toby has always dreamed of going to Harvard, but the family has suffered a financial set back. He decided to work part-time after high school and attend a two-year commuter college with the hope of transferring later to the state university. Toby is coping by:

    a. confrontation   c. withdrawal
    b. compromise   d. displacement

67. Alex was hiking in the mountains one day and came across two men who were hiking together. One of the men spontaneously put his arm around the other man's shoulder as they laughed at a joke. Alex thought, "Those men must be homosexuals." It is likely that Alex was using the mechanism of:

    a. projection   c. reaction formation
    b. regression   d. displacement

68. Ben was a professor at a small college. He had completed the courses and most of the work on his dissertation, but was having trouble with his dissertation committee. Members were accusing him of poor scholarship and doubting his ability. Ben treated his students in a very insulting manner, and accused them of being "dumb" and not qualified to attend college. Ben may be using displacement or:

    a. reaction-formation   c. projection
    b. denial   d. intellectualization

69. Maude secretly enjoys pornographic magazines and videos. She joined a community group, the purpose of which was to try to eradicate pornography. She spends many hours giving speeches in her area about the dangers of pornography. Maude is using the defense mechanism:

    a. projection   c. regression
    b. reaction formation d. denial

70. Joey is 4 years old. He is toilet trained and eats his meals with his parents. He has recently acquired a baby sister. He is no longer toilet trained as he cries for his bottle. Joey has turned to _____ to lower his anxiety because of the baby.

    a. regression   c. denial
    b. repression   d. reaction formation

71. A pre-medical student became intoxicated one night and went around his neighborhood cutting the tails off of dogs. He completed medical school and eventually became a world famous surgeon. _____ enabled him to rechannel basic aggressive drives into socially acceptable behavior.

    a. displacement   c. intellectualization
    b. sublimation   d. identification

72. Whenever Penny gets frustrated at school she wants to strike back at her teacher, but she knows she can't do that. She comes home yells at her dog and kicks and throws things about her room. _____ is Penny's method of coping.

    a. regression   c. sublimation
    b. reaction formation d. displacement

Answers for this section:

63.	b (454)	67.	a (461)	71.	b (464)
64.	b (458)	68.	c (461)	72.	d (464)
65.	d (459)	69.	b (463)		
66.	b (459)	70.	a (462)		

Fill-in-the-Blank Questions: Recalling What You Have Learned

By now, there should be a considerable amount of new information about Stress and Adjustment in long-term memory. The following questions of recall rather than recognition will show if you are becoming more comfortable with the material.

1.   Any effort to cope with stress is called _____.

2.   _____ is an adjustment demand that creates a state of tension or threat.

3.   The feeling that one must speed up, intensify, or change the direction of behavior or live up to a higher standard of performance is called _____.

4.   When a person is prevented from reaching a goal, the person feels _____.

5.   _____ arises with the simultaneous existence of incompatible demands, opportunities, needs, or goals.

6.   The simultaneous attraction to two appealing possibilities is called an _____/_____ conflict.

7.   The result of facing a choice between two undesirable possibilities is called an _____/_____ conflict.

8.   An _____/_____ conflict arises when one is simultaneously attracted to and repelled by the same thing.

9.   Acknowledging a stressful situation directly and attempting to find a solution or attain a goal is called _____.

10. Deciding on a more realistic solution or goal when an ideal solution is not practical is called _____.

11. _____ is the avoiding of a situation when other forms of coping are not practical.

12. Self-deceptive techniques for reducing stress are called _____ _____.

13. Refusing to acknowledge a painful or threatening reality is called _____.

14. _____ is the attributing of one's repressed motives, feelings, or wishes to others.

15. Taking on the characteristics of someone else to avoid feeling incompetent is the process of _____.

16. Reverting to childlike behavior and defenses is called _____.

17. When we think abstractly about stressful problems as a way of detaching ourselves from them we are _____.

18. When we exaggerate ideas and emotions that are the opposite of repressed beliefs or feelings, we are using _____ _____.

19. Shifting repressed motives and emotions from an original object to a substitute object is called _____.

20. _____ is the redirecting of repressed motives and feelings into more socially acceptable channels.

Answers for this section:

1.	adjustment (448)	11.	withdrawal (459)
2.	stress (449)	12.	defense mechanisms (460)
3.	pressure (452)	13.	denial (460)
4.	frustrated (452)	14.	projection (461)
5.	conflict (454)	15.	identification (462)
6.	approach, approach (454)	16.	regression (462)
7.	avoidance, avoidance (455)	17.	intellectualizing (463)
8.	approach, avoidance (455)	18.	reaction formation (463)
9.	confrontation (458)	19.	displacement (464)
10.	compromise (459)	20.	sublimation (464)

Understanding and Applying the Facts

As you previously did with recognition-type questions, you will now move to a higher level of recall. The following questions will determine if you understand the facts.

21. The stressfulness of various situations can be determined by the amount of _____ they require.

22. The SRRS scale was developed by Holmes and Rahe in 1967 to measure how much _____ a person has undergone in any given period.

23. Petty annoyances, irritations, and frustrations that give rise to stress are called _____ by Lazarus (1981).

24. Andrew is writing a book on a tight deadline. Although he is making progress, he feels considerable stress. The source of that stress is **most** likely to be _____.

25. You are on your way to your 8:00 a.m. class. You are in danger of being late. You know you have to cross a railroad track and, sure enough, the signals go on and here comes a long train. You feel _____.

26. During the war in Vietnam, a considerable number of men had the choice between leaving the country or being drafted. They were faced with an _____/_____ conflict.

27. Bill's father wants him to pursue a military career which upsets his mother. His mother wants him to go to medical school. Bill is faced with a _____ _____/_____ conflict.

28. If a person feels an overwhelming need to be competent, adequate, and successful at "everything," Aaron Beck would say that the person is a likely candidate for _____.

29. Confrontation, compromise, and withdrawal are all forms of _____ _____.

30. Divorce might be considered a form of _____ coping called _____.

31. Avoidance of all similar situations is the greatest danger of _____.

32. _____ - _____ is the central factor in the use of defense mechanisms.

33. To enter into the use of other defense mechanisms, one must first use _____ and _____.

34. When we use _____ we attribute characteristics that we do not like about ourselves to others. In doing so it lowers our level of _____.

35. George would not allow his wife to attend a concert in a distant city with a female friend. He felt that there would be too much "temptation." George had had several affairs with other women, but managed to keep his actions secret. George was using the defense mechanism of _____.

36. Alex was totally opposed to smoking. He constantly "lectured" against smoking to acquaintances and friends alike, put up large "no smoking" signs at meetings, and had a party where he segregated the smokers into a small room. Alex was a user of marijuana. Possibly he was using the defense mechanism _____ _____.

37. Whenever Kate, age 16, got into a stressful situation she would go to her room, lock the door, curl up in a fetal position on her bed and suck her thumb. She was displaying _____.

38. Joanne had a high school teacher she greatly admired. She began to dress like the teacher, bought music tapes and books her teacher mentioned liking, and began to mimic her teacher's mannerisms. The defense mechanism, here, is _____.

39. If your child is having trouble with the children in the new neighborhood and you discuss this problem in terms of the sociology of small groups you are _____.

40. If you come home after a frustrating day at work, kick the dog, and scream at your wife, you are using _____.

41. Jamie wants to be with Marcie. He has many "thoughts" about what he would do if he could be with her, and he feels a little guilty about his thoughts. He wrote a love poem and dedicated it to Marcie. The defense mechanism _____ was a partial solution to his problem.

42. In the third stage of Selye's General Adaptation Syndrome, people can be the victims of _____.

43. The third stage in reacting to the stress of unemployment is, according to Powell and Driscoll (1973), a period of _____ and _____.

44. Victims of man-made and natural catastrophes feel the need to describe their experiences over and over again in the _____ stage of reaction to such disasters.

45. Psychologists find it difficult to agree on what constitutes good _____.

Answers for this section:

21.	change (450)	34.	projection, anxiety (461)
22.	stress (450)	35.	projection (461)
23.	"hassles" (452)	36.	reaction formation (463)
24.	pressure (452)	37.	regression (462)
25.	frustration (452)	38.	identification (462)
26.	avoidance, avoidance (455)	39.	intellectualizing (463)
27.	double approach, avoidance (456)	40.	displacement (464)
28.	depression (457)	41.	sublimation (464)
29.	direct coping (458, 459)	42.	"burnout" (465)
30.	direct, withdrawal (459)	43.	vacillation, doubt (468)
31.	withdrawal (460)	44.	recovery (471)
32.	self-deception (460)	45.	adjustment (471, 472)
33.	repression, denial (461)		

Testing Yourself For Mastery

The following terms and concepts are found in boldface or italics in the chapter. The time has come to determine if you can define and discuss your new learning in your own words, then check your work against the text.

adjustment

stress

hassles

pressure

frustration

delays

lack of resources

losses

failures

discrimination

conflict

approach/approach conflict

approach/avoidance conflict

avoidance/avoidance conflict

double approach/avoidance conflict

hardiness

direct coping

confrontation

compromise

withdrawal

defense mechanisms

denial

repression

projection

identification

regression

intellectualization

reaction formation

displacement

sublimation

alarm reaction

resistance

exhaustion

Integrating Your Newly Learned Information

Now that you have recognized, recalled, and given definition to Stress and Adjustment, you are ready to try to integrate your knowledge in a definitive discussion through short-answer questions.

1. List the sources of stress that are common to all people. (449-454)

2. What are the 5 basic sources of frustration that are common to most, if not all, people. (454)

3. What is the nature of conflict and why is it so troublesome? (454)

4. How do people impose stress upon themselves? (457)

5. Why do people enter into defensive coping? (460)

6. If you suspect someone is using reaction formation rather than voicing a normal opposition to something, what is the clue that makes this defense mechanism a strong possibility? (463)

7. Although Hans Selye's General Adaptation Syndrome has been criticized, what is the major factor about prolonged, severe stress that may account for its role in physiological disorders? (466)

8. Briefly discuss at least two sources of extreme stress. (468, 469)

9. Since psychologists cannot seem to agree on what constitutes a well-adjusted person, consider making up your own definition. (471)

Applications

You have worked through a section of recognition-type questions to determine if you can apply information to real-life situations. It is time to try to respond to some applications. Some are based upon those questions. Answers to this section will not be given. Your questions concerning these applications will serve as a basis for classroom discussion and ideas for class projects throughout the course.

1. Choose a person you know very well; someone whose behavior you have observed for a long time, and one you considered "well adjusted" before you studied this chapter. Evaluate that person's behavior on the basis of the three criteria proposed by Morris (1990). Be specific about each behavior observed in the category to which it applies.

2. Choose another person you know very well, but this time choose a person you consider to be "maladjusted." Evaluate that person's behavior against Morris' criteria.

3. There was a gas explosion that destroyed an entire building and damaged many others on the main street of a small town at the rush hour. Two people were killed and many were injured. This would cause extreme stress. Identify the three stages that people in the area experienced and describe the typical behavior in each stage.

4. You will be studying about abnormal behavior in the next chapter. Before you do, give some extra thought to the defense mechanisms. What dangers, if any, do you see for a person who uses projection and/or reaction formation to an extreme. After you have studied abnormal behavior, check your response to this exercise and see if you were correct in any of your assumptions.

5. Do you, personally, experience an excessive amount of stress? Analyze your behavior and try to determine if any of your stress is self-imposed.

6. You were exposed to the idea that frustration sometimes results in aggression. Make a list of the behaviors you enter into when you get frustrated.

7. Look at your list from question #6. How many of your behaviors are constructive? How many are destructive to you or to others?

8. What can you say about a 30-year-old woman who pouts when she doesn't get "her way?"

9. Do you now know any reasons why people would break down security gates in an exclusive apartment complex? Use technical terminology in your answer.

10. Alicia has arthritis, psoriasis, asthma, an ulcer, may be developing into an alcoholic and is overweight. She is constantly plagued by "the common cold" and her blood pressure is dangerously high. Her husband criticizes her constantly, telling her she is ugly, the house is dirty, and she never does anything right. She often complains about being depressed. What would Hans Selye say about Alicia's situation?

Return to Chapter Summary

Now that you have concluded these exercises, you should go back and reread the chapter summary in your textbook. It provides you with a framework that integrates all of this newly-learned information. By reviewing the chapter summary, you will strengthen the many connections between the various new pieces of information.

ABNORMAL BEHAVIOR

12

Chapter Objectives

After you have read and studied this chapter, you should be able to:

1. Distinguish between the standards for defining abnormal behavior from the view of society, the individual, and the mental health professional.
2. Summarize historical attitudes toward abnormal behavior.
3. State the four current models of abnormal behavior and explain the diasthesis-stress model.
4. Explain how DSM-III-R classifies mental disorders.
5. Describe and compare the anxiety disorders.
6. Recognize the characteristics of the psychophysiological disorders and the somatoform disorders.
7. Characterize three different types of dissociative disorders.
8. Distinguish between the two basic kinds of affective disorders and how they may interact with each other.
9. Define and give examples of the psychosexual disorders.
10. State DSM-III-R's view of homosexuality.
11. Define personality disorder. Describe four kinds of personality disorders.
12. Describe four types of schizophrenic disorders and identify possible causes of the disorder.

Multiple-Choice Questions: Recognizing What Your Have Learned

These questions ask only that you recognize what you have learned. When you recognize a correct answer, you have accessed that information in memory. A knowledge of facts serves as a framework for later analysis and problem solving.

Remembering the Facts

This group of multiple-choice questions requires that you simply recognize facts from your text book.

1. The view that abnormal behavior is the result of unconscious conflicts is known as the _____ model.

    a. biological   c. psychoanalytic
    b. cognitive   d. diasthesis

2. The _____ model says that abnormal behavior is the result of faulty learning.

    a. behavioral   c. biological
    b. diasthesis   d. cognitive

3. Abnormal behavior is the result of maladaptive ways of thinking according to the _____ model.

    a. diasthesis   c. biological
    b. psychoanalytic   d. cognitive

4. A sudden, unpredictable feeling of intense fear or terror is characteristic of:

    a. posttraumatic stress disorder   c. obsessive-compulsive disorder
    b. panic attack   d. agoraphobia

5. A condition in which episodes of anxiety, sleeplessness, and nightmares are the result of some disturbing event in the past is called:

    a. panic attack   c. conversion disorder
    b. somatoform disorder   d. posttraumatic stress disorder

6. A disorder in which a person must think disturbing thoughts and perform senseless rituals is called:

a. obsessive-compulsive disorder   c. somatization disorder
b. agoraphobia   d. conversion disorder

7. Compulsive avoidance behavior is associated with _____ disorder.

a. posttraumatic stress   c. phobic
b. conversion   d. dissociative

8. Excessive unreasonable fear attached to an apparently harmless stimulus is called a/an:

a. obsession   c. compulsion
b. phobia   d. revulsion

9. Excessive unreasonable fear directed at a specific situation or object is called:

a. a simple phobia   c. agoraphobia
b. a complex phobia   d. an obsession

10. Excessive fear of being alone and of leaving home and being in public places is called:

a. simple phobia   c. repression
b. agoraphobia   d. regression

11. When people are afraid to be with other people they are said to:

a. be shy   c. have agoraphobia
b. have an obsession   d. have social phobia

12. Disorders in which there is an apparent physical disorder for which there is no organic basis are called:

a. psychosomatic   c. somatoform disorders
b. psychophysiological disorder   d. hypochondriasis

13. A disorder characterized by recurrent vague somatic complaints without a physical cause is called:

   a.   a somatization disorder   c.   a conversion disorder
   b.   a somatoform disorder   d.   schizophrenia

14. A _____ disorder is one in which a dramatic specific disability has no physical cause and is related to psychological problems.

   a.   dissociative   c.   conversion
   b.   hypochondriacal   d.   phobic

15. When a person interprets small insignificant symptoms as signs of serious illness in the absence of organic symptoms the condition is called:

   a.   psychosomatic disorder   c.   conversion disorder
   b.   hypochondriasis   d.   dissociative disorder

16. When a genuine physical disorder has a psychological cause, the diagnosis is called _____ disorder.

   a.   a dissociative   c.   a psychosomatic disorder
   b.   a psychophysiological disorder d.   depersonalization

17. A _____ disorder is one in which some aspect of the personality seems fragmented from the rest.

   a.   dissociative   c.   schizophrenic
   b.   personality   d.   manic

18. When a person feels unreal and unconnected to his or her body, the diagnosis is:

   a.   fugue   c.   personality disorder
   b.   schizophrenia   d.   depersonalization disorder

19. Conditions in which there is a disturbance of emotional state are called:

   a.   effective disorders   c.   affective disorders
   b.   mania   d.   defective disorders

20. When a person experiences periods of both depression and mania, the condition is known as:

   a. fugue   c. personality disorder
   b. bipolar disorder   d. dissociative disorder

21. The condition is called _____ when a person is overly excited and hyperactive.

   a. phobia   c. depression
   b. disorganized   d. mania

22. Unconventional objects or situations that cause sexual arousal in some people are called:

   a. pedophilias   c. sexual deviations
   b. paraphilias   d. paranorms

23. The reliance on nonhuman objects as the preferred or exclusive method of achieving sexual excitement is called:

   a. paraphilism   c. fetishism
   b. pedophilia   d. sexual dysfunction

24. _____ is dressing in the clothing of the opposite sex to achieve sexual arousal.

   a. Paraphilism   c. Transsexualism
   b. Transvestism   d. Exhibitionism

25. The desire to watch others having sexual relations or to spy on nude people is called:

   a. voyeurism   c. menage a trois
   b. inhibition   d. masochism

26. _____ is the compulsion to expose one's genitals to achieve sexual arousal.

   a. Sadoism   c. Voyeurism
   b. Transvestism   d. Exhibitionism

27. Obtaining sexual gratification from aggression is called:

a. masochism
b. sadomasochism
c. transvestism
d. transsexualism

28. The desire to have sexual relations with children as the preferred or exclusive method of achieving sexual arousal is termed:

a. pedophilia
b. child molesting
c. paraphilia
d. sexual deviation

29. The desire to become a member of the opposite sex is called:

a. pedophilia
b. transvestism
c. transsexualism
d. transgenderism

30. A _____ personality disorder is one in which a person is withdrawn and lacks feeling for others.

a. paranoid
b. schizoid
c. dependent
d. passive-aggressive

31. A person who cannot make decisions independently and cannot tolerate being alone is likely to have:

a. a passive-aggressive personality disorder
b. depression
c. a narcissistic personality
d. a dependent personality disorder

32. Expressing anger by covert means is a characteristic of:

a. the narcissistic personality
b. dependent personality disorder
c. the passive-aggressive personality
d. schizophrenia

33. _____ personality disorder is characterized by an exaggerated sense of self-importance and the need for constant admiration.

a. Dependent
b. Dissociative
c. Narcissistic
d. Passive-aggressive

34. Sensory experiences in the absence of external stimulation are called:

a. delusions
b. hallucinations
c. illusions
d. allusions

35. _____ are false beliefs about reality with no basis in fact.

a. Allusions
b. Illusions
c. Hallucinations
d. Delusions

36. Disorganized, catatonic, paranoid, and undifferentiated are all types of:

a. schizophrenia
b. depression
c. bipolar disorders
d. somatoform disorders

Answers for this section:

1.	c (486)	10.	b (491)	19.	c (498)	28.	a (505)
2.	a (486)	11.	d (491)	20.	b (499)	29.	c (505)
3.	d (486)	12.	c (493)	21.	d (498)	30.	b (506)
4.	b (489)	13.	a (493)	22.	b (504)	31.	d (507)
5.	d (489)	14.	c (493)	23.	c (504)	32.	c (507)
6.	a (490)	15.	b (494)	24.	b (504)	33.	c (508)
7.	c (490)	16.	b (495)	25.	a (504)	34.	b (510)
8.	b (490)	17.	a (495)	26.	d (504)	35.	d (510)
9.	a (491)	18.	d (497)	27.	b (505)	36.	a (512, 513)

Understanding the Facts

Now that you have found that you can recognize facts from Abnormal Behavior, the next step is to determine if you understand the meaning of newly-learned information. These multiple-choice questions require a higher level of thinking. They will help you establish more solid connections and provide practice in dealing with higher level concepts.

37. During the middle ages, abnormal behavior was considered:

    a. to arise from natural causes
    b. to be the work of demons
    c. as a medical problem
    d. an imbalance in body fluids

38. The first real reforms in the treatment of the mentally ill occurred in the late 18th century under the direction of:

    a. Dorothea Dix   c. Phillippe Pinel
    b. Anton Mesmer   d. Jean-Martin Charcot

39. Which of the following is **not** a purpose of DSM-III-R?

    a. to describe various kinds of abnormal behavior
    b. to classify various kinds of abnormal behavior
    c. to standardize diagnosis of abnormal behavior
    d. to outline the causes of abnormal behavior

40. Anxiety disorders include all but which of the following?

    a. phobias   c. hyponchondriasis
    b. panic attack   d. obsessive-compulsive disorder

41. A person with chest pain, dizziness, fainting, sweating, and difficulty breathing, along with feelings of intense fears is **most** likely a victim of:

    a. phobias   c. fugue
    b. hypochondriasis   d. panic attack

42. Attempts to "wash away" contaminating thoughts would be indicative of:

    a. panic attack   c. agoraphobia
    b. obsessive-compulsive disorder   d. conversion disorder

43. Although abnormal behavior is difficult to define, all but which of the following conditions serves as a useful criteria for definition?

    a. self-defeating behavior
    b. distortion of reality
    c. danger to self and others
    d. shyness and unpopularity

44. People who avoid crowds, busy streets, elevators, and tunnels may be suffering from:

    a.   simple phobia   c.   social phobia
    b.   agoraphobia   d.   compulsions

45. Social phobias usually begin:

    a.   in middle adulthood   c.   in infancy
    b.   in early childhood   d.   during adolescence

46. Which of the following is **not** true of phobic disorders?

    a.   There is paralyzing fear in the absence of any real danger.
    b.   Phobias are closely linked to feelings of anxiety.
    c.   The person suffering from a phobia considers the fear reasonable.
    d.   A phobia is a fear of something most people find bearable.

47. If a person visits one doctor after another looking for one that will agree that there is a serious illness when no illness is present, the likely diagnosis is:

    a.   hypochondriasis   c.   phobia
    b.   conversion disorder   d.   obsessive-compulsive disorder

48. All but which of the following is classified by DSM-III-R as a somatoform disorder?

    a.   hypochondriasis   c.   somatization disorder
    b.   conversion disorder   d.   fugue

49. *La belle indifference* is a characteristic of:

    a.   depression   c.   hypochondriasis
    b.   conversion disorder   d.   amnesia

50. It is often easy to determine that there is no organic cause for a *glove anaesthesia* because:

    a.   the patient is extremely concerned about the condition
    b.   the patient admits readily that the condition is attention-getting
    c.   the symptoms are anatomically impossible
    d.   the patient can relate the nature of the conflict

51. DSM-III-R categorizes psychophysiological disorders according to:

  a. the part of the body that is affected
  b. the degree of anxiety present
  c. a list of all of the serious diseases
  d. the level of impairment caused by the disease

52. Which of the following is **not** classified by DSM-III-R as a dissociative disorder?

  a. depersonalization disorder   c. depression
  b. fugue   d. multiple personality

53. Which of the following statements about multiple personality disorder is **not** true?

  a. It is a rare disorder.
  b. Two personalities emerge at the same time.
  c. The various personalities are distinct people.
  d. The different personalities may have different IQ's.

54. Which of the following is **widely** accepted as an explanation for multiple personality disorder?

  a. it is a natural progression from the development of phobias
  b. it is an elaborate kind of play acting
  c. it is a mild form of schizophrenia
  d. it develops as a response to childhood abuse

55. It may be that multiple personality is extreme use of which of the following defense mechanisms?

  a. reaction formation   c. projection
  b. repression   d. regression

56. If a person suddenly feels that he or she has left the body or that actions are mechanical, the diagnosis might be:

  a. somatization disorder   c. depression
  b. depersonalization disorder   d. schizophrenia

57. Which of the following is **not** classified as an affective disorder by DSM-III-R?

  a. schizophrenia   c. mania
  b. depression   d. bipolar disorder

58. Which of the following statements about the differences between bipolar disorder and unipolar depression is **not** true?

a. Bipolar disorder is less common than depression.
b. Bipolar disorder is equally prevalent in men and women.
c. Bipolar disorder is more common in women than depression.
d. Bipolar disorder has a stronger biological component than depression.

59. _____ viewed depression as excessive and irrational grief.

a. Behavior theory   c. Aaron Beck
b. Dorothea Dix   d. Sigmund Freud

60. According to _____, feelings of worthlessness and incompetence may result in depression.

a. Aaron Beck   c. behavior theory
b. psychoanalytic theory   d. Alfred Adler

61. In 1986, which of the following was dropped from the DSM-III-R list of disorders?

a. panic disorder   c. homosexuality
b. sexual dysfunction   d. voyeurism

62. One of the most serious of the paraphilias is:

a. sadomasochism   c. transsexualism
b. pedophilia   d. exhibitionism

63. Which of the following statements about transvestism is **not** true?

a. It occurs equally in males and females.
b. There is no explanation for it.
c. There is no evidence of hormonal abnormality.
d. There is no evidence of genetic abnormality.

64. Which of the following statements about personality disorder is **not** true?

a. Personality disorder may coexist with other disorders.
b. A person with a personality disorder may become depressed.
c. People with personality disorders are harmless.
d. A person with personality disorder may develop sexual problems.

65. People with _____ are suspicious and distrustful, hypersensitive to threat, refuse to accept blame or criticism, and are secretive, devious, scheming, and argumentative.

   a.   schizoid personality disorder
   b.   a passive-aggressive personality
   c.   paranoid schizophrenia
   d.   paranoid personality disorder

66. People who fear that they will be rejected or abandoned by important people in their lives might develop:

   a.   passive-aggressive personality disorder
   b.   dependent personality disorder
   c.   schizophrenia
   d.   multiple personality

67. Self absorption, grandiose sense of self-importance, fantasies of unlimited success, and a need for constant attention and admiration are all characteristics of:

   a.   antisocial personality disorder
   b.   undifferentiated schizophrenia
   c.   narcissistic personality disorder
   d.   bipolar disorder

68. Disordered thought and communication, inappropriate emotions, bizarre behavior and loss of touch with reality are characteristics of _____ disorders.

   a.   schizophrenic   c.   dissociative
   b.   multiple personality   d.   attention-deficit hyperactivity

69. Bizarre symptoms such as giggling, grimacing, and frantic gesturing along with disregard for social conventions is characteristic of:

   a.   dissociative disorder   c.   disorganized schizophrenia
   b.   catatonic schizophrenia d.   undifferentiated schizophrenia

70. Extreme suspiciousness and complex delusions are characteristic of:

   a.   paranoid personality disorder   c.   schizoid personality disorder
   b.   paranoid schizophrenia   d.   undifferentiated schizophrenia

71.   "Highly distractible," "fidgety," "impulsive," and "in constant motion" describe:

a.   ADAH   c.   ADHD
b.   childhood autism   d.   anorexia nervosa

Answers for this section:

37.	b (485)	46.	c (490)	55.	c (497)	64.	c (506)
38.	c (485)	47.	a (494)	56.	b (497)	65.	d (506)
39.	d (487)	48.	d (493, 494)	57.	a (510)	66.	b (507)
40.	c (489, 491)	49.	b (494)	58.	c (500)	67.	c (508)
41.	d (489)	50.	c (494)	59.	d (500)	68.	a (510)
42.	b (490)	51.	a (495)	60.	a (501)	69.	c (512)
43.	d (483, 484)	52.	c (496)	61.	c (503)	70.	b (513)
44.	b (491)	53.	b (496)	62.	b (505)	71.	c (514)
45.	d (491)	54.	d (497)	63.	a (504)		

Applying the Facts

The learning of facts and concepts is of little value unless it can be applied and employed to solve problems. The next group of multiple-choice questions reflects applications of your learning.

72.   Abraham and his family survived the devastating flood in New York State in the 1970's. They moved to another geographic area, but through the years they continue to have episodes of anxiety, sleeplessness, and nightmares. They are the victims of:

a.   panic attack   c.   agorophobia
b.   posttraumatic stress disorder   d.   dissociative disorder

73.   Ingrid will not take a bath in a tub that she knows a man has used unless the tub is scrubbed before her use. She must also have a new bar of soap. Ingrid's problem is:

a.   simple phobia   c.   social phobia
b.   agoraphobia   d.   compulsion

74. Ralph refused to go to a scenic mountain overlook area for a picnic with his friend. When prodded for a reason, Ralph admitted that he knew he would jump off the mountain if he came near the edge. Ralph's problem is:

   a. agoraphobia   c. simple phobia
   b. obsessive-compulsive disorder   d. dissociative disorder

75. Mac has occasional pain in his left knee. He went to a doctor and found that the pain is the result of a minor skiing accident that happened years ago. The doctor assured him that the pain was nothing serious, but Mac did not believe the doctor and continues to see other physicians in an attempt to get relief. Mac has become a victim of:

   a. conversion disorder   c. hypochondriasis
   b. an obsession   d. psychophysiological disorder

76. Ed was an infantryman in Vietnam. His right hand is paralyzed. Doctors can find no nerve damage to explain the paralysis. Ed is most probably suffering from:

   a. a conversion disorder   c. posttraumatic stress disorder
   b. fugue   d. dissociative disorder

77. Bobby was found, by the state patrol, walking along a highway on a cold winter night. He had been missing since late autumn and he was 200 miles from home. He was not married. He said his name was Jim and his wife was to meet him at the next intersection. That is all the information Bobby could give to the patrolman about his life. Bobby was a victim of:

   a. an obsession   c. fugue
   b. affective disorder   d. depersonalization disorder

78. Alicia is "down in the dumps" most of the time lately. She is having a difficult time dealing with her husband's criticism of her. Although she participates in several activities outside her home, she finds no joy in anything. She feels that she is ugly and has serious feelings of failure. She knows she drinks too much, but right now alcohol seems to be the only relief. Alicia's situation is **most** likely to be classified as:

   a. normal depression   c. bipolar disorder
   b. clinical depression   d. agoraphobia

314

79. Vivian appeared to be very ambitious. On occasion she was known to get up at 4:00 a.m., clean the house, do the laundry, play 18 holes of golf, and end the day with a dinner party for 12 people. Then she would disappear. She would stay in the basement and drink for as long as two weeks. Vivian's diagnosis was **most** likely:

    a. mania
    b. bipolar disorder

    c. depersonalization disorder
    d. clinical depression

80. Andrea decided to hang her laundry outside rather than use the dryer since it was such a beautiful day. When she went to bring the laundry in she found that all of her personal undergarments had been stolen. The person who stole the undergarments was likely exhibiting:

    a. transvestism
    b. sexual dysfunction

    c. voyeurism
    d. fetishism

81. Sally worked as a maid in a moderately wealthy household. She was quiet and mannerly and honest. Over a period of time she had asked for several raises in pay and her requests were granted, but the last time she tried for an increase she was told that she would have to remain at the same level. Sally accepted the rejection and continued to work, but her employer increasingly found household items broken or misplaced. There is a chance that Sally had a _____ personality disorder.

    a. dependent
    b. passive-aggressive

    c. schizoid
    d. paranoid

Answers for this section:

72.	b (489)	77.	c (496)	
73.	a (491)	78.	a (498)	
74.	b (490)	79.	b (499)	
75.	c (494)	80.	d (504)	
76.	a (494)	81.	b (507)	

Fill-in-the-Blank Questions: Recalling What You Have Learned

By now, there should be a considerable amount of new information about Abnormal Behavior in long-term memory. The following questions of recall rather than recognition will show if you are becoming more comfortable with the material.

Remembering the Facts

1. The view that people are biologically predisposed to a disorder will tend to exhibit that disorder when particularly affected by stress is called the _____ - _____ model of abnormal behavior.

2. The _____ model views abnormal behavior as the result of maladaptive ways of thinking.

3. _____ disorder is one in which anxiety or the avoidance of anxiety motivates abnormal behavior.

4. An unpredictable feeling of intense fear or terror is called _____ _____.

5. When a person must think disturbing thoughts and perform senseless rituals, the diagnosis is _____ - _____ disorder.

6. Anxiety, sleeplessness, and nightmares as a result of some disturbing event in the past are characteristic of _____ _____ disorder.

7. A phobia directed at a specific situation or object is called _____ phobia.

8. Excessive fear of being alone or of leaving home and being in public places is called _____.

9. _____ disorder is characterized by recurrent vague somatic complaints without physical cause.

10. In a _____ disorder there is a dramatic specific disability that has no physical cause.

11. When a person interprets a small and insignificant symptom as a sign of serious illness in the absence of any organic symptoms the condition is called _____.

12. A _____ disorder is one in which there is genuine physical pathology with a psychological cause.

13. When some aspect of the personality seems fragmented from the rest, the condition is known as _____ disorder.

14. When a person feels unreal and unconnected to his or her body the condition is _____ disorder.

15. Overwhelming feelings of sadness, apathy, guilt and self-reproach indicate
    _____.

16. _____ is characterized by over excitability and hyperactivity.

17. When a person experiences both depression and mania the condition is
    _____ disorder.

18. The inability, in men, to achieve or keep an erection is termed _____
    disorder.

19. Loss or impairment of ordinary physical responses of sexual function is termed
    _____ _____.

20. The inability, in women, to become sexually aroused or reach orgasm is called
    _____ _____ _____ disorder.

21. A psychosexual dysfunction involving lack of sexual interest is termed
    _____ _____ _____.

22. Unconventional objects or situations that cause sexual arousal in some people are
    termed _____.

23. _____ is reliance on nonhuman objects of achieving sexual arousal.

24. The desire to watch others have sexual relations or to spy on nude people is called
    _____.

25. _____ expose their genitals in public to achieve sexual arousal.

26. _____ dress in the clothing of the opposite sex to achieve sexual
    gratification.

27. _____ obtain sexual gratification from aggression.

28. The desire to have sexual relations with children is called _____.

29. Rejection of one's biological gender and the desire to become a member of the
    opposite sex is called _____.

30. A _____ personality disorder is one in which a person is withdrawn and
    lacks feeling for others.

31. In the _____ personality disorder a person is inappropriately suspicious and mistrustful of others.

32. If a person cannot make decisions independently and cannot tolerate being alone the condition is called _____ personality disorder.

33. The _____ - _____ personality disorder is one in which the person's anger is expressed by covert means.

34. The _____ personality has an exaggerated sense of self-importance and needs constant admiration.

35. The _____ personality displays a pattern of violent, criminal, unethical, and exploitive behavior and cannot feel affection for others.

36. Sensory experiences in the absence of external stimulation are called _____.

37. _____ are false beliefs about reality with no basis in fact.

38. Bizarre and childlike behaviors are common in _____ schizophrenia.

39. Disturbed motor behavior is prominent in _____ schizophrenia.

40. Extreme suspiciousness and complex, bizarre delusions characterize _____ schizophrenia.

41. When there are clear schizophrenic symptoms that don't meet the criteria for another type, schizophrenia is termed _____.

42. _____ - _____ _____ disorder is characterized by inattention, impulsiveness, and hyperactivity.

Answers for this section:

1. diasthesis stress (487)
2. cognitive (486)
3. anxiety (489)
4. panic attack (489)
5. obsessive-compulsive (490)
6. posttraumatic stress (489)
7. simple (491)
8. agoraphobia (491)
9. somatization (493)
10. conversion (493)
11. hypochondriasis (494)
12. psychophysiological (495)
13. dissociative (495)
14. depersonalization (497)
15. depression (498)
16. mania (498)
17. bipolar (499)
18. erectile (503)
19. sexual dysfunction (503)
20. female sexual arousal (503)
21. inhibited sexual desire (503)

22. paraphilias (504)
23. fetishism (504)
24. voyeurism (504)
25. exhibitionists (504)
26. transvestites (504)
27. sadomasochists (505)
28. pedophilia (505)
29. transsexualism (505)
30. schizoid (506)
31. paranoid (506)
32. dependent (507)
33. passive-aggressive (507)
34. narcissistic (508)
35. antisocial (508)
36. hallucinations (510)
37. delusions (510)
38. disorganized (512)
39. catatonic (512)
40. paranoid (513)
41. undifferentiated (513)
42. attention-deficit hyperactivity (514)

Understanding and Applying the Facts

As you previously did with recognition-type questions, you will now move to a higher level of recall. The following questions will determine if you understand the facts.

43. Although psychological abnormality is difficult to define, it is useful to consider abnormal behavior as self _____.

44. People's behavior may be considered abnormal because their perception of _____ is distorted.

45. Penny, always worried about someone breaking in her house checks the doors in her house 25 times to be sure they are locked before she goes to bed. Penny has a/an _____ and checking the doors is a/an _____.

46. Phobic disorders are closely linked to feelings of _____.

47. Arthur, in his first freshman semester in college, kept putting off taking a required speech course because he knew he had to speak in front of an audience if he took the course. The thought of taking the course caused him extreme anxiety. Arthur suffered from _____ phobia.

48. According to the psychoanalytic view, phobias are the result of use of the defense mechanism _____.

49. Irving was in a minor automobile accident. He was not seriously injured, but he could not walk. His right foot was paralyzed. Doctors could find no corresponding nerve damage. Irving was having difficulty dealing with the pressures of college and really wanted to make money to support his interest in sports cars. It is likely that Irving's affliction was a _____ disorder.

50. Repeated assurances by the medical profession that a serious illness does not exist have little effect on a/an _____.

51. Irving, whose foot was paralyzed, showed very little concern and even appeared to be cheerful about the condition. This attitude is called _____ _____ _____ by psychologists.

52. Alicia has ulcers, asthma, psoriasis, and arthritis. She is in constant conflict with her husband and is unhappy with her job. It is **most** likely that her afflictions would be classified as _____ disorders.

53. It is very possible that Senator Ted Kennedy's delay in reporting the 1969 accident at Chappaquiddick resulted from _____.

54. Contrary to the popular view, _____ _____ disorder is extremely rare.

55. _____ _____ is a widely accepted factor in the development of multiple personality disorder.

56. Alice, a widow, was watching television one evening when she had the feeling that her left leg and foot were not a part of her body. She was in the process of selling her home and attempting to move to another state. But no progress was being made toward the sale. She felt she had lost control of the situation. If this episode had occurred again or had become more intense, Alice might have been classified as having a/an _____ disorder.

57. Feelings of utter failure and a tendency to blame the self for everything are two of the symptoms of _____.

58. Elizabeth is hyperactive and extremely flamboyant in dress and mannerisms. She has great plans for the future, but does not carry them out. She often calls her brother-in-law long distance and talks for long periods, but does not stay on one topic for more than a few seconds. It is possible that Elizabeth is afflicted with _____.

59. Inhibited sexual desire is more common among (women, men) and may play a part in _____ percent of all sexual dysfunctions.

60. Involuntary muscle spasms in the outer part of the vagina that makes intercourse impossible is called _____ _____.

61. Fetishists are almost always (women, men).

62. _____ humiliate or physically harm their sex partners, while _____ cannot enjoy sex without accompanying emotional or physical pain.

63. Approximately 88 percent of the victims of _____ are girls whose mean age is 9/12 years.

64. A person who is suspicious and mistrustful for no reason, hypersensitive to threat, will not accept deserved blame or criticism, is guarded, secretive, devious, scheming, and argumentative would likely be diagnosed with _____ personality disorder.

65. Pete conceals most of the anger he feels. He is not doing well in college and is frustrated because he can't be comfortable with campus life. One night he poured a gallon of black enamel over the sign at the entrance to his campus. Pete is displaying characteristics of _____ - _____ personality disorder.

66. "The pathological _____ cannot sustain his or her self-regard without having it fed constantly by the attention of others," Wolfe (1978).

67. Greg is a college professor who runs a small business on the side. He is charming and witty and bright. He has found ways to use his campus office and telephone to conduct his business and has "charmed" many of his students into being customers. Greg exhibits features of the _____ personality.

68. Joan was watching television one evening when the picture disappeared and was replaced with the face of Jesus Christ telling her to kill herself and how to do it. She was found wandering in the rain in her night clothes on the streets of a large city. She was hospitalized. Joan was having _____ and it is **most** likely she was diagnosed _____ schizophrenic.

69. Angie, who worked as an attendant in the psychiatric section of the hospital was working in an area near a patient who was mute and immobile. Suddenly the patient jumped out of bed, shouted, and picked a chair and threw it, narrowly missing Angie. Angie's patient was **most** likely a _____ schizophrenic.

70. If an identical twin becomes schizophrenic, the chances are about _____ percent that the other twin will become schizophrenic.

71. Research suggests that schizophrenia may be related to excess amounts of the neurotransmitter _____ in the central nervous system.

72. Amphetamines increase the amount of _____ in the brain and increase the severity of schizophrenics symptoms.

73. The incidence of schizophrenia is (<u>higher, lower</u>) in the lower-class than in other social classes.

74. ADHD is present at birth, but becomes a serious problem when the child
_____ _____ _____.

75. The most frequent treatment for ADHD is the drug _____.

76. Distance, withdrawal, peculiar speech patterns, strange motor behavior, repeated body movements, and lack of social interaction are all characteristics of a serious childhood disorder know as _____.

77. (<u>Men, Women</u>) are most likely to suffer from substance abuse and antisocial disorder, while (<u>men, women</u>) are more likely to suffer from depression, agoraphobia, simple phobia, and somatization disorders.

Answers for this section:

43.	defeating (483)	61.	men (504)
44.	reality (484)	62.	sadists, masochists (505)
45.	obsession, compulsion (490)	63.	pedophilia (505)
46.	anxiety (490)	64.	paranoid (506)
47.	social (491)	65.	passive-aggressive (507)
48.	displacement (491)	66.	narcissist (507)
49.	conversion (494)	67.	antisocial (508)
50.	hypochondriac (494)	68.	hallucinations, paranoid (510-513)
51.	*la belle indifference* (494)	69.	catatonic (512)
52.	psychophysiological (495)	70.	50 (513)
53.	amnesia (496)	71.	dopamine (513)
54.	multiple personality (496)	72.	dopamine (513)
55.	childhood abuse (497)	73.	higher (514)
56.	depersonalization (497)	74.	goes to school (515)
57.	depression (498)	75.	Ritalin (515)
58.	mania (498)	76.	autism (515)
59.	women, 40 (503)	77.	men, women (517)
60.	functional vaginismus (504)		

Testing Yourself for Mastery

The following terms and concepts are found in boldface or italics in the chapter. The time has come to determine if you can define and discuss your new learning in your own words, then check your work against the text.

psychoanalytic, behavioral, cognitive,
biological, and diasthesis-stress models of
abnormal behavior

anxiety disorder

panic attack

posttraumatic stress disorder

obsessive-compulsive disorder

phobic disorder

phobia

simple phobia

agoraphobia

social phobia

somatoform disorders

somatization disorder

conversion disorder

hypochondriasis

psychophysiological disorder

dissociative disorders

amnesia

multiple personality

depersonalization disorder

affective disorders

depression

mania

bipolar disorder

sexual dysfunction

erectile disorder

female sexual arousal disorder

inhibited sexual desire

inhibited sexual excitement

orgasm

inhibited orgasm

paraphilias

fetishism

voyeurism

exhibitionism

transvestism

sadomasochism

pedophilia

transsexualism

personality disorders

schizoid personality disorder

paranoid personality disorder

dependent personality disorder

passive-aggressive personality disorder

narcissistic personality disorder

antisocial personality disorder

schizophrenic disorders

hallucinations

delusions

disorganized schizophrenia

catatonic schizophrenia

paranoid schizophrenia

undifferentiated schizophrenia

attention-deficit hyperactivity disorder (ADHD)

autism

Integrating Your Newly Learned Information

Now that you have recognized, recalled, and given definition to Abnormal Behavior, you are ready to try to integrate your knowledge in a definitive discussion through short-answer questions.

1. Contrast historical views with contemporary criteria for determining if behavior is abnormal. (484-487)

2. Present at least one characteristic each of the four current models of abnormal behavior. (486, 487)

3. Describe DSM-III-R and give at least one criticism of it. (487, 488)

4. How would a behaviorist explain anxiety disorders? (491)

5. How would a psychoanalyst explain somatoform disorders? (494)

6. How would cognitive theory explain the cause of depression? (501)

7. What are 2 or 3 explanations for sexual dysfunction? (503, 504)

8. Although there is no single reason to account for pedophilia, what are some of the common reasons for a person engaging in pedophilia? (505)

9. As yet, the cause (or causes) of schizophrenia is not known, present one or two possible explanations for its development. (513, 514)

10. Discuss some of the problems involved in determining gender differences in abnormal behavior. (515-518)

Applications

You have worked through a section of recognition-type questions to determine if you can apply information to real-life situations. It is time to try to respond to some applications. Some are based upon those questions. Answers to this section will not be given. Your questions concerning these applications will serve as a basis for classroom discussion and ideas for class projects throughout the course.

1.   Ingrid cannot take a bath in a tub she knows a man has used. She also must have a new bar of soap. Ingrid is afraid she will get pregnant. When she discussed the problem with a close friend she had fleeting memories of a bathtub and a male cousin when she was very young, and her mother's memory came into prominence. How would you diagnose Ingrid's problem? Do you suppose she actually believes she could get pregnant in a tub a man used? Explain.

2.   Ed, the infantryman who served in Vietnam, had a paralyzed right hand. There was no nerve damage to be found. In talking with a counselor, Ed remembered that he had thrown a grenade with his right hand and killed what he perceived to be innocent people. How would you classify Ed's disorder? Try to explain why his hand is paralyzed.

3.   The owner of an exclusive women's shoe shop came to work one morning and found the shop had been burglarized. The thief was apprehended. Police officials found hundreds of pairs of shoes in the thief's apartment, all categorized according to color, shade, and style. The thief was not married and lived alone. Do you think there is an abnormality here? If so, what is it?

4.   As long as he could remember, Alfred's wife complained of being sick. She felt faint or had pains that she could not adequately describe. She was often too sick or weary to go any place and most often did not cook his meals. She often had dizzy spells and complained of abdominal pains. Alfred took her to doctors, but nothing could be found to explain these symptoms. Can you diagnose Alfred's wife's disorder?

5. Lillian found two dark spots on her skin. She went to the doctor to confirm that she had skin cancer. The spots were normal, but she was not convinced. She announced that she was going to continue to see doctors until she found one that was competent to help her. Where would Lillian fit in DSM-III-R?

6. Patti was severely abused as a child. When she was 12 she was often seen socializing with her friends, laughing and talking and having a good time, all the while maintaining a straight-A grade average. Her clothes were always neat and clean. Soon people noticed that she would isolate herself, be absent from school and show disregard for her appearance. Her grades began to drop. She was insolent and uncooperative. After a time, she would return to the happy child she once was. What might the diagnosis be? Is it a common disorder?

7. Abby was taking a course in abnormal psychology. To give credence to her professor's lecture she told of her own affliction and how she would charge airplane tickets to her credit card and fly all over the country. When she came home she would become depressed and worry about how she would pay her bills. She told of the medication that seemed to help. Abby had to quit college and be hospitalized before the term was over. What is Abby's problem? How would you feel if someone in your class related such a personal experience? What do you suppose was the reaction of the class to Abby's disclosure?

8. Barbara's baby appeared normal at first. When he was about 9 months old she and the baby's father noticed that their son did not want their closeness and affection. He did not even want to be picked up. As he grew older he did not develop normal speech. He merely repeated most words said to him. He did not play with his toys in a normal way. They took the baby to a doctor when they first noticed this strange behavior. What was the diagnosis and what is the cause?

Return to Chapter Summary

Now that you have concluded these exercises, you should go back and reread the chapter summary in your textbook. It provides you with a framework that integrates all of this newly-learned information. By reviewing the chapter summary, you will strengthen the many connections between the various new pieces of information.

THERAPIES

13

Chapter Objectives

After you have read and studied this chapter, you should be able to:

1. Differentiate between insight therapies, behavior therapies, cognitive therapies, and group therapies.
2. Discuss the criticisms of psychoanalysis.
3. Explain how client-centered and rational-emotive therapists interpret causes of emotional problems. Describe the therapeutic techniques of each approach.
4. Summarize the behavior therapist's interpretation of disorders. Describe aversive conditioning, desensitization, and modeling.
5. Describe stress-inoculation therapy, Beck's cognitive therapy, and Gestalt therapy.
6. List the advantages and disadvantages of group therapies. Identify five current approaches to group therapy.
7. Discuss the effectiveness of insight therapy and behavior therapy.
8. Outline the available biological treatments and discuss the advantages and disadvantages of each.
9. Summarize the inadequacies of institutionalization. List the alternatives to institutionalization.

Multiple-Choice Questions: Recognizing What You Have Learned

These questions ask only that you recognize what you have learned. When you recognize a correct answer, you have accessed that information in memory. A knowledge of facts serves as a framework for later analysis and problem solving.

Remembering the Facts

This group of multiple-choice questions requires that you simply recognize facts from your textbook.

1. The treatment of behavioral and emotional disorders using psychological techniques is called:

   a. insight
   b. psychoanalysis

   c. transference
   d. psychotherapy

2. _____ is a type of psychotherapy that helps the client achieve greater understanding of personal motives, expectations, and means of coping.

   a. Insight therapy
   b. Gestalt

   c. Stress-inoculation therapy
   d. Rational-emotive therapy

3. Freud developed this technique and based it on the attempt to uncover people's unconscious motives, feelings, and desires.

   a. client-centered therapy
   b. desensitization

   c. psychoanalysis
   d. psychotherapy

4. The uninhibited disclosure of thoughts and fantasies as they occur to the client is termed:

   a. conscious association
   b. free association

   c. catharsis
   d. insight

5. The development of warm feelings toward one's therapist is termed:

   a. free transference
   b. free association

   c. positive transference
   d. empathy

6. When a client displaces hostility for a parent or other authority figure to one's therapist, the term used is:

a. denial
b. negative transference

c. negation
d. reverse transference

7. The awareness of how and why we feel and act as we do is called:

a. intuition
b. discernment

c. perceptiveness
d. insight

8. Client-centered or person-centered therapy was developed by:

a. Carl Rogers
b. B.F. Skinner

c. Albert Bandura
d. Aaron Beck

9. Therapeutic approaches based primarily on the application of principles of conditioning are called _____ therapy.

a. insight
b. cognitive

c. behavior
d. rational-emotive

10. When client and therapist set reinforcements for reaching behavioral goals they are engaged in:

a. desensitization
b. behavioral conditioning

c. operant modeling
d. behavior contracting

11. Techniques aimed at eliminating undesirable behavior by teaching the person to associate them with pain and discomfort are called:

a. aversive conditioning
b. aversion conditioning

c. negative reinforcement
d. adversive conditioning

12. A therapy designed to gradually reduce anxiety about a particular object or situation is called:

a. cognitive change
b. desensitization

c. unsensitization
d. emotive alteration

13. When patients earn reinforcements for desired behavior and exchange them for desired items or privileges, the technique is called:

   a. tokenism
   b. positive economy

   c. token economy
   d. symbolic reward

14. _____ is a type of learning in which a person observes someone else performing a desired behavior.

   a. Copying
   b. Modeling

   c. Imitation
   d. Simulation

15. Changing the client's perception of his or her life situation as a way of modifying behavior is emphasized in _____ therapy.

   a. cognitive
   b. rational-emotive

   c. stress-inoculation
   d. Beck's cognitive

16. A directive cognitive therapy based on the idea that a person's problems are caused by irrational assumptions is called:

   a. SIT
   b. Gestalt therapy

   c. RET
   d. an insight therapy

17. Useful patterns of self-talk are employed to help clients to cope with stressful situations in:

   a. stress reduction therapy
   b. RET

   c. Gestalt therapy
   d. stress-inoculation therapy

18. Helping a person to identify and change inappropriately negative and self-critical thought patterns is the central characteristic of:

   a. Beck's cognitive therapy
   b. rational-emotive therapy

   c. aversive conditioning
   d. person-centered therapy

19. _____ can produce convulsions and temporary coma, but is used to alleviate severe depression.

   a. Aversive conditioning
   b. RET

   c. Desensitization
   d. ECT

20. Which of the following is rarely used in treatment of severe mental disorders?

    a.   antipsychotic drugs   c.   lithium
    b.   psychosurgery   d.   Prozac

21. Techniques for reducing long-term consequences of mental illness by facilitating an individual's readjustment to family and community life is called _____ prevention.

    a.   primary   c.   tertiary
    b.   third-rank   d.   secondary

Answers for this section:

1.	d (524)	7.	d (526)	13.	c (530)	19.	d (543)
2.	a (524)	8.	a (528)	14.	b (532)	20.	b (544)
3.	c (524)	9.	c (530)	15.	a (533)	21.	c (550)
4.	b (525)	10.	d (530)	16.	c (533)		
5.	c (525)	11.	a (531)	17.	d (533)		
6.	b (526)	12.	b (531)	18.	a (535)		

Understanding the Facts

Now that you have found that you can recognize facts from Therapies, the next step is to determine if you understand the meaning of newly-learned information. These multiple-choice questions require a higher level of thinking. They will help you establish more solid connections and provide practice in dealing with higher level concepts.

22. For emotional disorders, traditional psychoanalysis is most effective in treating:

    a.   low income clients   c.   potentially autonomous people
    b.   severely disturbed people   d.   schizophrenia

23. A crucial step in psychoanalysis is:

    a.   negative transference   c.   relaxation
    b.   euphoria   d.   catharsis

24. Some psychologists feel that traditional psychoanalysis is outdated because:

a. potentially autonomous people are rare in contemporary society
b. now it is more difficult to find rules for behavior than to break them
c. upper class women no longer need professional assistance
d. positive transference is unethical

25. The cardinal rule in person-centered therapy is for the therapist to:

a. express conditional positive regard
b. have less empathy than the client
c. foster positive transference
d. express unconditional positive regard

26. Client-centered therapy is emphatically:

a. nondirective   c. directive
b. interpretive   d. confrontational

27. Unlike traditional Freudian analysts, contemporary therapists:

a. have abandoned time-limited frameworks
b. discount early-child events as formative experiences
c. give clients more direct guidance and feedback
d. are less symptom oriented

28. Practitioners of which of the following therapies do not need to know how or why people behave as they do?

a. behavior therapies   c. cognitive therapies
b. psychoanalysis   d. RET

29. A type of therapy in which client and therapist decide on behavioral goals and the type of reinforcement the client will receive when those goals are reached is called:

a. behavior modification   c. behavior contracting
b. operant contracting   d. client-centered contracting

30. Which of the following approaches has been used with some success in treating alcoholism, obesity, and smoking?

a. aversive conditioning   c. RET
b. desensitization   d. modeling

31. Which of the following procedures has been effective in modifying the behavior of institutionalized patients who are considered resistant to other forms of treatment?

   a. aversive conditioning   c. token economies
   b. stress inoculation   d. desensitization

32. In _____, the therapist first establishes a hierarchy of fears.

   a. behavior contracting   c. aversive conditioning
   b. RET   d. desensitization

33. The heart of desensitization is:

   a. relaxation   c. aversion
   b. insight   d. cognition

34. Bellack, Hersen, and Turner (1976) found that a combination of _____ and positive reinforcement is successful in helping schizophrenic patients learn appropriate behavior.

   a. aversion   c. modeling
   b. densensitization   d. tokens

35. Cognitive psychologists believe that _____ cause psychological problems for people.

   a. misconceptions   c. childhood experiences
   b. habits   d. conflicts

36. Rational-emotive therapists are famous for:

   a. empathy   c. not "babying" their clients
   b. "babying" their clients   d. being non-directive

37. Dysfunctional beliefs are identified and confronted vigorously in:

   a. RET   c. Beck's cognitive therapy
   b. stress-inoculation therapy   d. Gestalt therapy

38. Rational-emotive therapy belongs in which of the following categories?

   a. insight   c. behavioral
   b. cognitive   d. group

39. Which of the following psychotherapies is especially useful for treating anxiety disorders?

    a.   drug therapy   c.   RET
    b.   Gestalt   d.   stress-inoculation

40. In _____ therapy a client is taught to suppress negative, anxiety producing thoughts and replace them with positive "coping thoughts."

    a.   stress-inoculation   c.   client-centered
    b.   psychoanalytic   d.   Gestalt

41. One of the most promising treatments for depression in recent years has been:

    a.   psychosurgery   c.   Gestalt therapy
    b.   Beck's cognitive therapy   d.   desensitization

42. People with unrealistic expectations who magnify their failure and make negative generalizations from little evidence would most benefit from:

    a.   psychoanalysis   c.   behavior contracting
    b.   RET   d.   Beck's cognitive therapy

43. People with interpersonal problems might benefit **most** from:

    a.   Gestalt therapy   c.   group therapy
    b.   tertiary prevention   d.   Beck's cognitive therapy

44. Lower cost, sharing, and social support are all advantages of:

    a.   Beck's cognitive therapy   c.   behavior therapy
    b.   group therapy   d.   deinstitutionalization

45. _____ feel(s) that most professionals treat people in a vacuum.

    a.   Family therapists   c.   B.F. Skinner
    b.   Biological therapists   d.   Fritz Perls

46. Helping a married couple to develop a schedule for exchanging specific caring actions would be a goal of a _____ - oriented therapist.

    a.   behaviorally   c.   cognitively
    b.   psychoanalytically   d.   humanistically

47. Who said, "Freud invented the couch because he could not look people in the eye?"

    a. Aaron Beck   c. Carl Rogers
    b. B.F. Skinner   d. Fritz Perls

48. Gestalt therapy is designed to make people:

    a. insightful   c. self-supporting
    b. less anxious   d. less selfish

49. What does Gestalt therapy have in common with psychoanalysis?

    a. It employs free-association.
    b. It uses people's dreams to help uncover information.
    c. It helps the client to resolve unconscious conflicts.
    d. It is especially helpful with the problems of upper middle-class women.

50. The current trend in psychotherapy is toward:

    a. drug therapy   c. eclecticism
    b. biological treatment   d. cognitive therapy

51. Desensitization is most effective with:

    a. sexual dysfunction
    b. conditioned avoidance responses
    c. people seeking profound self-understanding
    d. depression

52. Insight therapy seems to be best suited:

    a. for people seeking relief from inner conflict and anxiety
    b. for people with phobias
    c. for relief from depression
    d. in cases where there is a specific behavioral problem

53. A major reason for using biological treatment is:

    a. because psychotherapy cannot help some clients
    b. to lower the cost of treatment
    c. to change clients' behavior so they can benefit from therapy
    d. because of the large number of professionals trained in this approach

54. The most common biological treatment in use today is:

a. ECT   c. insulin shock
b. psychosurgery   d. drugs

55. _____ is most often used for cases of prolonged and severe depression.

a. RET   c. Psychosurgery
b. ECT   d. Lithium

56. A treatment for prolonged and severe depression that reduces memory impairment and confusion is called:

a. unilateral ECT   c. bilateral ECT
b. psychosurgery   d. chlorpromazine therapy

57. Biological treatment is almost always used for treating:

a. bipolar disorder   c. schizophrenia
b. tardive dyskinesia   d. anxiety panic

58. Which of the following statements about prefrontal lobotomy is **not** true?

a. Lobotomies can work with one person and fail completely with another.
b. In the last 25 years there has been a major increase in the use of prefrontal lobotomy.
c. Lobotomies can produce permanent undesirable side effects.
d. Sometimes lobotomies are used for pain control and terminal illness.

59. Which of the following statements about reserpine and phenothiazines is **not** true?

a. They were not available before the mid-1950's.
b. They reduce hallucinations and delusions.
c. They alleviate anxiety and aggressive behavior.
d. They are minor tranquilizers.

60. Research with animals indicates that phenothiazines inhibit functioning of the:

a. thalamus   c. endocrine system
b. hypothalmus   d. reticular formation

61. It appears that virtually all antipsychotic drugs block _____ receptors in the brain.

    a. visual   c. dopamine
    b. auditory   d. anxiety

62. The most serious side effect of antipsychotic drugs is:

    a. blurred vision   c. constipation
    b. tardive dyskinesia   d. mood swings

63. MAOI's and tricyclics are used to alleviate symptoms of:

    a. bipolar disorder   c. schizophrenia
    b. migraine headaches   d. depression

64. Which of the following statements about Prozac is **not** true?

    a. In 1991, the FDA took it off the market.
    b. It works by acting on the substance serotonin.
    c. It has not been proved that Prozac causes violent behavior.
    d. At first, it appeared that Prozac had fewer side effects than older antidepressants.

65. Which of the following is not a drug, but a naturally occurring salt that helps level out wide mood swings?

    a. Prozac   c. lithium
    b. tricyclia   d. Thorazine

66. Which of the following statements about lithium carbonate is **true**?

    a. It is used to treat symptoms of schizophrenia.
    b. It takes effect very quickly.
    c. It is effective in treating multiple personality.
    d. It is effective 75 percent of the time.

67.   Which of the following occurrences created a favorable climate for
       deinstitutionalization?

       a.   the advent of antipsychotic drugs in the 1950's
       b.   advances in techniques of psychosurgery
       c.   the development of drugs that have no side effects
       d.   refinements of ECT procedures

68.   It has been estimated that there may be _____ homeless persons living on
       American streets on any given night.

       a.   450,000   c.   600,000
       b.   1 million   d.   250,000

69.   Which of the following statements about gender difference in treatments is **true**?

       a.   Men are more willing than women to admit they have a problem.
       b.   Women are more likely than men to be in psychotherapy.
       c.   Psychotherapy is more socially accepted for men.
       d.   In one study, 60 percent of people seeing the therapists were men.

Answers for this section:

22.	c (527)	34.	c (533)	46.	a (537)	58.	b (545)
23.	a (526)	35.	a (533)	47.	d (537)	59.	d (545)
24.	b (527)	36.	c (533)	48.	c (537)	60.	b (545)
25.	d (528)	37.	a (533)	49.	b (537)	61.	c (545)
26.	a (528)	38.	b (533)	50.	c (543)	62.	b (546)
27.	c (530)	39.	d (535)	51.	b (542)	63.	d (546)
28.	a (530)	40.	a (534)	52.	a (542)	64.	a (546)
29.	c (530)	41.	b (535)	53.	c (543)	65.	c (547)
30.	a (531)	42.	d (535)	54.	d (545)	66.	d (547)
31.	c (531)	43.	c (535)	55.	b (543)	67.	a (548)
32.	d (531)	44.	b (536)	56.	a (544)	68.	c (549)
33.	a (532)	45.	a (536)	57.	c (543)	69.	b (552)

Applying the Facts

The learning of facts and concepts is of little value unless it can be applied and
employed to solve problems. The next group of multiple-choice questions reflects
applications of your learning.

70. It was 1920. Annabelle had recently married into a wealthy banking family in Philadelphia. She was experiencing considerable anxiety about some childhood memories and was in conflict about having children. She sought professional help. That assistance was most likely:

a. desensitization
b. RET
c. psychoanalysis
d. person-centered therapy

71. Trammel was an alcoholic. He tried to support himself by doing yard work and odd jobs. He was often arrested for his drunkenness. He agreed to take a special drug that induced nausea and vomiting if he attempted to drink alcohol. The treatment for Trammel was:

a. desensitization
b. aversive conditioning
c. Gestalt therapy
d. RET

72. Douglas finally got the job that he wanted. He was to begin in two months, but he had a serious conflict about accepting the job. He had a phobia: he could not get on an elevator. Which of the following treatments would be most advantageous to Douglas given the time limit?

a. stress-inoculation therapy
b. psychoanalysis
c. Beck's cognitive therapy
d. desensitization

73. Doris has some serious dental problems, but is so afraid of the dentist that she will not go in spite of the consequences. Which of the following might be of **most** help for Doris?

a. Gestalt therapy
b. modeling
c. stress-inoculation therapy
d. client-centered therapy

74. Brenda has noticed that life is not fair and she won't accept it. She sees no reason why she shouldn't be liked by everyone. She believes that she should have A's in all of her classes because she works so hard. She makes such logical plans for herself and her boyfriend and sees no reason why he won't carry them out. She has become quite depressed. The approach of which of the following would be of **most** help for Brenda?

a. Albert Ellis
b. Fritz Perls
c. Carl Rogers
d. Sigmund Freud

344

75. Alice is scheduled to take the state licensing board exams for her certification as a registered nurse. Although she completed requirements for her degree, she has developed a high level of anxiety because of the exam and is afraid she will not pass it no matter how she tries to prepare for it. She has decided to seek professional help. Which of the following should you recommend for Alice?

    a.   Beck's cognitive therapy   c.   psychoanalysis
    b.   desensitization   d.   stress-inoculation therapy

76. If you were seriously depressed and had decided to seek professional help, which of the following psychotherapies would be **most** promising as a way to help you?

    a.   Gestalt therapy   c.   psychoanalysis
    b.   Beck's cognitive therapy   d.   client-centered therapy

77. Ginger is in a therapeutic setting for the purpose of making her more aware of her feelings. Her therapist tells her to talk about herself in the first person. It sounds like Ginger is in:

    a.   Beck's cognitive therapy   c.   Gestalt therapy
    b.   marital therapy   d.   client-centered therapy

78. If you were suffering from prolonged and severe depression, which of the following treatments might be the best for you?

    a.   lithium   c.   institutionalization
    b.   psychosurgery   d.   ECT

Answers for this section:

70.	c (527)	73.	b (532)	76.	b (535)
71.	b (531)	74.	a (533)	77.	c (537)
72.	d (531)	75.	d (533)	78.	d (543)

Fill-in-the-Blank Questions: Recalling What You Have Learned

By now, there should be a considerable amount of new information about Therapies in long-term memory. The following questions of recall rather than recognition will show if you are becoming more comfortable with the material.

Remembering the Facts

1. Treatment of behavioral and emotional disorders using psychological techniques is called _____.

2. _____ therapy is aimed at having the client achieve greater understanding of personal motives and expectations.

3. Freud's technique of uncovering the client's unconscious motives, feelings, and desires is called _____.

4. _____ _____ is the uninhibited disclosure of thoughts and fantasies as they occur to the client.

5. _____ _____ is the development of warm feelings toward one's therapist.

6. The displacement of hostility felt for an authority figure to one's therapist is called _____ _____.

7. An awareness of how and why we feel and act as we do is called _____.

8. Client-centered or person-centered therapy was developed by _____.

9. _____ therapy is an application of the principles of operant conditioning.

10. When client and therapist set reinforcements for reaching behavioral goals the technique is termed _____ _____.

11. A _____ _____ is a technique in which patients earn reinforcements for desired behavior and exchange them for desired items or privileges.

12. Through _____ _____ clients learn to eliminate undesirable behavior patterns by associating them with pain and discomfort.

13. _____ gradually reduces anxiety about a particular object or situation.

14. A person learns by observing someone else perform a desired behavior in _____.

15. Emphasis on changing the client's perceptions of his or her life situation as a way of modifying behavior defines _____ therapies.

16. _____ - _____ therapy is based on the idea that a person's problems are caused by irrational assumptions.

17. _____ - _____ therapy trains clients to cope with stress by learning more useful patterns of self-talk.

18. _____ cognitive therapy identifies and changes negative and self-critical thought patterns.

19. Couples can be helped in improving their communication and interactions through _____ therapy.

20. _____ therapy emphasizes the wholeness of the personality and attempts to reawaken people to their emotions.

21. To alleviate severe depression, a mild electric current is passed through the brain for a short period. This procedure is called _____ therapy.

22. _____ is the term for brain surgery that is rarely used in the treatment of severe mental disorders.

23. Mental health care provided in the local community rather than in institutions is called _____.

24. Programs emphasizing early detection of maladaptive behavior and prompt treatment in high-risk groups is called _____ prevention.

Answers for this section:

1. psychotherapy (524)
2. insight (524)
3. psychoanalysis (524)
4. free association (525)
5. positive transference (525)
6. negative transference (526)
7. insight (526)
8. Carl Rogers (528)
9. behavior (530)
10. behavior contracting (530)
11. token economy (530)
12. aversive conditioning (531)
13. desensitization (531)
14. modeling (532)
15. cognitive (533)
16. rational-emotive (RET) (533)
17. stress-inoculation (533)
18. Beck's (535)
19. marital (536)
20. Gestalt (537)
21. electroconvulsive (ECT) (543)
22. psychosurgery (544)
23. deinstitutionalization (548)
24. secondary (550)

Understanding and Applying the Facts

As you previously did with recognition-type questions, you will now move to a higher level of recall. The following questions will determine if you understand the facts.

25.   Psychoanalysis and client-centered therapies are categorized as _____ therapies.

26.   Behavior contracting, aversive conditioning, densensitization, and modeling are categorized as _____ therapies.

27.   RET, stress-inoculation, and Beck's approach are categorized as _____ therapies.

28.   Family therapy, marital therapy, and Gestalt therapy are categorized as _____ therapies.

29.   If you had unlimited funds, plenty of time to spare, wanted to work through old conflicts that are interfering with your life, and were a middle-aged person in the late 1930's, you would probably turn to _____.

30.   Edgar is lucky. He has scheduled appointments with Dr. M. Scott Peck for some help in working through some troubling personal conflicts. Dr. Peck is helping him to cope with current problems brought on by these conflicts, talks with Edgar face-to-face, and takes an active role in his therapy. Dr. Peck is **most** likely a _____ _____.

31.   The goal of therapy as viewed by Carl Rogers is to help clients to become _____ _____.

32.   Client-centered therapy use a (directive, nondirective) approach.

33.   Reflections of client's statements is a major characteristic of _____ - _____ therapy.

34.   Madeline wanted someone to talk to. She had many decisions to make, and also had made some serious mistakes. When she tried talking with friends and family members she found them quick to judge and to tell her what she ought to do. She took a psychology course and decided that the therapy developed by _____ is the one she should pursue.

35.   Behavior therapies concentrate on _____ behavior.

36. Betty is obese. She wants to try to lose weight without someone trying to find out *why* she is obese. Also, her time is rather limited. She chose _____ _____.

37. In cases where aversive conditioning may be harmful, two other behavioral techniques are _____ and _____.

38. Linda has an IQ of 120, but has always thought of herself as "dumb." That misconception is keeping her from doing well in college. _____ - _____ therapy might be helpful for Linda.

39. Rational-emotive therapists are very (directive, nondirective).

40. Changing one's thoughts when one is engaged in self-talk from negative to "coping" thoughts is called _____ - _____ therapy.

41. _____ _____ believes that depression results from negative patterns of thought that people develop about themselves.

42. Lower cost and social support are two advantages of _____ therapy.

43. To help partners recognize the ways they have been misinterpreting each other's communication, Aaron Beck developed _____ _____ therapy.

44. _____ therapy can be done with individuals, but is more frequently done in a group setting.

45. You may be ignoring some important sensory information and you may also need to be more in touch with your feelings. You want to feel more complete. You might join a _____ group.

46. _____ _____, in 1952, concluded that individual psychotherapy was no more effective against neurotic disorders than no therapy at all.

47. According to Smith and Glass (1977), the typical therapy client is better off than _____ percent of untreated controls.

48. In addition to their effectiveness with depression, cognitive therapies appear promising for treating _____ disorders.

49. _____ is a mental disorder than has a strong biological component. Therefore, treatment is virtually always _____.

349

50. _____ ECT is a recent development in which the current is passed through the nondominant hemisphere.

51. ECT, although controversial, is used for good reason with _____ _____ people.

52. _____ _____ are rarely performed today.

53. Antipsychotic drugs are especially helpful in reducing _____ and _____.

54. David's wife has been schizophrenic for many years. She has never been institutionalized. Institutionalization was not necessary because of the use of _____ _____.

55. Although antipsychotic drugs are extremely helpful, there are side effects. The most serious side effect is _____ _____.

56. A controversial drug used to treat depression is _____.

57. _____ is a naturally occurring substance that is frequently used to treat bipolar disorder and is effective about _____ percent of the time.

58. Large state mental hospitals are examples of _____.

59. Because of the introduction of antipsychotic drugs, _____ is now possible.

60. Many released mental patients have ended up on the streets because of _____.

61. Action taken after the Hyatt Regency Hotel disaster in Kansas City in 1981 is an example of _____ prevention.

Answers for this section:

25.	insight (524)	44.	Gestalt (537)
26.	behavior (530-532)	45.	Gestalt (537)
27.	cognitive (533-535)	46.	Hans Eysenck (538)
28.	group (535-537)	47.	75 (539)
29.	psychoanalysis (527)	48.	anxiety (543)
30.	neo-Freudian (528)	49.	schizophrenia, biological (543)
31.	fully functioning (528)	50.	unilateral (543)
32.	non-directive (528)	51.	suicidally depressed (544)
33.	client-centered (528)	52.	prefrontal lobotomies (545)
34.	Carl Rogers (528)	53.	hallucinations, delusions (545)
35.	overt (530)	54.	antipsychotic drugs (545)
36.	aversive conditioning (531)	55.	tardive dyskinesia (546)
37.	desensitization,modeling (531, 532)	56.	Prozac (546)
38.	rational-emotive (533)	57.	lithium, 75 (547)
39.	directive (533)	58.	institutionalization (547)
40.	stress-inoculation (533)	59.	deinstitutionalization (548)
41.	Aaron Beck (535)	60.	deinstitutionalization (548)
42.	group (536)	61.	primary (550)
43.	cognitive marital (537)		

Testing Yourself For Mastery

The following terms and concepts are found in boldface or italics in the chapter. The time has come to determine if you can define and discuss your new learning in your own words, then check your work against the text.

psychotherapy

insight therapy

psychoanalysis

free association

positive transfer

negative transfer

insight

client-centered or person-centered therapy

behavioral therapies

behavioral contracting

token economy

aversive conditioning

desensitization

modeling

cognitive behavior therapy

rational-emotive therapy

stress-inoculation therapy

Beck's cognitive therapy

group therapy

family therapy

marital therapy

Gestalt therapy

biological treatment

electroconvulsive therapy

psychosurgery

antidepressant drugs

lithium

tardive dyskinesia

deinstitutionalization

primary prevention

secondary prevention

tertiary prevention

Integrating Your Newly Learned Information

Now that you have recognized, recalled, and given definition to Therapies, you are ready to try to integrate your knowledge in a definitive discussion through short-answer questions.

1. Differentiate between insight therapies, behavior therapies, and cognitive therapies incorporating only the main goal of each in your answer. (524-535)

2. How does the neo-Freudian approach differ from traditional or orthodox psychoanalysis? (524-528)

3. Discuss two or three contemporary trends in psychotherapy. (529, 530)

4. How does a therapist justify using pain and discomfort in treating problem behavior? (531)

5. What is the outstanding characteristic of rational-emotive therapy that differentiates it from client-centered therapy? (533)

6. Why does Aaron Beck's cognitive therapy appear to be promising in dealing with depression? (535)

7. Discuss at least one advantage and one disadvantage of family therapy. (536, 537)

8. Is Gestalt therapy suited for people who are "sick?" Why or Why not? (537)

9. Present at least one piece of evidence that psychotherapy is effective. (538, 539)

10. Present two central reasons for using biological treatment of mental disorders. (543-547)

11. Has deinstitutionalization failed? Discuss. (548, 549)

Applications

You have worked through a section of recognition-type questions to determine if you can apply information to real-life situations. It is time to try to respond to some applications. Some are based upon those questions. Answers to this section will not be given. Your questions concerning these applications will serve as a basis for classroom discussion and ideas for class projects throughout the course.

1. Think of a personal problem you have. Everyone has problem situations, whether or not they are serious. Write down the nature of your problem. Choose from the therapies discussed in the chapter one that you think might best assist you in solving that problem.

2. You have a close friend who may be developing an alcoholic problem. She has several psychophysiological disorders and has become depressed. Much of her stress originates from her perceptions of an overly-critical husband who is lowering her self-esteem. She has asked you where she might find some help. What would you suggest she do?

3.   Andy is working for a mental health facility as an aide. He has had several undergraduate psychology courses. He has been asked to come up with some ideas to improve the personal habits of several patients on a ward. What technique might Andy suggest?

4.   Martin is 10 years old and very much afraid of dogs. He was severely bitten by a dog when he was 2 years old. His parents would like him to lose this fear. There are two techniques in behavior therapy that might help Martin. What are they?

5.   Your friend has been severely depressed for a long time. Suicide has been discussed. He has not responded to psychotherapy. What treatment might be the only hope?

6.   Amy is suffering from serious depression. Tricyclics have been prescribed for her. Her condition has improved, but what must she and her doctor pay attention to while she is using these drugs?

7.   Vivian, who was a manic-depressive in the 1950's died as a result of her alcoholism. What treatment might have helped her if she were alive today?

8.   Many people were injured and two people were killed in a gas explosion in a small town. They were victims of a man-made catastrophe and the injured and bystanders showed the symptoms characteristic of this type of trauma. What should the community mental health organizations have done immediately after the mishap?

Return to Chapter Summary

Now that you have concluded these exercises, you should go back and reread the chapter summary in your textbook. It provides you with a framework that integrates all of this newly-learned information. By reviewing the chapter summary, you will strengthen the many connections between the various new pieces of information.

SOCIAL PSYCHOLOGY 14

Chapter Objectives

After you have read and studied this chapter, you should be able to:

1. Describe the process by which we form first impressions of other people. Identify three factors that influence person perception.
2. Explain three aspects of attribution and explain attribution errors.
3. Explain the dynamics of interpersonal attraction.
4. Identify the components of attitudes. Discuss the relationship between attitude and behavior.
5. Explain how attitudes are acquired.
6. Explain the theory of cognitive dissonance. List ways to reduce cognitive dissonance.
7. Explain the origin of prejudice and discrimination and how prejudice can be reduced.
8. Discuss the dynamics of attitude change and the process of persuasion.
9. Define risky shift and polarization. Summarize the conditions under which groups are effective and ineffective in solving problems.
10. Explain how culture, conformity, compliance, and obedience exert social influence.
11. Identify the four types of social action.
12. Identify the theories of leadership.

13. Discuss the concerns of organizational behavior and the role of the industrial/organizational psychologist.

Multiple-Choice Questions: Recognizing What You Have Learned

These questions ask only that you recognize what you have learned. When you recognize a correct answer, you have accessed that information in memory. A knowledge of facts serves as a framework for later analysis and problem solving.

Remembering the Facts

This group of multiple-choice questions requires that you simply recognize facts from your textbook.

1. A set of beliefs or expectations about something is called a/an:

   a. concept   c. schema
   b. attitude   d. value

2. When we meet a person for the first time, we fit the person into ready made:

   a. categories   c. ranks
   b. schemata   d. classes

3. The extent to which early information about someone weighs more heavily than later information on our impression of that person is called:

   a. early judgement   c. first impression
   b. the recency effect   d. the primacy effect

4. When a person's expectation about another elicits behavior from the second person that confirms the expectation the process is called:

   a. self-fulfilling prophecy   c. stereotyping
   b. self-attribution   d. biasing

5. A/an _____ is a set of characteristics presumed to be shared by all members of a social category.

   a. attribution   c. bias
   b. stereotype   d. judgement

6. _____ theory addresses the question of how people make judgements about the causes of behavior.

   a. Distinctiveness
   b. Consistency
   c. Proximity
   d. Attribution

7. The extent to which a behavior is present only when a particular stimulus is also present is called:

   a. attribution
   b. proximity
   c. distinctiveness
   d. consistency

8. The extent to which a particular event produces the same behavior each time it is present is termed:

   a. consistency
   b. accordance
   c. consonance
   d. consensus

9. _____ is the extent to which everyone in a given situation is behaving in the same way.

   a. Agreement
   b. Consistency
   c. Consensus
   d. Homogeneity

10. _____ tends to make people overemphasize personal causes for other people's behavior and to underemphasize those causes for their own behavior.

    a. Interpersonal error
    b. Fundamental attribution error
    c. Defensiveness
    d. Proximity

11. The tendency to attribute success to our own efforts or qualities and failure to external factors is called:

    a. defensive attribution
    b. fundamental defense
    c. scapegoating
    d. inconsistency

12. "Bad things happen to bad people and good things happen to good people" is the attribution error of the:

    a. fairness hypothesis
    b. uninformed
    c. just-world hypothesis
    d. fantasy-prone person

13. How close two people live to each other is called:

    a. similarity   c. vicinity
    b. proximity   d. propinquity

14. The principle that relationships are based on trading rewards among partners is called:

    a. barter   c. reciprocity
    b. equity   d. exchange

15. _____ is the fairness of exchange when every partner receives the same proportion of outcomes to investments.

    a. Equity   c. Fair exchange
    b. Equalization   d. Equivalence

16. The quality of genuine closeness and trust achieved in communication with another person is called:

    a. closeness   c. intimacy
    b. familiarity   d. companionship

17. A/an _____ is a relatively stable organization of beliefs, feelings, and behavior tendencies directed toward some object such as a person or group.

    a. value   c. personal position
    b. attitude   d. presumption

18. _____ is the tendency for an individual to observe the situation for cues about how to react.

    a. Self-observation   c. Self-monitoring
    b. Self-consciousness   d. Expectation

19. An unfair, intolerant, or unfavorable attitude toward a group of people is called:

    a. discrimination   c. stereotyping
    b. prejudice   d. bias

20. _____ is an unfair act or series of acts taken toward a group of people or individual members of the group.

   a. Prejudice
   b. Bias

   c. Exclusion
   d. Discrimination

21. A personality pattern characterized by rigid conventionality, respect for authority, and hostility toward those who defy norms is called a/an _____ personality.

   a. dissonant
   b. authoritarian

   c. authoritative
   d. dominant

22. Perceived inconsistency between two cognitions is called:

   a. cognitive dissonance
   b. cognitive confusion

   c. inharmoniousness
   d. cognitive disagreement

23. _____ is the process by which others individually or collectively affect one's perceptions, attitudes, and actions.

   a. Cultural influence
   b. Assimilation

   c. Obedience
   d. Social influence

24. _____ is a belief that most members of a society accept as true and self-evident.

   a. Group truism
   b. Social agreement

   c. Cultural truism
   d. Cultural assimilation

25. Voluntarily yielding to social norms even at the expense of one's own preference is called:

   a. obedience
   b. conformity

   c. peer pressure
   d. compliance

26. _____ is a change of behavior in response to an explicit request from another person or group.

   a, Compliance
   b. Obedience

   c. Conformity
   d. Altruism

27. A change of behavior in response to a command from another person, typically an authority figure is called:

    a. compliance
    b. submission
    c. obedience
    d. deference

28. The loss of personal sense of responsibility in a group is called:

    a. deidentification
    b. deindividuation
    c. irresponsibility
    d. the *snowball effect*

29. Helping behavior that is not linked to personal gain is called:

    a. selflessness
    b. benevolence
    c. philanthropy
    d. altruism

30. _____ is the greater willingness to take risks in decision making in a group than as independent individuals.

    a. Risk taking
    b. The risky shift
    c. Polarization
    d. Groupthink

31. The shift in attitudes by members of a group toward more extreme positions than the ones held before group discussion is called:

    a. polarization
    b. risky shift
    c. dichotomization
    d. opposite alignment

32. The theory that leadership is a result of personal qualities and traits that qualify one to lead others is called:

    a. chosen leadership
    b. the great leader theory
    c. the eminence theory
    d. the great person theory

33. The _____ effect is the principle that subjects will alter their behavior because of a researcher's attention and not because of a specific experimentation.

    a. Milgram
    b. Hawthorne
    c. Western Electric
    d. Mayo

Answers for this section:

1.	c (560)	10.	b (565)	19.	b (571)	28.	b (586)
2.	b (560)	11.	a (565)	20.	d (571)	29.	d (586)
3.	d (561)	12.	c (565)	21.	b (572)	30.	b (589)
4.	a (562)	13.	b (565)	22.	a (578)	31.	a (589)
5.	b (562)	14.	d (568)	23.	d (580)	32.	d (591)
6.	d (563)	15.	a (568)	24.	c (580)	33.	b (592)
7.	c (563)	16.	c (568)	25.	b (582)		
8.	a (564)	17.	b (570)	26.	a (583)		
9.	c (564)	18.	c (571)	27.	c (584)		

Understanding the Facts

Now that you have found that you can recognize facts from Social Psychology, the next step is to determine if you understand the meaning of newly-learned information. These multiple-choice questions require a higher level of thinking. They will help you establish more solid connections and provide practice in dealing with higher level concepts.

34.   Which of the following is **not** a function of schemata?

   a.   They play a crucial role in how we interpret and remember information.
   b.   They allow us to make inferences about other people.
   c.   They keep us from making errors about people's intentions.
   d.   They might cause us to remember things about people we never actually observed.

35.   Early impressions of a person create a context of how later information about that person is evaluated. This is a function of:

   a.   stereotyping   c.   the self-fulfilling prophecy
   b.   prejudice   d.   the primacy effect

36.   One of the dangers of the primacy effect is that it can lead to:

   a.   forming a prejudice   c.   cognitive dissonance
   b.   altruism   d.   attribution error

37. The primacy effect can be weakened or even nullified in all but which one of the following conditions?

    a.   Warn people to beware of first impressions.
    b.   Interpret information about others slowly.
    c.   Expect to have a bad impression of a person we meet for the first time.
    d.   Interpret information about others carefully.

38. When first impressions of people are governed by a stereotype we:

    a.   pay attention to facts that are inconsistent with the stereotype
    b.   ignore facts that are inconsistent with the stereotype
    c.   remember things about people accurately
    d.   remember things about people nonselectively

39. Which of the following can easily become the basis for self-fulfilling prophecy?

    a.   attribution   c.   altruism
    b.   prejudice   d.   stereotypes

40. Which of the following is **not** one of the three kinds of information about behavior that we rely on in determining its cause according to Harold Kelly (1967)?

    a.   consistency   c.   distinctiveness
    b.   stereotype   d.   consensus

41. When making an attribution you are guessing about:

    a.   the true causes of a particular action
    b.   the biases involved in your observation
    c.   the excuses made for a particular action
    d.   another person's deception

42. When students do well, teachers are more likely to assume responsibility for their performance than when students do poorly. This is an example of:

    a.   simple bias   c.   defensive attribution
    b.   fundamental attribution error   d.   self-fulfilling prophecy

43. When a crime is committed we might wonder if the victim "asked for it." This is an example of:

    a.   defensive attribution   c.   fundamental attribution error
    b.   the just-defense hypothesis   d.   the just-world hypothesis

44. It may be that the most important factor in determining attraction is:

a. similarity
b. proximity
c. propinquity
d. physical attractiveness

45. In the Festinger, Schachter, and Back (1950) investigation of the effects of proximity on friendship in a housing project, it was found that:

a. the proximity effect is due to simple convenience
b. residents did not make friends in the project
c. 50 percent said their best friends lived down the hall
d. 44 percent of residents were most friendly with their next-door neighbors and only 10 percent said their best friends lived down the hall

46. Which of the following is the physical attractiveness stereotype?

a. what is beautiful is also presumed to be "dumb"
b. what is beautiful is also presumed to be good
c. what is beautiful is also presumed to be a bore
d. what is beautiful is also presumed to be shallow

47. We value similarity and sometimes exaggerate its extent among our friends because of all but which **one** of the following?

a. It keeps us from being prejudiced.
b. It strengthens our convictions.
c. It boosts our self-esteem.
d. It helps us to clarify information and reduce uncertainty about social situations.

48. When people's attraction seems to be founded on their differences, their critical qualities are:

a. their diversity
b. their values
c. opposites
d. complements

49. The reward theory of attraction is based on:

a. proximity
b. similarity
c. exchange
d. intimacy

50. Which of the following statements about reward theory of attraction is **true**?

a. As long as both parties find interactions more rewarding than costly their exchanges will continue.
b. People do not "keep score" in their interactions in early stages of the relationship.
c. Exchanges need not be equitable.
d. Usually the person who gains the most does not feel guilty.

51. According to Jourard (1964), intimate communication is based on:

a. equity
b. shared values
c. self-disclosure
d. reciprocity

52. In intimate communication, the relationship will suffer if:

a. not enough is revealed
b. too much is revealed too soon
c. someone is too eager to make a personal response
d. shocking information is revealed

53. La Piere's (1934) study on the relationship between attitudes and behavior concluded that:

a. attitudes are reliable predictors of behavior
b. behavior is not linked to a person's intentions
c. attitudes are not reliable predictors of behavior
d. intentions are a direct product of a person's attitudes

54. Attitudes do not predict behavior well among people who:

a. have strong prejudices
b. are low in self-monitoring
c. do no self-monitoring
d. are high in self-monitoring

55. Which of the following is **not** listed as a factor in attitude development?

a. early, direct personal experience
b. genetic factors
c. imitation
d. television and newspapers

56. Prejudicial beliefs are almost always:

    a. discriminatory   c. a prelude to hostility
    b. caused by frustration   d. stereotypes

57. People who try to simplify and organize social thinking as much as possible exemplify which of the following theoretical sources of prejudice?

    a. cognitive sources of prejudice
    b. frustration-aggression theory
    c. authoritarian personality
    d. conformity in society

58. Which of the following plans has succeeded in reducing prejudice?

    a. school desegregation
    b. contact between groups
    c. educating the public with films and literature
    d. working together in cooperation and interdependence

59. Why do advertisers create ads that annoy us?

    a. because they attract our attention
    b. because they are more memorable
    c. because we find them humorous
    d. because they surprise us

60. According to the communication model of persuasion which of the following is **not** manipulated in an effort to get you to change your attitudes?

    a. attention   c. message
    b. medium   d. source

61. The credibility of a source is **most** important when:

    a. we pay close attention to the message
    b. we have high interest in the message
    c. we are not inclined to pay attention to the message itself
    d. humor is used

62. According to Miller and Campbell (1959), it is better to present your own view second in a two-sided argument if:

a. the audience cannot discern a difference between the first and second argument
b. a short-time elapses between the first and second argument
c. there is no time between the first and second argument
d. a long time elapses between the first and second positions

63. The most important factors in changing attitudes are those that have to do with the:

a. medium
b. audience
c. message
d. source

64. Which of the following results is **true** when people are enticed by reward to engage in attitude discrepant behavior?

a. When rewards are large, dissonance is at a minimum and attitude change is small.
b. Larger rewards cause greater dissonance which lowers the chance for attitude change.
c. When rewards are small, dissonance is at a minimum and attitude change is small.
d. The larger the reward, the larger the change in attitude.

65. One technique for understanding other cultures is:

a. cultural mores
b. cultural assimilators
c. norms
d. values

66. According to Asch (1951), the likelihood of conformity increases with group size until _____ confederates are present.

a. 6
b. 8
c. 4
d. 10

67. According to Allen and Levine (1971), conformity can be reduced by:

a. having just one "ally" in the group
b. having an "ally" that shares the subject's viewpoint in the group
c. having two "allies" in the group
d. having three confederates break the majority agreement

68. Once a person has granted a small request that person is more likely to comply with a larger request. This is known as the _____.

    a.   lowball procedure   c.   foot-in-the-door technique
    b.   door-in-the-face technique   d.   compliance method

69. In Milgram's experiments on obedience it was found that:

    a.   only 3 percent of the subjects delivered the entire series of shocks
    b.   when responsibility for an act is shared, obedience is much greater
    c.   when responsibility for an act is shared, obedience lessens
    d.   an insignificant number of subjects complied with the experimenter commands

70. It is a fact that people act differently in the presence of others than they would by themselves. The striking and frightening instance of this is:

    a.   mob behavior   c.   stereotyping
    b.   prejudice   d.   the bystander effect

71. When a dominant and persuasive person convinces people to act the result is called:

    a.   deindividuation   c.   the snowball effect
    b.   protection   d.   anonymity

72. The most important situational variable in helping behavior is:

    a.   the degree of altruism of the bystander
    b.   the degree of ambiguity
    c.   people who score high on the need for approval
    d.   the presence of other people

73. Because of polarization, if you want a group to ensure that a problem will be resolved in a cautious, conservative direction:

    a.   initiate groupthink
    b.   be sure the group members are cautious and conservative
    c.   tell group members that you want a cautious and conservative resolution
    d.   choose the group leader on the basis of great person theory

74. Bad decisions such as resulted in the Bay of Pigs invasion, the Watergate cover up, and the Challenger disaster appear to have resulted from:

a. groupthink   c. group cohesiveness
b. great person theory   d. the transactional view

75. Most historians and psychologists now regard great person theory of leadership as naive because:

a. Adolph Hitler was not a great person
b. there are not enough extraordinary people to assume positions of influence
c. it ignores social and economic factors
d. no time is ever "right" for the emergence of a leader

76. Which of the following concepts would be of the most interest to an I/O psychologist?

a. great person theory   c. mob behavior
b. the Hawthorne effect   d. Fielder's contingency model

Answers for this section:

34.	c (561)	45.	d (565)	56.	d (572)	67.	a (582)
35.	d (561)	46.	b (566)	57.	a (573)	68.	c (583)
36.	a (562)	47.	a (567)	58.	d (575)	69.	b (584)
37.	c (562)	48.	d (567)	59.	b (576)	70.	a (585)
38.	b (562)	49.	c (568)	60.	a (577)	71.	c (586)
39.	d (562)	50.	a (568)	61.	c (577)	72.	d (587)
40.	b (563)	51.	c (568)	62.	d (578)	73.	b (589)
41.	a (564)	52.	b (568)	63.	b (578)	74.	a (590)
42.	c (565)	53.	c (570)	64.	a (579)	75.	c (591)
43.	d (565)	54.	d (571)	65.	b (581)	76.	b (593)
44.	b (565)	55.	b (571)	66.	c (582)		

Applying the Facts

The learning of facts and concepts is of little value unless it can be applied and employed to solve problems. The next group of multiple-choice questions reflects applications of your learning.

77. Virginia is very talkative and outspoken. We label her an extrovert. Later, we "remember" that she is very sociable, but we have never seen examples of her sociability. We are using a/an _____ to interpret Virginia's behavior.

    a.   stereotype   c.   primacy observation
    b.   expectation   d.   schema

78. You have an appointment to be interviewed for your first job after graduating from college. You have never met your interviewer. You know you must make a good first impression because you have studied the research of:

    a.   Solomon Asch   c.   Fritz Heider
    b.   Stanley Milgram   d.   Leon Festinger

79. During the 1970's men who wore their hair long were often suspected of being "hippies." Which of the following social forces was operating?

    a.   prejudice   c.   stereotyping
    b.   primacy effect   d.   self-fulfilling prophecy

80. Your favorite sports are tennis and golf. On Saturday you played tennis and won every set. You won because of your superior ability. On Sunday, you played golf, but came into the clubhouse with the highest score of your foursome. The greens had not been properly groomed and the weather was too humid. You are displaying:

    a.   self-fulfilling prophecy   c.   just-world hypothesis
    b.   fundamental attribution error d.   defensive attribution

81. Alice liked Joe and went on several dates with him. Joe was pleased. He liked Alice very much. But Alice soon turned down dates with Joe when she found out he was drinking too much. Joe then disliked Alice immensely. This is an example of:

    a.   reverse intimacy   c.   reward theory of attraction
    b.   equity fairness   d.   proximity

82. Gigi wanted to be a lifeguard at a country club, but was told that the club only hires men for that job. This shows that:

    a.   the club was discriminating, but not necessarily prejudiced
    b.   prejudice and discrimination occur together
    c.   the club was unfair to and intolerant of women
    d.   the club president had an authoritarian personality

83. You are a social psychologist. You visited Los Angeles after the riot in the spring of 1992. You knew that, in addition to the political and economic factors operating in the situation there was also:

a. group decision making   c. groupthink
b. deindividuation and protection   d. the bystander effect

84. Joanie was leaving the classroom building late one afternoon. She was carrying some important papers in her hand. The area seemed deserted. The wind caught her papers and scattered them in all directions. A lone male student appeared and picked up every piece of paper. This illustrates:

a. the snowball effect   c. deindividuation
b. protection   d. the bystander effect

85. Tom is the chairperson of the psychology department at your university. He is conducting meetings with the goal of making some important curriculum changes. He has some strong opinions about what should be done, but he is not promoting his ideas in the meetings. He is asking the group for their ideas and opinions. Tom is trying to avoid:

a. discrimination   c. the risky shift
b. groupthink   d. cohesiveness

Answers for this section:

77. d (561)   82. a (572)
78. a (561)   83. b (586)
79. c (562)   84. d (587)
80. d (565)   85. b (590)
81. c (568)

Fill-in-the-Blank Questions: Recalling What You Have Learned

By now, there should be a considerable amount of new information about Social Psychology in long-term memory. The following questions of recall rather than recognition will show if you are becoming more comfortable with the material.

Remembering the Facts

1. A set of beliefs or expectations about something is called a/an _____.

2.	The extent to which early information about a person weighs more heavily than later information in influencing one's perception of that person is called the _____ effect.

3.	In the _____ - _____ _____ an expectation about another person elicits behavior from that person that confirms the expectation.

4.	A set of characteristics presumed to be shared by all members of a social category is called a/an _____.

5.	_____ theory addresses the question of how people make judgements about the causes of behavior.

6.	The extent to which a behavior is present only when a particular stimulus is present is known as _____.

7.	_____ is the extent to which a particular event produces the same behavior each time it is present.

8.	_____ is the extent to which everyone in a given situation is behaving in the same way.

9.	People tend to overemphasize personal causes for other people's behavior and underemphasize those causes for their behavior. This phenomenon is called _____ _____ _____.

10.	When we attribute success to our own efforts or qualities and failure to external factors we are engaged in _____ attribution.

11.	The assumption that bad things happen to bad people and good things happen to good people is called the _____ - _____ hypothesis.

12.	Social psychologists use the term _____ to indicate how close people live to each other.

13.	_____ theory is the term used for relationships that are based on trading rewards among partners.

14.	The fairness of the exchange achieved when every partner receives the same proportion of outcomes to investment is called _____.

15.	_____ is the genuine closeness and trust achieved in communication with another person.

16. A/an _____ is the relatively stable organization of beliefs, feelings, and behavior directed toward some object, person, or group.

17. When people observe a situation for cues about how to react they are displaying _____ - _____.

18. _____ is an unfair, intolerant, or unfavorable attitude toward a group of people.

19. An unfair act taken toward a group of people or individual members of the group is called _____.

20. A person with a/an _____ personality is rigidly conventional, respects authority, and is hostile to those who defy norms.

21. The perceived inconsistency between two cognitions is called _____ _____.

22. _____ _____ is the process by which others affect one's perceptions, attitudes, and actions.

23. A/an _____ _____ is a belief that most members of a society accept as true and self-evident.

24. Voluntarily yielding to social norms even at the expense of one's own preferences is called _____.

25. _____ is a change of behavior in response to an explicit request from another person or group.

26. A change of behavior in response to a command from an authority figure is called _____.

27. _____ is the loss of personal sense of responsibility in a group.

28. Helping behavior that is not associated with personal gain is called _____.

29. Individual helpfulness tends to decrease as the number of bystanders to an emergency increases. This is called the _____ _____.

30. There is greater willingness to take risks in decision making in a group than as independent individuals. This is called the _____ _____.

31. _____ is a shift in attitudes by members of a group towards more extreme positions than the ones held before group discussions.

32. Leadership is a result of personal qualities that qualify one to lead others. This is the _____ _____ theory.

33. The area of psychology that is concerned with behavior in the work place is called _____/_____ psychology.

34. A situation where subjects will alter behavior because of researchers' attention and not necessarily because of any specific experimentation is labeled the _____ effect.

Answers for this section:

1. schema (560)
2. primacy (561)
3. self-fulfilling prophecy (562)
4. stereotype (562)
5. attribution (563)
6. distinctiveness (563)
7. consistency (564)
8. consensus (564)
9. fundamental attribution error (565)
10. defensive (565)
11. just-world (565)
12. proximity (565)
13. exchange (568)
14. equity (568)
15. intimacy (568)
16. attitude (570)
17. self-monitoring (571)

18. prejudice (571)
19. discrimination (571)
20. authoritarian (572)
21. cognitive dissonance (578)
22. social influence (580)
23. cultural truism (580)
24. conformity (582)
25. compliance (583)
26. obedience (584)
27. deindividuation (586)
28. altruism (586)
29. bystander effect (587)
30. risky shift (589)
31. polarization (589)
32. great person (591)
33. industrial organizational (592)
34. Hawthorne (592)

Understanding and Applying the Facts

As you previously did with recognition-type questions, you will now move to a higher level of recall. The following questions will determine if you understand the facts.

35. If we interpret information about other people slowly and carefully the _____ _____ can be weakened or nullified.

36. "Emotional, excitable, home oriented, and gentle." This description is often a _____ for women.

37. Jordan has never been able to keep a job very long. He believes that the economy is to blame along with the fact that employers never really give him a chance. His friend Mike has the same problem, but Jordan knows that Mike is incompetent and quite lazy. Jordan is committing _____ _____ error.

38. Elaine did very well in her fine arts course and she knew it was because she has talent, but she had great difficulty passing psychology. That was because her instructor did not explain the concepts very well. Elaine's bias is _____ _____.

39. We can defend ourselves against the implied possibility that misfortune could happen to us by giving in to the _____ - _____ hypothesis.

40. When people's attraction seems to be founded on "differentness," the critical qualities are probably not opposites, but _____.

41. Aronson's (1992) gain-loss theory of attraction suggests that increases in rewarding behavior influence attractiveness more than _____ rewarding.

42. A relationship is based on _____ when one person gets "out of it" is equal to what the other gets "out of it."

43. Shirley and Pete have begun to discuss what they hope for, many of their past experiences, their goals, where they have failed, and many of their favorite memories. They have achieved _____ communication.

44. _____ - _____ is only possible when you trust the listener.

45. During the campaign days for the 1992 presidential election, Jack was in constant conflict with his friends who were mostly Democrats. He was a Republican and would not keep his thoughts to himself even though he was outnumbered. Jack is a low _____ - _____.

46. According to Hartmann and Husband (1971), children without experiences of their own rely on _____ in forming their social attitudes.

47. To _____ is to treat an entire group in an unfair way.

48. Rigidly conventional, hostile to those who defy norms, submission to authority, and cynical about human nature all describe the _____ personality.

49. To be persuaded, you must first _____ _____.

50. The four elements of the communication model of persuasion are the _____, _____, _____, and _____.

51. In choosing a medium it is good to know that _____ appears to be best suited to getting others to understand complex arguments while _____ is more effective in persuading an audience once it has understood an argument.

52. People with low _____ - _____ are more easily influenced when a message is complex and hard to understand.

53. Roy stole some videotapes from his friend Mark. There was no way Mark would find out. But stealing from a friend caused Roy some discomfort, so he thought about all the trouble Mark had given him. Roy decided that Mark was not a friend after all. Roy had to resolve _____ _____.

54. The mobile territory a person maintains in interactions with others is called _____ _____.

55. If a person born in 1920 were to go the the beach today, that person might be shocked when viewing the swimming attire of the 90's. The shock would come from the fact that a former _____ is being violated.

56. When a task is difficult or poorly defined, conformity tends to be (lower, higher)

57. In an ambiguous situation, individuals are (more, less) willing to conform to that of the majority.

58. For a person of relatively low status in a group, the fear of _____ motivates conformity to group behavior.

59. Phil was going door-to-door attempting to sell subscriptions to cable TV. He began his conversation with the prospective client by stating that the cable company would be in the neighborhood to check the lines and that they wanted residents to know the company was there. Actually, Phil's sole purpose was to sell. He was using the _____ - _____ - _____ - _____ effect.

60. If you are thinking of buying a new car you should beware of the _____ procedure.

61. In the Milgram experiment on obedience, the "learner" was actually a _____ in the experiment.

62. Obedience is _____ with a command.

63. _____ is social influence in its most direct and powerful form.

64. Of all of the research cited in this chapter, the experiments of _____ _____ are the **most** likely to be considered unethical by the APA today.

65. If a thousand people start destroying property in a riot situation, those participating feel that they will not be arrested because the large group provides _____.

66. Whatever the cause of the Los Angeles riots in the spring of 1992, a social psychologist would most likely say that _____ contributed strongly to the violent, antisocial behavior.

67. One strongly dominant and persuasive person in a group can convince people to act through the _____ effect. When a few people are convinced to act, those few will convince others.

68. The bystander effect says that as the number of passive bystanders increases, the likelihood _____ that anyone of them will help someone in trouble.

69. You just found that you got an A on your last psychology test. Another student stopped you in the parking lot and asked your help in getting the keys out of her locked car. You said you'd be glad to help. In this case, it is likely that your _____ enhanced your willingness to help unless, of course, you are _____.

70. You hope that there won't be many strangers in the vicinity if you ever need help in an emergency. You feel this way because now you understand the _____ effect.

71. The time-honored assumption that groups make more conservative decisions than individuals was shown to be incorrect with the 1961 experiment of James Stoner who discovered the phenomenon of the _____ _____.

72. Fraser (1971), found that groups that start out risky will become more risky during their deliberations, and groups that tend to be cautious will become more cautious. This is an example of _____.

73. Group cohesiveness can undermine the quality of group decision making. Group cohesiveness can lead to _____.

74. Fred Fiedler's _____ model of leadership provides a viable alternative to great person theory which has fallen from the favor of social psychologists.

75. According to Fiedler's model of leadership, the most effective style depends on three factors: the _____, the _____ between the leader and the group, and the leader's ability to exert great or little _____.

76. Elton Mayo's experiment at a Western Electric plant in the 1920's demonstrated that there is not a simple, direct relationship between working conditions and worker productivity. The findings of Mayo's work are known as the _____ effect.

77. To keep workers on a long assembly line feeling that they are a part of an indentifiable group, _____ _____ _____ have been implemented.

Answers for this section:

35. primacy effect (562)
36. stereotype (562)
37. fundamental attribution (565)
38. defensive attribution (565)
39. just-world (565)
40. complements (567)
41. constant (567)
42. equity (568)
43. intimate (568)
44. self-disclosure (568)
45. self-monitor (571)
46. television (571)
47. discriminate (572)
48. authoritarian (572)
49. pay attention (575)
50. source, message, medium, audience (577)
51. writing, videotape (578)
52. self-esteem (578)
53. cognitive dissonance (578)
54. personal space (580)
55. norm (581)
56. higher (582)

57. more (582)
58. rejection (582)
59. foot-in-the-door (583)
60. lowball (583)
61. confederate (584)
62. compliance (584)
63. obedience (584)
64. Stanley Milgram (584)
65. anonymity (586)
66. deindividuation (586)
67. snowball (586)
68. decreases (587)
69. mood, altruistic (588)
70. bystander (587)
71. risky shift (589)
72. polarization (589)
73. groupthink (590)
74. contingency (591)
75. task, relationship, power (591)
76. Hawthorne (592)
77. autonomous work groups (593)

<u>Testing Yourself For Mastery</u>

The following terms and concepts are found in boldface or italics in the chapter. The time has come to determine if you can define and discuss your new learning in your own words, then check your work against the text.

social psychology

primacy effect

self-fulfilling prophecy

stereotype

attribution theory

distinctiveness

consensus

consistency

fundamental attribution error

defensive attribution

just-world hypothesis

proximity

exchange

equity

intimacy

attitude

self-monitoring

prejudice

discrimination

frustration-aggression theory

authoritarian personality

cognitive dissonance

social influence

cultural truism

personal space

conformity

compliance

obedience

altruistic behavior

deindividuation

bystander effect

risky shift

polarization

great person theory

cohesiveness

groupthink

industrial/organizational (I/O) psychology

Hawthorne effect

Integrating Your Newly Learned Information

Now that you have recognized, recalled, and given definition to Social Psychology, you are ready to try to integrate your knowledge in a definitive discussion through short-answer questions.

1. How do we decide whether a person's behavior is internally or externally caused? Use Harold Kelly's explanation in your answer. (563)

2. Explain the biases in interpreting the causes of behavior that occur because of defensive attribution and the just-world hypothesis. (564, 565)

3. Discuss two factors in interpersonal attraction. (565-569)

4. Cite the findings of one research investigation on the relationship between attitudes and behavior. (570, 571)

5. List the sources of prejudice and present one way that prejudice can be reduced. (572, 573)

6. List the factors in the process of persuasion. (575-578)

7. Cite the results of one of Solomon Asch's studies on the effects of conformity. (582)

8. List and define the specific techniques used to get people to comply with another person's request. (583, 584)

9. Obedience is a necessary phenomenon in social interaction, but what did the results of Stanley Milgram's experiments on obedience tell us about the danger of obedience? (584, 585)

10. How does a social psychologist account for the violent, antisocial behavior sometimes shown by groups? (585, 586)

Applications

You have worked through a section of recognition-type questions to determine if you can apply information to real-life situations. It is time to try to respond to some applications. Some are based upon those questions. Answers to this section will not be given. Your questions concerning these applications will serve as a basis for classroom discussion and ideas for class projects throughout the course

1. Think of one or two personal situations in which you have used defensive attribution and the just-world hypothesis to explain your behavior.

2. The next time you take a classroom test, listen to your professor when the grades are returned and see if you can detect defensive attribution on the part of your professor.

3. Ben had just moved into a new condominium and found that he was having frequent conversations with his next-door neighbor. He asked his neighbor if he would keep an eye on his home while he was out-of-town. Then, the neighbor asked Ben if he would take him to the repair shop to pick up his car. Ben and his neighbor made arrangements to have dinner together. What factors of interpersonal attraction are operating here?

4. The next time you are in a social group that is displaying attitudes that are different from your own, do some self-observation and decide if you are low or high on self-monitoring and note the results of the interactions.

5. Shirley and Tom had taken their first trip abroad. When they were in France they noticed that people came very close to them if they happened to ask a question of strangers. Shirley and Tom felt uncomfortable. Explain why the travelers were uncomfortable.

6. Virginia was in the process of organizing a fund raiser for the symphony. She asked her friend Lola if she would be the hostess for 6 tables of bridge at her home. Lola refused, but when Virginia asked Lola to bring two other bridge players to another person's home for a fund raiser, Lola consented to do so. What technique of compliance was Virginia using?

7. When a lone student arrived to "rescue" Joanie's papers that were blown about the campus, there were no other people in the vicinity. What factor in "helping behavior" was operating in that situation? What do you think would have happened to Joanie's papers if they had been blown away while students were in the process of going from one class to another?

8. Think of a situation in which you have the opportunity to observe a leader in action. Analyze that situation and decide which of the presented theories of leadership applies. Is it a vote for the great person theory or is there some other explanation?

Return to Chapter Summary

Now that you have concluded these exercises, you should go back and reread the chapter summary in your textbook. It provides you with a framework that integrates all of this newly-learned information. By reviewing the chapter summary, you will strengthen the many connections between the various new pieces of information.

APPENDIX
MEASUREMENT
AND STATISTICAL
METHODS

Chapter Objectives

After you have read and studied this chapter, you should be able to:

1. Identify the properties of the four scales of measurement and the situations in which each should be used.
2. Identify the three measures of central tendency and describe the kind of information provided by each.
3. Define frequency distribution. Construct a frequency histogram and a frequency polygon.
4. List the properties of the normal curve, and contrast these with skewed and bimodal distributions.
5. Identify two measures of variability.
6. Explain the purpose of a scatter plot.
7. Explain the function of a correlation coefficient and how to interpret positive and negative correlations.
8. Define the term "significance" and explain its relationship to probability.

Multiple-Choice Questions: Recognizing What You Have Learned

These questions ask only that you recognize what you have learned. When you recognize a correct answer, you have accessed that information in memory. A knowledge of facts serves as a framework for later analysis and problem solving.

Remembering the Facts

This group of multiple-choice questions requires that you simply recognize facts from your textbook.

1. A _____ scale is a set of categories for classifying objects.

    a. nominal   c. ordinal
    b. ratio   d. interval

2. When a measurement scale indicates order or relative position according to some criterion it is called a/an _____ scale.

    a. ratio   c. ordinal
    b. nominal   d. interval

3. A scale with equal distance between points or values, but without a true zero is called a/an _____ scale.

    a. ordinal   c. ratio
    b. interval   d. nominal

4. A _____ scale has equal distance between points or values and includes a true zero.

    a. ratio   c. ordinal
    b. nominal   d. interval

5. Under certain conditions scores congregate around some middle value. Statisticians call this:

    a. correlation   c. averaging
    b. variability   d. central tendency

6. If you divide the sum of values by the total number of cases, you have calculated a:

   a. median
   b. standard deviation

   c. mean
   d. mode

7. The point that divides a set of scores in half is called the:

   a. median
   b. range

   c. mode
   d. mean

8. The point at which the largest number of scores occurs is the:

   a. range
   b. mode

   c. median
   d. standard deviation

9. A count of the number of scores that falls within each of a series of intervals is known as a:

   a. range
   b. frequency occurrence

   c. frequency distribution
   d. scatter plot

10. A bar graph that shows frequency distributions is called a:

    a. scatter plot
    b. frequency histogram

    c. frequency polygon
    d. range curve

11. A _____ curve is a hypothetical, bell-shaped distribution that occurs when a normal distribution is plotted as a frequency polygon.

    a. skewed
    b. bimodal

    c. frequency
    d. normal

12. The difference between the largest and smallest measurements in a distribution is called the:

    a. average deviation
    b. standard deviation

    c. range
    d. discrepancy

13. The statistical measure of variability in a group of scores or other values is called the:

    a. standard deviation
    b. average deviation

    c. variance
    d. range

14. A _____ is a diagram showing the association between two sets of scores.

    a. histogram   c. scatter plot
    b. significance diagram   d. polygon

15. A statistical measure of the strength of association between two variables is called a:

    a. normal distribution   c. measure of variance
    b. correlation coefficient   d. measure of central tendency

16. The probability that results obtained were due to chance is called:

    a. significance   c. prediction
    b. odds   d. luck

Answers for this section:

1.	a (600)	5.	d (601)	9.	c (602)	13.	a (606)
2.	c (600)	6.	c (601)	10.	b (603)	14.	c (608)
3.	b (600)	7.	a (601)	11.	d (604)	15.	b (609)
4.	a (601)	8.	b (602)	12.	c (606)	16.	a (610)

Understanding the Facts

Now that you have found that you can recognize facts from Measurement and Statistical Methods, the next step is to determine if you understand the meaning of newly-learned information. These multiple-choice questions require a higher level of thinking. They will help you establish more solid connections and provide practice in dealing with higher level concepts.

17. Statistics enables psychology to be a/an _____ science.

    a. exact   c. quantitative
    b. nominal   d. qualitative

18. In order to measure anything we must first assign to it the proper:

    a. definition   c. quantity
    b. scale   d. ratio

19. The **least** informative scale of measurement is the _____ scale.

   a. ordinal   c. interval
   b. ratio   d. nominal

20. The **most** informative scale of measurement is the _____ scale.

   a. ratio   c. interval
   b. nominal   d. ordinal

21. The nominal scale is more of a way of _____ than _____.

   a. measuring, identifying   c. classifying, measuring
   b. classifying, qualifying   d. measuring, classifying

22. We do not know the distance between items on a/an _____ scale.

   a. interval   c. ordinal
   b. ratio   d. nominal

23. The word "ranking" signifies that we are using a/an _____ scale.

   a. ratio   c. nominal
   b. interval   d. ordinal

24. A ruler that is broken off at the bottom is analogous to a/an _____ scale.

   a. nominal   c. ordinal
   b. interval   d. ratio

25. A thermometer is an example of a/an _____ scale.

   a. interval   c. nominal
   b. ordinal   d. ratio

26. An intelligence test uses a/an _____ scale.

   a. ordinal   c. nominal
   b. ratio   d. interval

27. The scale that includes a true zero is the _____ scale.

   a. ratio   c. nominal
   b. interval   d. ordinal

28. The mean, median, and mode of a distribution are called the distribution's central tendency. They are also called:

   a. variances
   b. ranges
   c. average
   d. ratios

29. In order to calculate the standard deviation for a set of scores, we must first calculate the:

   a. median
   b. mean
   c. mode
   d. range

30. In a distribution of a set of scores, 50 percent of those scores fall above the _____ and 50 percent fall below.

   a. mean
   b. range
   c. mode
   d. median

31. The highest point on a frequency polygon is the:

   a. median
   b. mode
   c. range
   d. mean

32. If there are two "bumps" in a frequency polygon, the distribution is:

   a. skewed
   b. normal
   c. bimodal
   d. biased

33. The way to put large numbers of scores in a distribution into more manageable groups is to select a set of _____.

   a. ranges
   b. boundaries
   c. spaces
   d. intervals

34. In constructing a frequency histogram or polygon, the intervals are marked on the _____ axis and the frequency is indicated on the _____ axis.

   a. horizontal, vertical
   b. vertical, horizontal
   c. short, high
   d. positive, negative

35. In normal distribution the mean, median, and mode:

   a. are skewed to the left
   b. are skewed to the right
   c. all have the same value
   d. all have different values

36. In a skewed distribution, the mean, median, and mode:

   a.   are difficult to calculate   c.   have the same value
   b.   have different values   d.   cannot be predicted

37. If you know that the mean is greater than the median, the frequency polygon:

   a.   is skewed to the left   c.   shows a linear relationship
   b.   is not significant   d.   is skewed to the right

38. The easiest measure of variation to compute is the:

   a.   normal mean   c.   range
   b.   standard deviation   d.   variance

39. To find out how measurements are distributed around the mean we would compute a:

   a.   standard deviation   c.   correlation coefficient
   b.   range   d.   mode

40. In a normal distribution _____ percent of the scores fall between one standard deviation above the mean and one standard deviation below the mean.

   a.   50   c.   70
   b.   68   d.   72

41. More than _____ percent of the scores in normal distribution fall between three standard deviations above the three standard deviations below the mean.

   a.   68   c.   4
   b.   27   d.   99

42. If the dots on a scatter plot form a straight line from lower left to upper right there is a _____ between the two sets of variables.

   a.   perfect negative correlation   c.   zero correlation
   b.   perfect positive correlation   d.   biased relationship

43. The configuration of a scatter plot for a moderate correlation would be a:

   a.   cigar shape   c.   curved line
   b.   straight line   d.   u-shaped curve

44. The limits of a correlation coefficient are:

    a. -1.0 to 2.0   c. +1.0 to -1.0
    b. unpredictable   d. insignificant

45. According to the classification in the text, which of the following correlation coefficients is considered **high**?

    a. 1.89   c. -.89
    b. .65   d. 2.50

46. Which of the following correlation coefficients could **not** occur?

    a. -1.50   c. .998
    b. .0002   d. -.50

47. A correlation smaller than plus or minus .20 is considered:

    a. negative   c. biased
    b. insignificant   d. causal

48. If the significance level for experimental results is .05, we know that:

    a. the correlation is not significant
    b. there was error based on sampling procedures
    c. in 95 chances out of 100 the results were due to experimental treatment
    d. in 95 chances out of 100 the results were due to chance

49. If there is a large difference between the scores of an experimental group and the scores of the control group:

    a. random effects still could have caused the results
    b. the difference can be attributed to manipulation of variables
    c. it is obvious that sampling procedures were inadequate
    d. the significance level is automatically .05

Answers for this section:

17.	c (600)	26.	d (601)	35.	c (605)	44.	c (609)
18.	b (600)	27.	a (601)	36.	b (605)	45.	c (609)
19.	d (600)	28.	c (601)	37.	d (606)	46.	a (609)
20.	a (601)	29.	b (607)	38.	c (606)	47.	b (609)
21.	c (600)	30.	d (607)	39.	a (606)	48.	c (610)
22.	c (600)	31.	b (601)	40.	b (607)	49.	a (610)
23.	d (600)	32.	c (605)	41.	d (607)		
24.	b (600)	33.	d (602)	42.	b (608)		
25.	a (601)	34.	a (603)	43.	a (608)		

Applying the Facts

The learning of facts and concepts is of little value unless they can be applied and employed to solve problems. The next group of multiple-choice questions reflects applications of your learning.

50. A service station owner concerned about foreign imports counts the number of domestic, Japanese, Swedish, French, and German automobile drivers who patronize his place of business. His measurement is based upon which of the following scales?

    a.   ordinal   c.   ratio
    b.   nominal   d.   interval

51. The football team at your college is number 20 in the nation. Which scale is being used here?

    a.   ratio   c.   ordinal
    b.   nominal   d.   interval

52. Your home town had twice as much rain for the summer months this year as it did last year. The meteorologists used a/an _____ scale.

    a.   ratio   c.   nominal
    b.   interval   d.   ordinal

53. The mean of the set of scores 3, 1, 5, 2, 3, 8, 3 is:

    a.   3   c.   3.57
    b.   3.02   d.   3.52

54. The mode of the set of scores 3, 1, 5, 2, 3, 8, 3 is:

    a.   3   c.   3.03
    b.   3.57   d.   2.52

55. The median of the set of scores 3, 1, 5, 2, 3, 8, 3 is:

    a.   3.03   c.   3
    b.   3.57   d.   2

56. The distribution 3, 1, 5, 2, 3, 8, 3 is:

    a.   skewed right   c.   normal
    b.   skewed left   d.   bimodal

57. The standard deviation of the distribution 3, 1, 5, 2, 3, 8, 3 is:

    a.   7   c.   2.127
    b.   3   d.   4.524

58. The range of the distribution 3, 1, 5, 2, 3, 8, 3 is:

    a.   2.127   c.   4.524
    b.   7   d.   3.57

59. In the distribution 3, 1, 5, 2, 3, 8, 3, the _____ and the _____ have the same value.

    a.   mode, median   c.   mean, range
    b.   mean, median   d.   mode, mean

60. Jeannie did a correlation between college grade-point average and the distance students live from a commuter campus. She obtained a correlation coefficient of -.0005. Which of the following is the correct interpretation of her results?

    a.   The closer students live to the campus, the higher their grades.
    b.   This type of data cannot be correlated.
    c.   There is no relationship between GPA and distance from campus.
    d.   Living far from the campus tends to lower grades.

61.   Jeannie plotted her data on a graph. Dots were scattered all over the paper. This showed that:

a.   she probably put the Y values on the wrong axis
b.   she probably put the X values on the wrong axis
c.   living close to the campus tends to raise GPA
d.   there is no relationship between GPA and distance from campus

Answers for this section:

50.	b (600)	53.	c (601)	56.	a (605)	59.	a (601)
51.	c (600)	54.	a (601)	57.	c (607)	60.	c (609)
52.	a (601)	55.	c (601)	58.	b (606)	61.	d (609, 610)

Fill-in-the-Blank Questions: Recalling What You Have Learned

By now, there should be a considerable amount of new information about Measurement and Statistical Methods in long-term memory. The following questions of recall rather than recognition will show if you are becoming more comfortable with the material.

Remembering the Facts

1.   The branch of mathematics that psychologists use to organize and analyze data is called _____.

2.   A/an _____ scale is a set of categories for classifying objects.

3.   The _____ scale indicates order or relative position of items according to some criterion.

4.   A/an _____ scale has equal distances between points or values, but does not have a true zero.

5.   The _____ scale has a true zero, and the distances between the points or values is equal.

6.   Scores tend to congregate around some middle value. In statistics, this is called _____ _____.